C++ Primer for
C Programmers

Other McGraw-Hill Books of Interest

ISBN	AUTHOR	TITLE
003355-2	Baker	*C Tools for Scientists and Engineers*
003358-7	Baker	*More C Tools for Scientists and Engineers*
026001-X	Hancock et al.	*The C Primer*
043152-3	Morgan, McGilton	*Introducing UNIX System V*
062885-8	Tare	*Data Processing in UNIX*
062879-3	Tare	*UNIX Utilities*
062884-X	Tare	*UNIX Utilities* (softcover)

C++ Primer for C Programmers

Jay Ranade

Saba Zamir

McGraw-Hill, Inc.
New York   St. Louis   San Francisco   Auckland   Bogotá
Caracas   Lisbon   London   Madrid   Mexico   Milan
Montreal   New Delhi   Paris   San Juan   São Paulo
Singapore   Sydney   Tokyo   Toronto

Library of Congress Cataloging-in-Publication Data

Ranade, Jay.
    C++ primer for C programmers / Jay Ranade, Saba Zamir.
       p.   cm.—(UNIX/C series)
    Includes bibliographical references and index.
    ISBN 0-07-911315-X (cloth : book/disk combo) :   —ISBN
0-07-051216-7 (paper : book/disk combo) :
    1. C++ (Computer program language)   I. Zamir, Saba, date.
II. Title. III. Series.
QA76.73.C153R36   1992
005.265—dc20   91-34950
                                           CIP

   3 4 5 6 7 8 9 0 DOC/DOC 9 7 6 5 4 3

P/N 911316-8
PART OF
ISBN 0-07-051216-7

The sponsoring editor for this book was Jerry Papke,
and the production supervisor was Donald F. Schmidt.
It was set in Century Schoolbook by Archetype, Inc.

Printed and bound by R. R. Donnelley & Sons Company.

This book is dedicated to the memory of my grandfather,
Pundit S.R.D. Ranade (1895–1957)

Jay

To the light in her eyes, and the life in her soul,
Who loves to be loved, who we love to hold,
Beautiful child—vibrant and wild—this one's just for you.

To Sheena Zamir

Saba

Contents

Part 2   The Power of C++   83

Preface

Although microcomputers have been in existence for quite some time, IBM's announcement of its PC in August, 1981 lent credibility to this piece of computing hardware. Now, the market had to determine which will become the primary programming language in that environment. COBOL had already established itself as the de facto standard language of application development for the IBM mainframes. However, it was not destined to be the language of choice for microcomputers. For lack of anything else, initial application development was all done in BASIC. Gradually, it was to be replaced by PASCAL, but that too had an ephemeral existence. And finally, it was C that took over in a giant stride, and made BASIC and PASCAL a thing of the past.

Since early 1987, C became the lingua franca of microcomputer developers. And we thought that the market has stabilized and no new language was in sight for a long time to come. But no! The age of object-oriented programming was in the offing. And C needed some serious enhancements to support that. In the meantime, the corridors of Bell Labs, which has more PhDs per square foot than any other place on the globe, were reverberating with the thoughts of Mr. Bjarne Stroustrup, who had been working on the superset of C, which came to be known as C^{++}. This new language had the object-orientation features which C lacked. C^{++} complemented C and created a superset on top of strong foundations already laid out by Dennis Ritchie's C. And thus, it was the dawn of a new era in microcomputer programming languages.

WHY THIS BOOK?

This is not the first book written on C^{++}, and definitely will not be the last one, either. But the authors found, after talking to many readers who had read other books on C^{++}, that although they were complete and encyclopedic in nature, they were not written for somebody who did not know C^{++}. If you already knew C^{++}, it did help to understand those books better. This book has a different audience. It is written for those people who do not know C^{++} at all. It is also written for those who do not know the principles of object orientation.

WHO THIS BOOK IS FOR

Primarily, this book is written for application developers who are already comfortable with C language and would like to learn C^{++}. Be aware that this book will not teach you C. It presupposes knowledge of C language on your part (although it does provide brief refreshers whenever necessary!). If you do not know C at all, we advise you to learn it before delving into the beauty of C^{++}. If you do have to learn C first, we advise you to read the following book:

Hancock, Les, et al., *The C Primer,* Third Edition, McGraw-Hill, 1991

A WORD ON THE STYLE USED

There are so many types of software, add-on boards, and hardware alternatives in the microcomputing environment that it is difficult to keep up with all of them. So you do not have enough time to learn new things. And authors are very well aware of that. So we have worked very hard (correction, very *very* hard) to keep the writing style simple. We sincerely hope that you will read this book for enjoyment. Learning C^{++} will be just a side effect of that.

In addition, we have used the time-tested methodology of learn-by-example in this book. For anything that leaves any room for doubt, there is an example or two. As a matter of fact, we build subsequent examples on top of previous ones. This way, you will see how a C^{++} application develops as you progress from one page to the next.

However, the authors would like to read your comments and advice. That will help us in incorporating such suggestions in the next edition. Please drop us a line at the following address:

Jay Ranade
P.O. Box 338
Grand Central Station
New York, NY 10163

WHAT ENVIRONMENT THIS BOOK IS FOR

Obviously, this book is for the PC environment. However, all the examples have been tested using Borland's Turbo C^{++} compiler. Although we have not tested these examples using any other compiler, they should work for them, too.

FINAL WORD

After reading this book you will not only learn C^{++}, but also its applicability in an object-oriented environment. The authors expect that after finishing this book, you will be able to design and code in C++ with a high degree of confidence and competence. But let us know if we have succeeded in this endeavor. A successor to this volume may be in the offing.

Jay Ranade
Saba Zamir

P. S.:   By the way, it should not take you more than an hour to completely understand a chapter. So, it should not take you more than 24 hours to finish the book. Good luck and enjoy C++.

JR and SZ

Acknowledgments

My thanks are due to Kyungjoo Suh for reviewing the manuscript and giving many useful suggestions in making it more readable. My thanks are also due to Mary Ritter whose constructive criticism was very helpful in writing some parts of the book. Sunita Engira and Ram Engira gave many suggestions on the flow of the text and the kind of examples that we hope have improved the quality of the book. My special regards to Alan Nash for his company and razor-sharp intellect, which keeps me on my toes when I am relaxing. My special thanks are also to Kizmin Reeves, my manager and Vice President at Merrill Lynch, whose projects always keep me on the leading edge of technology. My thanks are due to Richard Breunich and Norman Stone for their support and encouragement.

And now the family members whose support and understanding is necessary if you are in the writing business. My thanks to my wife Ranjna for letting me work late and on the weekends, and to my mother for supplying many cups of fine English tea when I encounter writer's block.

And my very special thanks to Gerald T. Papke, Senior Editor at McGraw-Hill, for his support.

Jay Ranade

Many thanks are due to Nevine Abdel-Wahab for sharing my concerns (in German) at the time that the book was still in its inception. Special thanks are due to her for being the special person that she is.

Special thanks are due to my parents, Iram and Zamir Ahmad (also known as Ammi and Abjani), for their love and support that came long distance and half-way around the world. I would also like to thank my aunt Khalida Azhar (also known as Khala Jaan), for her love that parallels that of a mother. Thanks are due to Ruby and Fauzi (who also happen to be the parents of the little girl that this book is dedicated to); Tazien and Naseem (long-distance support, yet once again); Tom Lorenzo (for those crazy war games that were played while this book was being written), and my husband, for coming through when it seemed like nothing else would.

Finally, I would like to thank my unborn child (unborn as of this writing), for those little kicks that are the sweetest little entertainment that can be had!

Saba Zamir

1

Introduction/Comparison to C

An Introduction to C++

1.1 INTRODUCTION

If you are a C programmer, then you must have a basic understanding of data types, storage classes, operators, control structures, functions, pointers, structures, and all of those other features that make C the versatile and powerful language that it is. You are now in a position to go one step further. You are now ready for C++.

C++ is a successor of C. It was invented by Bjarne Stroustrup of AT&T Bell Laboratories in the mid-1980s. It builds upon the facilities provided by C, and provides new features that are significant improvements on C. C++ is expected to be the dominant software development platform of the future; it may even ultimately replace C.

1.2 AN ANALOGY

We will present a simple analogy that will help you understand the key concept in C++—the *class mechanism*. Then this analogy will be expanded to introduce the concept of a *derived class*. The discussion will continue with an explanation of *virtual functions*.

We will conclude with a synopsis that will help you understand the concept of *object-oriented programming*. It is this powerful new programming tool that makes C++ the language of the future.

1.3 CLASSES

Assume that you are a busy manager in a large company, and you have not one but two secretaries: Mary and John. If these employees could be represented by numbers (after all, each employee is assigned an employee number), then we could represent them in C in the form of a structure. Recall how a structure is defined in C—it is a compound data type that gathers together, in a fixed pattern, different atoms of information that comprise a given entity. In our example, we can name this given entity "secretary"—this would be the structure tag name. The members of this structure would be mary and john. This is how the declaration would look:

```
struct secretary
    {
    int mary;
    int john;
    };
```

Mary and John perform three functions: They type, file, and answer phones. Their function prototypes can be represented in C as follows:

```
void type(int);
void file(int);
void answer_phones(int);
```

For the sake of simplicity, we will assume that the functions above return no value, that is, they are of type *void,* and are passed one argument of type *int.*

A typical C program that contains the above structure declaration and function prototypes could look something like this:

```
void type(int);       /* function prototype area */
void file(int);
void answer_phones(int);

struct secretary      /* structure declaration */
    {
    int mary;
    int john;
    };

main()
{
    .
    .
    .
    type(..);
    .
    file(..);
    .
```

```
        answer_phones(..);
              .
}


void type(..)
{
        .
}


void file(..)
{
        .
}


void answer_phones(..)
{
        .
}
```

In our program, mary and john are grouped together in a structure called secretary. Some functions that perform various tasks are also declared and defined.

Now suppose there are other functions in the program:

```
void type(int);
void file(int);
void answer_phones(int);

void write_programs(int);
    .
    .
```

Secretaries do not write programs! We would like to somehow group together the functions that can be performed by the members of the structure secretary with its members mary and john. C++ allows us to do so by declaring the relevant functions within the structure declaration itself:

```
struct secretary
    {
    int mary;
    int john;

    void type(int);
    void file(int);
    void answer_phones(int);
    };
```

Functions declared within a structure are called *member functions*. In C, structure variables that are of the type specified in the tag name are defined as follows:

```
struct secretary a;
```

The above statement defines `a` as a structure of type `secretary`. In C++, structure variables are defined as follows:

```
secretary a;
```

The above statement defines `a` as a structure of type `secretary`. In C, structure members can be referenced using the . operator:

```
a.mary = 5000;
```

The structure member `mary` of structure `a` is set to 5000.

In C++, members are referenced the same way:

```
a.mary = 5000;
```

Member functions are also referenced using the . operator:

```
a.type(5000);
```

The above statement invokes the function `type()`, which was declared as a member function of the structure of type `secretary`, and passes it an argument of type `int`. This conforms with the function prototype declaration.

The interesting thing to note in the declaration

```
struct secretary
    {
    int mary;
    int john;

    void type(int);
    void file(int);
    void answer_phones(int);
    };
```

is that the structure members `mary` and `john` can be accessed by any function in the program. One of these members could even be passed as an argument to the function `write_programs()`! However, you are quite particular as to the functions that Mary and John are to perform. You don't want them to write_programs. (They don't want to write_programs either!) All you want them to do is file, type, and answer_phones. C++ allows you to restrict the access of the members of a structure to specific functions only. Restrictions such as these can be specified by declaring a *class* instead of a *struct*, and incorporating the key words *private* and *public* in the class declaration:

```
class secretary
    {
    private:
    int mary;
    int john;

    public:
    void type(int);
    void file(int);
    void answer_phones(int);
    };
```

The keyword `private` is followed by a colon, and then `mary` and `john` are declared. The keyword `public` is also followed by a colon, and then the function prototypes are declared. The keyword `private` specifies that members declared as such can be accessed only by the functions that are declared in their class. In C++, this is known as *data hiding*—the data for the members declared as private is hidden from all functions but those that are declared in their class. The keyword `public` specifies that members are accessible from anywhere within program scope. Functions that are public can work with any variable in the program, unless that variable has been declared as a private member of some other class.

Thus, the functions `type()`, `file()`, and `answer_phones()` only can access the private members that belong to their class: `mary` and `john`. The function `write_programs()` cannot access `mary` or `john`, since it is not a member of the class `secretary`.

```
write_programs(mary);     /* won't work */
```

The default specification for a class is `private`. The following declaration is equivalent to the one you just saw:

```
class secretary
    {
    int mary;
    int john;

    public:
    void type(int);
    void file(int);
    void answer_phones(int);
    };
```

Classes with different tag names can have member functions of the same name. Hence, it is necessary to specify the class to which a member function belongs when it is defined. This is done by prefixing the function name with the class name and the scope resolution operator: ::. This operator resolves the scope of the class to which a particular function belongs. This operator is required; since different classes may have functions with the same name, it helps identify the function by class type. For example, the function type() would be defined as follows:

```
void secretary::type(int mary)
{
        .
        <code for function type()>
        .
}
```

The definition above states that the function type() is a member function of the class secretary, it returns no value, and it expects to be passed an argument of type int.

The interesting thing to note here is that class members other than mary and john can be passed to this function as well, as long as they have not been declared as private members of some other class. This is because this function is declared in the public area of the class declaration. However, mary and john cannot be passed as arguments to any function other than type(), file(), and answer_phones().

Functions can be defined within a program after they have been declared. C++ allows function definitions within the declaration as well:

```
class secretary
    {
    int mary;
    int john;

    public:
    void type(int)   {..code for type()..}
    void file(int)   {..code for file()..}
    void answer_phones(int)   {..code for answer_phones()..}
    };
```

Notice the absence of the semicolon after each definition. Member functions larger than one or two lines are usually defined outside of the class body. The reasons for this will become clear later on in this book.

Let's stop for a moment and think about what we have learned so far. What we just described is the concept of *classes* and *information hiding* in C++. Classes offer a method for grouping together variables and functions that can be performed on these variables. They also provide a mechanism for restricting access to specific data. Restrictions such as these have many benefits. If something is not filed or typed correctly, you know right away that Mary or John is to blame. However, someone else is responsible if the programs are full of bugs! You are able to localize problems, and thereby fix them quickly and efficiently. We are now in a position to take the next step forward—we will now describe the concept of *derived classes*. Let's go back to where we left off in our analogy.

1.4   DERIVED CLASSES

The company is growing. Work is piling up on your desk. Mary and John are capable secretaries, but the workload is just too much. It seems that you need to hire another secretary. You put an ad in the paper.

As you skim through the pile of resumés on your desk, you find one that catches your eye. This woman's name is Priscilla, and she is bright indeed! Not only does she know how to file, type, and answer_phones, she also knows how to add numbers! This person performs all of the functions that we grouped under the class type secretary, plus one more: add_numbers. Priscilla gets the job—her title: accounting secretary.

Let's take a look at the original declaration of the class secretary:

```
class secretary
    {
    int mary;
    int john;

    public:
    void type(int);
    void file(int);
    void answer_phones(int);
    };
```

C++ allows us to derive the class accounting_secretary from secretary. This results in the derived class "*inheriting*" members of the class that it derives from. Here's the declaration:

```
class accounting_secretary:public secretary
    {
    int priscilla;

    public:
    void add_numbers(int);
    };
```

The class accounting_secretary is called the *derived class* and secretary is called the *base class*. The keyword public precedes the name of the base class, and indicates that the public members of secretary are also to be the public members of accounting_secretary. Thus, accounting_secretary inherits the public members of secretary. At the same time, accounting_secretary has a member function that is unique to it: add_numbers().

The interesting thing to note here is that members of the derived class do not have access to the private members of their base class. Private members mary or john cannot be passed as arguments to the function add_numbers() because they are private members of the base class. C++ does provide a *friend* mechanism to gain access to private members of a base class, but a discussion of this topic will be reserved for later chapters.

The foremost benefit to be derived from *"inheritance"* is that code for the functions that the derived class inherits from the base class does not have to be rewritten, and therefore it does not have to be retested. This allows for the reuse of existing code to create a new type. One class is used as a building block for another.

Let's take a breather and review what we have learned so far:

1. We learned how to declare classes, and the reasons for doing so.

2. We learned how to derive one class from another, and the benefits in doing so.

Now we are ready to take the next step forward, which brings us one step closer to understanding the powerful tool called *object-oriented programming*. The next step consists in understanding what C++ calls *virtual functions*.

1.5   VIRTUAL FUNCTIONS

Take another look at the declarations for secretary and accounting_secretary:

```
class secretary
    {
    int mary;
    int john;

    public:
    void type(int);
    void file(int);
    void answer_phones(int);
    };

class accounting_secretary:public secretary
    {
    int priscilla;

    public:
    void add_numbers(int);
    };
```

As mentioned previously, Priscilla knows how to type, file, answer_phones, and add_numbers. However, the way Priscilla files documents is different from Mary and John. We will modify our declaration for `accounting_secretary` accordingly:

```
class accounting_secretary:public secretary
    {
    int priscilla;

    public:
    void add_numbers(int);
    void file(int);
    };
```

Within the program, each `file()` function can be defined as follows:

```
void secretary::file(int mary)
{
        .
        <code for file() that belongs to class secretary>
        .
}

void accounting_secretary::file(int priscilla)
{
        .
        <code for file() that belongs to class accounting_secretary>
        .
}
```

Sometimes we want to execute the `file()` function defined for the base class. At other times, we want to execute the `file()` function defined for the derived class. Now, the question is, how can we invoke the correct function without explicitly having to state which one it is? The answer is through the use of a *pointer*, which is made to point to the class whose function is to be executed. Take a look at the fragment of code below, and you will understand exactly how this works:

```
// Declare class secretary:
class secretary
    {
    int mary;
    int anna;

    public:
    void type(int);
```

```
        virtual void file(int);  // Notice use of keyword virtual
        void answer_phones(int);
        };
// Declare derived class:
class accounting_secretary:public secretary
        {
        int priscilla;

        public:
        void add_numbers(int);
        void file(int);  // Notice no use of keyword virtual
        };

// Define functions with common names:
void secretary::file(int mary)
{
     ..<Code for file() in secretary>..
}

void accounting_secretary::file(int priscilla)
{
     ..<Code for file() in accounting_secretary>..
}

// Code for main():
main()
{
secretary a;            // a is class of type secretary
accounting_secretary b; // b is class of type accounting_secretary
int arg1, arg2;         // arguments that are sent to functions
secretary *ptr;  // ptr is a pointer to class of type secretary

arg1 = 5000;
ptr = &a;        // set ptr to address of base class
ptr->file(arg1); // execute  secretary::file()

arg2 = 6000;
ptr = &b;        // set ptr to address of derived class
ptr->file(arg2); // execute  accounting_secretary::file()
}
```

Let's step through this program and see what happened. We start off by declaring the base and derived classes. In the declarations, notice:

1. The use of //. In C, we can insert comments anywhere in our code using the notation /* comment */. In C++, one line comments can be inserted using the double slash: // comment. The traditional style (/*...*/) can also be used.

2. The use of the word *virtual*. This keyword indicates that the function `file()` can have different versions for different derived classes. However, the programmer does not have to worry about which function to invoke— the compiler takes care of these details at run time. Thus, the selection of the appropriate function that is to be executed is *dynamic*, as opposed to *static*.

Next, we see the definition of the functions declared. The function that has different versions must be declared as virtual in the base class. It can (but need not) be redefined for each derived class. It is necessary to define the function for the class in which it is first declared. In other words, the following function definition must exist:

```
void secretary::file(..)
{

}
```

Next, we see the `main()` function which drives all of the other functions, just like in C. Within `main()`, variables a and b of the class types `secretary` and `accounting_secretary`, and a pointer to a class of type `secretary` is declared. This is a pointer to the base class. `ptr` is set to point to a using the address of (&) operator. The statement

```
ptr->file(arg1);
```

executes the function that belongs to the class that `ptr` is pointing to. Therefore, the statement

```
ptr->file(arg1);
```

results in `secretary::file(int)` being executed. The statement

```
ptr->file(arg2);
```

results in `accounting_secretary::file(int)` being executed.

This topic will be discussed in greater detail in later chapters in this book. For now, we just want you to get a feel for what C++ is about.

1.6 OBJECT-ORIENTED PROGRAMMING

We have now covered the three main concepts that are the building blocks for *object-oriented programming:*

1. The *class mechanism*, which allows *"encapsulation"* of different data types and operations that can be performed by them. This mechanism allows data hiding and management of access privileges.

2. *Derivation of classes*, or *inheritance*, that allows the reuse of existing code, with minor variations, to create a new type.

3. *Dynamic selection* by the compiler, instead of the programmer, of the appropriate function that is to be executed, based on the object that is being pointed to.

An *"object"* is created via the class mechanism. A second object can be derived from the first. A third can be created from a combination of the two, and so on. Access privileges of one object to another can be restricted, as required. Exactly which object is executed at any particular time is the compiler's problem, not the programmer's. This is the power of an object-oriented language.

Object-oriented programs are easier to change, maintain, and reuse, at the cost of perhaps being a little more difficult to design. C++ is an object-oriented programming language, and incorporates the three features just described, plus a host of other features that make it a better C.

We will briefly touch upon the basic similarities and differences between the two languages in the next chapter. This will help you feel comfortable with the basics and confident that you will be able to assimilate the knowledge that you will gain in subsequent chapters. The remainder of the book will present brief references to C and detailed explanations of features specific to C++. Parallel examples in both languages will be presented whenever necessary. They will help you truly appreciate the power that C++ has to offer over C.

C++ Versus C—
Basic Similarities and Differences

2.1 INTRODUCTION

In this chapter, we will describe the features of C++ that are derived from C. For those of you who are experienced C programmers, you will notice little or no difference between the syntax rules that you are familiar with, and those of C++. The basic constructs are the same, since, after all, C++ is a direct descendant of C. In C++ terminology, if C is a class, then C++ is derived from it! However, we recommend that you do read this chapter; it will help you feel comfortable and confident as you proceed to the next chapter. Instances of how C++ improves on classical C concepts will also be described.

This chapter is meant to be a brief introduction to the language only; the topics touched upon here will be covered in detail in the remainder of the book. For now, we just want to get you started.

2.2 SOURCE-CODE NAMING CONVENTIONS

Different operating systems have varying rules for the names of C and C++ programs. You should consult your system manual for rules that are applicable to your system. Generally speaking, C programs are postfixed with a ".c" and C++ programs are postfixed with a ".C". For example, your first C program may have been called "test_1.c". Along the same lines, your first C++ program can be called "test_1.C".

2.3   WHICH COMPILER?

All programs in this book have been compiled and run using the Turbo C++ compiler Version 2.0, in an MS-DOS environment on an IBM Personal Computer. This compiler understands C programs if they are postfixed with a .c, and C++ programs if they are postfixed with a .cpp. We will use this same convention throughout the book. Remember, however, that C++ is a portable language. If you are working with some other operating system or compiler, simply refer to the relevant documentation for applicable instructions. More likely than not, the programs will compile and execute exactly as they would on our system. The code and output should remain the same.

2.4   CREATION AND EXECUTION OF A PROGRAM

One of the basic assumptions of this book is that you are somewhat familiar with C and know how to compile and run programs written in that language. If this assumption is true, then you must know that before a program can be run, it has to be typed using your favorite (or nonfavorite) editor and then stored in a file. Once the file has been created, it is compiled, linked and run, as required by the particular implementation that is being used. Some implementations allow the above steps to be performed by typing commands at the operating-system command-line prompt. Other systems allow the whole process to be implemented via menus and dialogue boxes. Our system is completely menu-driven, and allows the user to edit, compile, and run programs using dialogue boxes within an integrated environment. For all others, simply "compile" and "run" as instructed by your system documentation.

2.5   COMPILE PROCESS FOR THE TURBO C++ MENU-DRIVEN SYSTEM

We will step through the edit, compile, and run process within the Integrated Development Environment that is provided by Borland's Turbo C++ Version 2.0 compiler. You may select options by positioning and clicking the mouse, if you have one. Or you may simply move the arrow keys to highlight the relevant option and press Return. We will adopt the latter method. Options may also be selected via their corresponding hot keys.

Assuming you have installed the Turbo C++ compiler correctly, type the following at the DOS system prompt:

```
C:> cd \tc
```

This will place you into the proper subdirectory. Continue as follows:

```
C:> tc
```

This will place you into the *Integrated Development Environment* (IDE), which contains windows, menus, dialogue boxes, and a status line at the bottom of the screen. Refer to Fig. 2.1 for a picture of this screen.

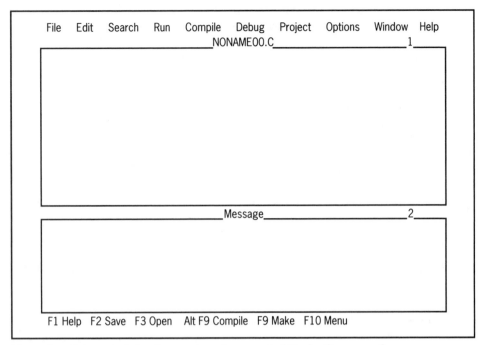

Figure 2.1   Integrated development environment of Turbo C++ compiler.

Press the F10 key. This will place you in the menu bar. Move the arrow key to File and press the Return key. This will open the File dialogue box. Refer to Fig. 2.2 for a picture of the screen.

Now move the arrow key to New, and press the Return key. A blank window will open up, and the cursor will be placed inside this window. Refer to Fig. 2.3. You are now ready to type in the source code.

Once done typing, press F10 to get back into the menu bar, select File, and then Save. The Save Editor File window will appear. Refer to Fig. 2.4 now.

Either accept the default name (noname001.c), or type in the name of your choice. Make sure that C programs are postfixed with a .c, and C++ programs are postfixed with a .cpp. Press Return. Now press the F10 key again and select Run. The Run dialogue box will appear. Refer to Fig. 2.5.

Select Run (or press its corresponding hot key Ctrl-F9). Doing so will automatically compile, link, and run your program. If there are any errors, then you will be informed as such in the Message Window portion of the screen. Refer to Fig. 2.6 for a sample error message.

Press the Enter key, and you will be placed back in the window that contains the source code. Modify the file, and press the F10 key to get back into the menu bar. Select Run at the menu bar, and then Run again within the dialogue box. The program will be recompiled. Assuming that there are no errors this time, the program will be automatically linked, and then executed.

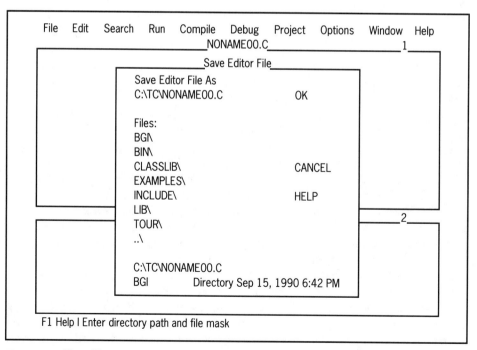

| IFilel | Edit | Search | Run | Compile | Debug | Project | Options | Window | Help |

_____NONAME00.C_____1_____

Open...   F3
New
Save

Print
Get info...
DOS shell
Quit   Alt X

_____Message_____2_____

F1 Help I Locate and open a file

Figure 2.2 File dialogue box.

| File | Edit | Search | Run | Compile | Debug | Project | Options | Window | Help |

_____NONAME00.C_____1_____

_____Save Editor File_____

Save Editor File As
C:\TC\NONAME00.C   OK

Files:
BGI\
BIN\
CLASSLIB\   CANCEL
EXAMPLES\
INCLUDE\   HELP
LIB\   2_____
TOUR\
..\

C:\TC\NONAME00.C
BGI   Directory Sep 15, 1990 6:42 PM

F1 Help I Enter directory path and file mask

Figure 2.3 New file set up.

18

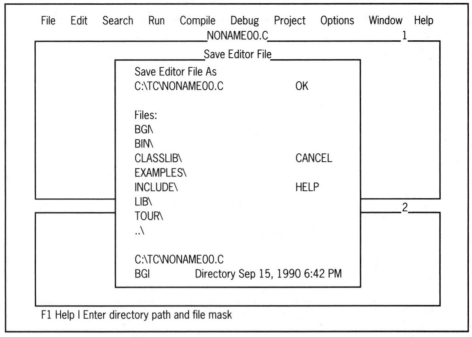

Figure 2.4 Save editor file.

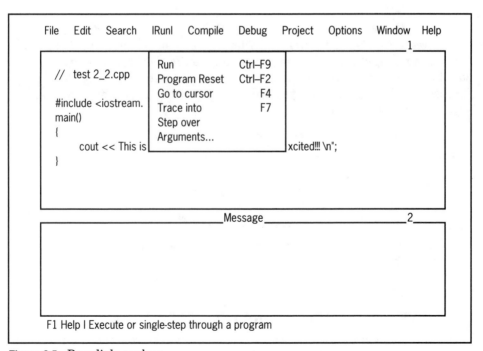

Figure 2.5 Run dialogue box.

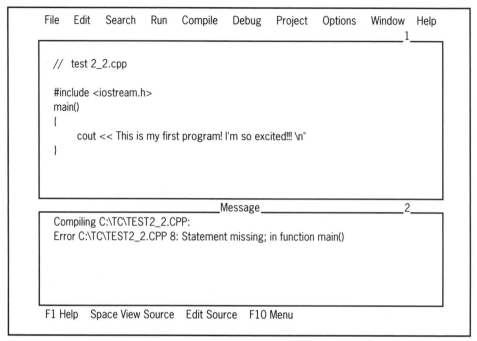

Figure 2.6 Sample error message.

In order to see the output, press the F10 key, select Window, and then User Screen (Alt F5). Refer to Fig. 2.7 for a picture of this dialogue box.

Selecting User Screen will place you outside the IDE, and display the output of the program. Refer to Fig. 2.8 for sample output of the program typed.

Press the Return key, and you will be back in the IDE. The following hot keys provide useful shortcuts:

Hot Key	Result
Alt F9	Compile
Ctrl F9	Run
F2	Save
Alt F5	Show user screen
Alt F3	Close current window
F6	Go to next window

The menu bar, dialogue boxes, windowing schemes, hot keys, etc. could vary for your compiler, but the basic procedure of selecting options and executing them will not be that much different from what you have just read.

2.6 COMPILE PROCESS FOR NON-MENU-DRIVEN SYSTEMS

Most C++ compilers typically use the command CC to compile the program. Let's compile a program that we will call source.cpp:

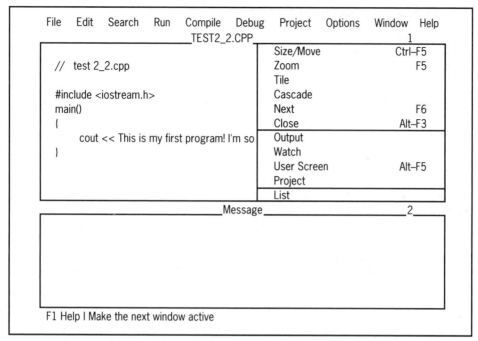

Figure 2.7 Window dialogue box.

```
C:> CC source.cpp
```

We can run this program simply by typing its name, without its prefix:

```
C:> source
```

In a UNIX environment, the name of the executable file will be a.out. Hence, you will type the following at the operating system prompt:

```
$ a.out
```

2.7   C++ AND C—SIMILARITIES

Now that we've got the generalities out of the way, let's get on with what this chapter is all about. First, features of C++ that are similar to C will be discussed.

```
C:\TC> tc
This is my first program! I'm so excited!!!
```

Figure 2.8 Sample output.

2.7.1   Fundamental data types

C++ contains the same fundamental data types as C:

```
char  short  int  long  float  double
```

The adjective *const* can be applied to any of the above data types to indicate that the value of the variable of this type cannot be changed, once it has been initialized:

```
const int age = 35;
```

You know how it is, some people just don't age beyond 35! In C++, a constant must be initialized when it is declared.

2.7.2   Operators

C++ contains the same arithmetic operators as C:

```
+ (plus)    - (minus)    * (multiply)   / (divide)
```

The comparison operators are carried over from C to C++:

```
== (equal to)    != (not equal to)  > (greater than)  < (less than)
<= (less than or equal to)    >= (greater than or equal to)
```

And so are the bitwise operators:

```
~ (complement)   & (and)   ^ (exclusive or)   | (inclusive or)
<< (logical left shift)    >> (logical right shift)
```

C++ adds quite a few operators on its own. You have already encountered three of these in Chap. 1:

```
:: (scope resolution)   << (put to)    >> (get from)
```

You will notice that the "put to" and "get from" operators are the same as the logical left shift and logical right shift operators. This is an example of "operator overloading" in C++. What this means is that an operator can be "overloaded" to mean different things at different times. We will touch upon this topic later on in this chapter.

The operators *new* and *delete* will be introduced later in the chapter.

2.7.3   Expressions

C++ forms expressions by combining one or more operators just like C. Following are valid expressions in C and C++:

```
a = a + b;
if (a < b)
     a = b;

if (a == b)
     a = "temp";
```

2.7.4 Control structures

C++ supports the same control structures as C. We can summarize these in pseudocode:

```
* if (this statement is true)
     {
     do this;
     and this;
     }
   else
     {
     do this;
     and this:
     }

* while (this condition is true)
     {
     do this;
     and this;
     }


* do
     {
     this;
     and this;
     }
     while (this condition is true);

* for (initialize counter; perform conditional test;
                                   reevaluate counter)
     {
     do this;
     and this;
     }

* switch (on integer expression)
     {
```

```
       case constant1:
            do this;
       case constant2:
            do this;
       default:
            do this;
       }
```

2.8   C++ AND C—DIFFERENCES

Now we will briefly describe those features of C++ that are not found in C. You were introduced to several of these features in Chap. 1.

2.8.1   Output

When you first started out to learn C, one of the first complete programs that you ever wrote probably looked something like this:

```
main()
{
     printf ("This is my first program! I'm so excited!!!\n");
}
```

Assuming that this nice little program was called test2_1.c, and using an IBM or IBM-compatible computer, it was compiled, linked, and executed as follows:

```
C:> cl test2_1.c
$ test2_1
 This is my first program! I'm so excited!!!
```

The equivalent of this program in C++, (we'll call it test2_2.cpp), is as follows (We are using the standard MS/DOS command "type" to display the file):

```
C:> type test2_2.cpp

#include <iostream.h>
main()
{
     cout << "This is my first program! I'm so excited!!!\n";
}
```

Compiling and running the code gives the following output:

```
This is my first program! I'm so excited!!!
```

The include file <iostream.h> contains the standard input and output facilities for C++. The name of this header file can vary with different compilers.

The operator "<<" (put to) writes the argument that follows it to the argument that precedes it. "cout" is defined as the standard output stream in <iostream.h>. Thus, the phrase

```
This is my first program! I'm so excited!!!
```

outputs to the terminal.

2.8.2 Input

C provides many functions that allow input of data, for example, getchar(), getc(), and gets(). C++ allows input of data through the input stream *cin*. Here's a program that demonstrates its use:

```
C:> type test2_3.cpp

#include <iostream.h>
main()
{
    int num;
    cout << "Please enter number: ";
    cin >> num;
    cout << "The number you entered was " << num  << "\n";
}
```

Compiling and running this program gives this output:

```
Please enter number: 7
The number you entered was 7
```

All variables that will be used in the program must be declared, just like in C. The variable num is declared of type int. We are prompted to enter a value via the statement

```
cout << "Please enter number: ";
```

Notice that the newline character "\n" is missing.

The number entered is read from the standard input stream cin, using the ">>" (get from) operator and output, as usual, via cout. Notice the use of three output operators to cout in the final statement.

2.8.3 Functions

Functions are invoked from anywhere in the program, similar to C. The function prototype which specifies the return value and type of arguments must be declared before main().

C++ adds the concept of function overloading. This allows functions that perform similar tasks, but work with different data types of objects, to have the same name. Take a look at this program:

```
C:> type  test2_4.cpp

void print(int);
void print(float);

#include <iostream.h>

main()
{
      int num = 5;            // num is int
      print(num);

      float num2 = 5.0;    // num2 is float
      print(num2);
}
void print(int num)
{
      cout << " Num is: " << num << "\n";

}
void print(float num2)
{
      cout << " Num is: " << num2 << "\n";
}
```

The output for this program looks as follows:

```
Num is 5
Num is 5
```

The compiler matches the argument type in the program to the function prototypes, and chooses the right function to call, based upon the data types involved.

C++ has the capability of overloading operators as well. For example, the operator "+" can be overloaded to mean "*". In the `<iostream.h>` file, the logical left shift operator << has been overloaded to mean "put to," and the logical right shift operator >> has been overloaded to mean "get from."

2.8.4   Pointer declaration and indirection

Pointers are declared and referenced similar to C:

```
int *ptr;      // ptr is pointer to int
ptr = &var;    // ptr now contains the address of the variable var
*ptr = 50;     // set var to 50, via ptr, i.e. through indirection
```

C++ adds the concept of a constant pointer:

```
char *const ptr2;   //ptr2 is a constant pointer to char
```

The declaration above declares ptr2 as a constant pointer to a char data type. The programmer cannot modify the address that ptr2 is initialized to:

```
ptr2 = &var2;  // ptr2 contains address of var2
ptr2 = &var3;  // won't work!!  ERROR
```

C++ also adds the concept of a pointer to a constant:

```
char const *ptr3;   //ptr3 is a pointer to a constant

ptr3 = &var3;  // ptr3 contains address of var3
ptr3 = &var4;  // ptr3 now contains address of var4 - that's ok too
var5 = 50;     // var5 initialized to 50;
*ptr3 = 60;    // trying to set var5 to 60 - won't work!!  ERROR
```

The last statement will generate an error because ptr3 is declared as a pointer to a constant. It can point to any variable of the correct data type, but the contents of what it is pointing to cannot be changed through indirection; they remain constant.

2.8.5   Structures and unions

C++ allows the declaration of structures similar to that in C. However, it adds the capability of declaring member functions as well. The analogy presented in Chap. 1 described this feature in detail.

2.8.6   Classes and derived classes

Classes and derived classes have also been discussed in Chap. 1.

2.8.7   References

C++ allows the use of a *reference,* which is simply another name of the variable that is being initialized. Following is a reference declaration:

```
int richard = 666;
int& rich = richard; // Notice use of "&", it follows variable type
```

The declaration above will result in `rich` being an alternative name for `richard`. If we add 2 to `rich`:

```
rich += 2:      // richard equals 668
```

we have, in effect, added 2 to `richard`. A reference must be initialized at the time that it is declared.

2.8.8   Constructors, destructors, new, and delete

A *constructor* is a member function in a declared class, and it dynamically initializes a variable of its class. It is distinguished from other member functions in that it has the same name as its class.

A *destructor* deallocates memory for a class member. A destructor also has the same name as its class, except that it is preceded by a tilde (~). Constructors and destructors are discussed in detail in later chapters.

2.9   REVIEW

In this chapter, we briefly reviewed some of the concepts introduced in Chap. 1, which described features such as *data encapsulation, inheritance,* and *dynamic run-time binding* of functions. These combined features make C++ more structured, expandable, and easier to maintain than non-object-oriented languages.

We also described non-menu- and menu-driven compilation processes for C++ programs. By now you should have a feel for the basic building blocks of C++.

Chapter

3

C++ Standards for Tokens and Control Structures

3.1 INTRODUCTION

In this chapter, we will describe some of the basic building blocks of C++ programs, i.e., the "tokens" that make up a program. Control structures, which utilize tokens to implement program logic, will be described next. Once again, this chapter will prove to be very easy reading for experienced C programmers, and a refresher for beginners.

3.2 TOKENS

A program comprises word-like units and whitespace—it is the whitespace that separates the word-like units. The word-like units are known as *tokens*. The combination of tokens and whitespace makes up a program, and allows the compiler to parse or break it up before it proceeds to the next step of the compilation process. A program is made up of one or more of the following components:

identifiers

constants

string-literals

operators

Tokens are separated by whitespace. Whitespace comprises blanks, tabs, newline characters, and comments. As we discuss each type, you will find that they are inherently similar to what you have encountered in C.

3.2.1 Keywords

The following words cannot be used as identifiers; they are reserved for C and C++:

auto	continue	enum	if	short	typedef
break	default	extern	int	sizeof	union
case	do	float	long	static	unsigned
char	double	for	register	struct	void
const	else	goto	return	switch	while

The following keywords have been added by C++:

class	friend	new	overload	protected	this
delete	inline	operator	private	public	virtual

Some compilers support additional keywords.

asm	template
catch	volatile

Now that you know the words that you cannot use as identifiers in your programs, let's discuss the rules for the names that you can create.

3.2.2 Identifiers

Identifiers are the names that you choose to give to variables, constants, functions, classes, and the like. The first character must be a letter, or an underscore. The remainder of the name may contain digits. Letters may be upper- or lower-case. The allowable length of the identifier name varies with different implementations. Our system allows up to 32 characters of significance; yours may not. Please refer to your compiler documentation for rules specific to your implementation.

3.2.2.1 Case sensitivity

As in C, C++ identifiers are case-sensitive. A variable declared as follows:

```
int variable;
```

is not the same as this one:

```
int Variable;
```

or this one:

```
int VARIABLE;
```

Here's a small program that illustrates what we have discussed so far:

```
C:> type test3_1.cpp

#include <iostream.h>     // necessary for use of cout

main()
{
    int  float;    // ERROR - invalid use of keyword as name
    int  sum;      // valid identifier name
    int  Sum;      // valid identifier name

    float = 2;
    Sum = 0;
    sum = 5;

    Sum = sum + float;

    cout << "Sum is  " << Sum << "\n";
}
```

Compiling this program gives the following message:

```
Error:    Expression syntax in function main()
```

This is because "float" is a keyword, and it cannot be used as the name of an identifier. This problem can be fixed by changing float to var1:

```
#include <iostream.h>     // necessary for use of cout

main()
{
    int var1;      // valid identifier name
    int sum;       // valid identifier name
    int Sum;       // valid identifier name

    var1 = 2;
    Sum  = 0;
    sum  = 5;

    Sum = sum + var1;

    cout << "Sum is " << Sum << "\n"
}
```

Compiling and executing the above code results in the correct output:

```
Sum is 7
```

3.2.3   Data types

Data types can be constant or variable. C++ contains the same data types as C:

integer

character

floating point

3.2.3.1   Integer data

An integer does not have a fractional part. Integer constants can be represented as decimal values, octal (by prefixing the number with a 0), or hexadecimal (number is prefixed with a 0x or 0X). Integer constants can be short, which is the default, or long, if they are suffixed with an *l* or an *L*. They can also be signed, which is the default, or unsigned, by suffixing with a *u* or a *U*. The unsigned and long prefixes can be used together to represent an unsigned long constant. The following declarations are valid:

```
int   i = 10;        // short integer, decimal
int   j = 10l;       // long integer constant
int   k = 10ul;      // unsigned long integer constant
```

3.2.3.2   Character data

A character is enclosed in single quotes:

```
char yes = 'y';      // character constant yes initialized to y
```

Character constants can comprise more than one character enclosed within the single quotes. These are the escape sequences, or combinations of characters that have special significance for the compiler. The following escape sequences are recognized by our compiler:

Escape Sequence	Action Taken by the Compiler
\a	Rings bell
\b	Backspace
\f	Formfeed
\n	Newline character (linefeed)
\r	Carriage return
\t	Tab (horizontal)
\v	Tab (vertical)
\\	Backslash

\'	Single quote
\"	Double quote
\?	Question mark
\nnn	Octal bit pattern, where nnn is an octal number
\xnn	Hexadecimal bit pattern, where xnn is a hexadecimal number

These escape sequences should be familiar to you; the new ANSI C standard provides the same sequences.

3.2.3.3   Floating point

Floating point data comprises an integer part, a decimal fraction, and optional suffixes. This type of data is declared as follows:

```
float half = 0.5;
```

Floating point data can also contain an exponential value, and is declared as follows:

```
float big_number = 465.012e3
```

A floating point constant is suffixed with an *f* or an *F:*

```
float constant_half = 0.5f;
```

A double-data type is similar to float, except that twice as much storage space is reserved for variables and constants of this type. A floating point constant is suffixed with an *f* or an *F:*

```
float constant_half = 0.5f;    // will always be 0.5
```

Constants such as these can also be suffixed with an *l* or an *L* to indicate that they are type long.

3.2.3.4   Const data types

The qualifier const can precede the declaration of any data type to indicate that the value of the variable cannot be changed. Thus const can be used as an alternative way to specify a constant. Following is a const declaration:

```
const ten 10;  // ten will always equal the value 10
```

3.2.3.5   Storage requirements

The compiler assigns storage to different data types based on their declaration. Table 3.1 summarizes storage requirements and permissible values for the data types discussed. Remember that these storage specifications are for our computer which uses 16 bits to store a word. If you are working on an

TABLE 3.1   Data Types and Storage Requirements

Data type	Declaration in C++	Storage Requirements	Permissible Values
Integers	int	16 bits	-32,768 to +32,768
Integers, short	short int	16 bits	-32,768 to +32,768
Integers, long	long int	32 bits	-2,147,483,648 to +2,147,483,647
Integers, unsigned	unsigned int	16 bits	0 to 65,535
Integer constants, long	Add suffix *l* or *L*	32 bits	-2,147,483,648 to +2,147,483,647
Integer constants, unsigned	Add suffix *u* or *U*	16 bits	0 to 65,535
Character	char	8 bits	ASCII code
Float	float	32 bits	3.4x10-38 to 3.4x10+38
Double	double	64 bits	1.7x10-308 to 1.7x10+308
Double, long	Add suffix *l* or *L*	80 bits	3.4x10-4932 to 1.1x10+4932

IBM or IBM-compatible PC, then the storage specifications will probably be the same.

3.2.3.6   String literals

A *string literal* is a collection of characters enclosed within double quotes. A string literal is terminated by the null character, '\0', just like in C. Following is an example:

```
char string[16] = "This is a string";   // string literal
```

Escape sequences can be freely interspersed between string literals. Take a look at this short program:

```
C:> type test3_2.cpp

#include <iostream.h>     // necessary to use cout

main()
{

char string[36] = "This is line 1 \n and this is line 2";

cout << string;

}
```

Compiling and running this program results in the following output:

```
This is line 1
 and this is line 2
```

Notice the space before the "and" on the second line of output. We inserted a space after the newline character \n so that you could differentiate it from the remainder of the string. There would be no space on the second line of output if it had been initialized as follows:

```
char string[36] = "This is line 1 \nand this is line 2";
```

3.2.4   Operators

Operators are symbols which indicate the computation that is to be performed on two or more variables or constants within an expression.

In C++, we find the same operators as C, plus a few more of its own. Take a look at the following program, which illustrates the use of the ones that are used more frequently:

```
C:> type test3_3.cpp

#include <iostream.h>         // necessary for cout

main()                        // function call
{
    int i, j;                 // comma operator
    int   i = j = 0;          // assignment operator
    int   k[5] = {1, 2, 3, 4, 5};  // array subscript
                              // assignment
                              // comma

    struct person
        {
        int age;
        char sex;
        } ;

    struct person anna;       // declare structure anna of
                              // type person
    struct person *ptr;       // indirection - pointer to stucture
                              // of type person

    for (j=0; j <= 5; j++)    // less than or equal to operator
                              // increment operator
    {
        k[j] = 0;             // array subscript
                              // assignment
    }
```

```
      anna.age  = 25;                   // dot operator
      anna.sex = 'F';                   // dot operator
      cout << "Age is " << anna.age << "\n";
      cout << "Sex is " << anna.sex << "\n";

      ptr = &anna;         // address of operator
                           // set pointer to address of structure
                           // anna

      ptr -> age = 30;                    // arrow operator
      cout << "Using Indirection now \n";
      cout << "Age is " << ptr->age << "\n";
      cout << "Sex is " << ptr->sex << "\n";

      anna.age += 25;      // add 25 to original value of anna.age

      cout << "Age is " << anna.age << "\n");
}
```

Compiling and running this program results in the following output:

```
Age is 25
Sex is F
Using Indirection now
Age is 30
Sex is F
Age is 55
```

In this program several of the most frequently used operators are used to perform different functions. You should be familiar with all of them. Now take a look at the complete list of operators that have been carried forward from C to C++:

Operator	Function
()	Function call
[]	Array subscript
.	Dot—Accesses member of structure or union
->	Arrow—Points to member of structure or union
!	Logical NOT condition
~	One's complement
–	Unary minus
++	Increments
––	Decrements
&	Gets the address of
*	Performs indirection
(type)	Type casts

sizeof	Gets size of variable or constant specified
*	Multiplies
/	Divides
%	Modulus—Gets the remainder
+	Adds
–	Subtracts
<<	Performs left shift at the bit level
>>	Performs right shift at the bit level
<	Evaluates less than condition
>	Evaluates greater than condition
<=	Evaluates less than or equal to condition
>=	Evaluates greater than or equal to condition
==	Evaluates equal to condition
!=	Evaluates not equal to condition
&	Performs Bitwise AND
^	Performs Bitwise XOR
|	Performs Bitwise OR
&&	Performs Logical AND
||	Performs Logical OR
?:	Conditional—Evaluates two expressions
=	Assigns value
,	Separates variables, constants, and expressions inside functions, control structures, etc.

An expression such as this:

```
a = a + b;
```

can be written as follows:

```
a += b;
```

Hence, the following set of operators can be derived as well:

*=	expression 1 = expression 1 * expression 2
/=	expression 1 = expression 1 / expression 2
%=	expression 1 = expression 1 % expression 2
-=	expression 1 = expression 1 - expression 2
<<=	expression 1 = expression 1 << expression 2
>>=	expression 1 = expression 1 >> expression 2
&=	expression 1 = expression 1 & expression 2
^=	expression 1 = expression 1 ^ expression 2
|=	expression 1 = expression 1 | expression 2

These operators are used by the preprocessor:

#	define a variable or constant, or include a file
##	concatenates two strings together

C++ adds the following to the above list:

::	Resolves scope
.*	Dereferences pointer to a class member
->*	Dereferences pointer to a class member
new	Initializes, assigns storage dynamically
delete	Deallocates storage assigned by new

Table 3.2 displays the associativity and precedence of C++ operators. *Precedence* refers to the order in which operators are evaluated. *Associativity* refers to the order in which operators that have the same precedence are evaluated.

The order of the operators, from top to bottom, indicates the precedence. The associativity is indicated in the right-hand column.

The operators introduced by C++ will be discussed in detail as they are encountered in subsequent chapters. For now, we just want you to feel comfortable that the majority of operators in C++ are the same as in C.

3.2.4.1   Operator overloading

Now that you know what operators you can work with in C++, let's briefly touch upon an interesting feature that is not available in C: *operator overloading*. (This feature will be discussed in detail in later chapters.)

Overloading allows you to redefine the meaning of operators. You have seen instances of operator overloading in the use of cout and cin. cout uses

TABLE 3.2   Associativity and Precedence of C++ Operators

Operators	Associativity
() [] -> :: .	Left to right
! ~ − ++ −− & *	Right to left
sizeof new delete .* ->* / %	Left to right
+ −	Left to right
<< >>	Left to right
< <= > >=	Left to right
== !=	Left to right
&	Left to right
^	Left to right
|	Left to right
&&	Left to right
||	Left to right
? conditional operator	Right to left
= += /= %= += -=	Right to left
&= ^= |= ,	Left to right

the left shift operator << to output a stream of data, while cin uses the right shift operator >> to accept input.

What is important to note at this point in time is that almost all of the operators described can be overloaded. (We will discuss the few exceptions in later chapters.) However, their precedence and associativity cannot be changed.

3.3   CONTROL STRUCTURES

C++ has the same control structures as C. These control structures utilize different combinations of tokens to perform the logic or devise the flow of control within a program. These structures are as follows:

The if and if-else statement

The while statement

The do-while statement

The for statement

The switch case construct

Each type will be briefly described via pseudocode. Their use will be illustrated in small C++ programs:

3.3.1   The if statement

The syntax of the if statement is as follows:

```
if (expression is true)
    {
    do this;
    and this;
    }
```

The else statement can be appended to the if:

```
if (expression is true)
    {
    do this;
    and this;
    }
else
    {
    do this;
    and this;
    }
```

The following program illustrates its use:

```
C:> type test3_4.cpp

#include <iostream.h>      // necessary for cout
main()
{
     int income;
     char meal_1[] = "Go out - Eat steak";
     char meal_2[]  = "Stay home - Eat spaghetti";

     income = 55;

     if (income > 50)
         {
         cout << meal_1 << "\n";
         }
     else
         {
         cout << meal_2 << "\n";
         }
}
```

Compiling and executing the program results in the following output:

```
Go out - Eat steak
```

3.3.2   The while statement

The syntax of the `while()` statement is as follows:

```
while (expression is true)
     {
     do this;
     and this;
     }
```

The following program illustrates its use:

```
C:> type test3_5.cpp

#include <iostream.h>            // necessary for cout

main()
{
     int income;
```

```
char meal_1[] = "Go out - Eat steak";
char meal_2[] = "Stay home - Eat spaghetti";

income = 150;

while (income > 50)
    {
    cout << meal_1 << "\n";
    income -= 45;
    }
cout << "Out of money! \n" << meal_2 << "\n";
cout << "I don't think I can stand another steak anyway!! \n"

}
```

Compiling and running the above program gives us the following output:

```
Go out - Eat steak
Go out - Eat steak
Go out - Eat steak
Out of money!
Stay home - Eat spaghetti
I don't think I can stand another steak anyway!!
```

3.3.3   The do-while statement

The syntax of the do-while statment is as follows:

```
do
    {
    this;
    and this;
    }
    while (expression is true);
```

The following program illustrates its use:

```
C:> type test3_6.cpp

#include <iostream.h>           // necessary for cout

main()
{
    int income, i;
    char have_fun_type[2][10] =
        {{" See play"},
         {" See movie"}};
```

```
        char out_of_choices[] = "Stay home - watch TV";

        i = 0;
        income = 115;
        do
            {
            cout << "Income is " << income
                    << have_fun_type[i] << "\n";
            i++;
            income -= 45;
            }
            while (income > 50);      // end do-while() construct

        cout << "Income is " << income << " "
                << out_of_choices << "\n";
    }
```

Compiling and running this program results in the following output:

```
Income is 115 See play
Income is 70 See movie
Income is 25 Stay home - watch TV
```

3.3.4   The for statement

The syntax of a `for` statement is as follows:

```
for (initialize variable; perform conditional test;
            reevaluate variable)
    {
    do this;
    and this;
    }
```

The following program illustrates its use:

```
C:> type test3_7.cpp

#include <iostream.h>            // necessary for cout

main()
{
    int income;
    char compulsion[] = "Spend money";

    for (income = 200; income > 20; income -= 45)
        {
```

```
        cout << "Income is " << income << " "
            << compulsion << "\n";
        }

    cout << "Income is " << income << "."
        << " Can't spend anymore. Have to wait till pay-day. \n";
}
```

Compiling and running the above program gives the following output:

```
Income is 200 Spend money
Income is 155 Spend money
Income is 110 Spend money
Income is 20. Can't spend anymore. Have to wait till pay-day.
```

3.3.5   The switch-case construct

The syntax of a switch-case construct is as follows:

```
switch(on integer expression)
    {
    case 1:
        {
        do this;
        and this;
        }
    case 2:
        {
        do this;
        and this;
        }
    default:
        {
        do this;
        and this;
        }
    }
```

The following program illustrates its use:

```
C:> type test3_8.cpp

#include <iostream.h>          // necessary for cout

main()
{
    int income;
```

```
    income = 200;

    while (income > 0)
    {                       // start while()
        switch(income)
        {                   // begin switch case construct
            case 200:
            {
            cout << "Income is " <<  income << "."
                << "Spend with abandon \n";
            income -= 100;
            break;
            }
            case 100:
            {
            cout << "Income is " << income << "."
                << "Spend with less abandon \n";
            income -= 75;
            break;
            }
            case 25:
            {
            cout << "Income is " << income << "."
                << "Spend only on lunch. \n";
            income -= 10;
            break;
            }
            default:
            {
            cout << "Income is << " << income << "\n"
                << "Stay home";
            }
        }   // end switch
    }   // end while()
}   // end main()
```

Compiling and running test5_4.cpp **gives the following output:**

```
Income is 200 Spend with abandon
Income is 100 Spend with less abandon
Income is 25 Spend only on lunch
Income is 15 Stay home
Income is 15 Stay home
```

We were obliged to hit the Control Break key to stop program execution. This is because once income falls below 25, it is neither incremented or decremented, and hence the default condition is executed forever, or at least until the break key is hit.

3.4 REVIEW

In this chapter, the fundamental building blocks required to write a C++ program were described. In particular, we

- Reviewed the keywords that have been carried forward from C to C++.

- Found a few new ones that have been added by C++.

- Described int, char, float, double and string data types. The rules for these data types are the same as in C.

- Reviewed the operators that have been carried forward from C to C++.

- Discovered a few new ones that have been added by C++.

- Finally, we put it all together through control structures. We realized that all C control structures have also been carried forward from C to C++.

So far, so good! C++ does not seem to be deviating too much from the C language that you are familiar with! But that's the whole point of Part 1 of this book. You need to feel comfortable with the basics of C++ before we get you into the real stuff! Your transition will be that much easier if the introduction serves to build a strong foundation.

Storage Classes and Scope in C++

4.1 INTRODUCTION

In the last chapter, we learned the different data types that exist in C++. In this chapter, the storage classes of these types will be discussed. A *storage class* implies the location in which the variable will be stored, and its duration or lifetime. An *object* is a location in memory that fixed or variable values can be stored in. Tied closely to storage class is *scope*. Scope is that part of a program in which the variable is active, or can be accessed.

A variable's storage class can be implied explicitly, by stating it as such, or implicitly—that is, it defaults to the storage class implied by its context. The following storage classes have been carried forward from C to C++:

automatic

static

external

register

You should be familiar with each type, as they exist in C programs. Their use will be illustrated in C++ programs.

4.2 AUTOMATIC DECLARATIONS

The keyword *auto* is used to declare automatic variables. Auto variables are implied by default, if the keyword auto does not precede their declaration. Take a look at the following sample declarations:

```
auto int  a;     // automatic variable
char b;          // automatic variable by default
```

Just like in C, the scope of an automatic variable is only for the block, or any blocks within that block, in which it appears. Take a look at the following example:

```
C:> type test4_1.cpp

#include <iostream.h>     // necessary for cout

main()
{
     int  i;              // auto variable by default
     int  j;              // auto variable by default

     cout << " i in outer block is " << i << "\n";
     cout << " j in outer block is " << j << "\n";
     cout << " k in outer block is " << k << "\n";

     {    //   inner block
          int  k;          // auto variable by default
          cout << " i in inner block is " << i << "\n";
          cout << " j in inner block is " << j << "\n";
          cout << " k in inner block is " << k << "\n";
     }

     //   outer block again
     cout << " i back in outer block is " << i << "\n";
     cout << " j back in outer block is " << j << "\n";
     cout << " k back in outer block is " << k << "\n";

}    // end main()

C:>
```

Compiling this program results in the following error messages:

```
Error:    Undefined symbol 'k' in function main()
Error:    Undefined symbol 'k' in function main()
```

This is because the variable k is auto by default. It is declared inside the inner block, and it exists, or can be accessed only within this block. The compiler does not know the value of k in the outer block, and hence generates error messages. The error can be fixed simply by declaring k in the outer block and deleting its declaration in the outer block. Upon doing so, recompiling and executing the program gives the following output:

```
i in outer block is 8886
j in outer block is 18
k in outer block is 0
i in inner block is 8886
j in inner block is 18
k in inner block is 0
i back in outer block is 8886
j back in outer block is 18
k back in outer block is 0
```

So where did the values 8886, 18, and 0 magically appear in the variables i, j, and k? Well, recall from your knowledge of C that if automatic variables are not initialized within their scope, they contain random or garbage values. The same rule holds true in C++. If the original declarations of i, j, and k are modified as follows:

```
        .
        .
int i = 1;
int j = 2;
int k = 3;
        .
        .
```

then the output changes as follows:

```
i in outer block is 1
j in outer block is 2
k in outer block is 3
i in inner block is 1
j in inner block is 2
k in inner block is 3
i back in outer block is 1
j back in outer block is 2
k back in outer block is 3
```

4.3   STATIC DECLARATIONS

Static variables are declared as such by preceding their declaration with the keyword *static*. Like automatic variables, these variables are also local to the function, block, or subsumed blocks within which they exist. However, there is one important difference. Their values persist, or "stick," even when the variables go out of scope. When the program comes back to the same function, processing proceeds with the last value that was stored in them. Static variables, in the absence of initializers, are automatically initialized to 0 or null. Take a look at the following program:

```
C:>  type test4_2.cpp

#include <iostream.h>      // necessary for cout

void sum(void);            // function prototype

main()
{
     static int j;  // static declaration

     sum();                // sum() increments j
     cout << "Inside main(), j is  " << j << "\n";
     sum();
     cout << "Inside main(), j is  " << j << "\n";

}

void sum(void)
{
     static int     j    // static declaration

     j = j+1;
     cout << "Inside sum() j is %d " << j <<  "\n";
}
```

Compiling and running the program results in the following output:

```
Inside sum() j is 1
Inside main() j is 0
Inside sum() j is 2
Inside main() j is 0
```

j is declared as a static variable inside the functions main() and sum(). Inside sum(), 1 is added to j, and thus it is set to 1. Then, processing goes back to main(), and we see that the value of j is 0. This is because the variable j in main() is out of scope in the function sum(). In the absence of explicit initializers, statics are set to 0. Hence the value 0 is output for the value of j in main(). Next, control is returned to sum(), and here the old value of 1 that was placed in j has not been lost (because it is static), and now j is set to 2. Inside main(), the value of j is still 0.

In C++, static members of classes have special rules associated with them. These will be discussed in detail when we discuss classes.

4.4   EXTERNAL DECLARATIONS

External variables differ from the prior two just described in that their scope is global instead of local. External variables in C++ behave similarly to their C counterparts. They can exist outside or inside functions, and are available to all functions that are within the same file (this is known as *file scope*). The value of external variables persists, just as static types. In the absence of explicit initializers, externals are also set to 0 or null. Take a look at the following program:

```
C:> type test4_3.cpp

#include <iostream.h>        // necessary for cout

int  i;                      // global extern declaration

void function_1(void);       // function prototype area
void function_2(void);

main()
{
    cout << " i inside main() is " << i << "\n";
    function_1();
}

void function_1(void)
{
    i = i + 1;
    cout << " i inside function_1() is " << i << "\n";
    function_2();
}

void function_2(void)
{
    i = i + 1;
    cout << " i inside function_2() is " << i << "\n";
}

C:>
```

Compiling and running this program results in the following output:

```
i inside main() is 0
i inside function_1() is 1
i inside function_2() is 2
```

i outputs as 0 in main(), since it was not explicitly initialized. Inside function_1(), it outputs as 1. There is no need for a declaration of i inside function_1(), since it has been declared globally outside of main(). Inside function_2(), it outputs as 2, since the value set in function_1() persists.

As in C, externals can be declared as extern inside the function in which they are used. The compiler would accept the following change to the original program:

```
        .
        .
void function_1(void)
{
    extern int i;
        .
        .
}

void function_2()
{
    extern int i;
        .
        .
}
```

The rule here is that the extern declaration should be outside and above the function that references it, but within the same source code file. The compiler will generate an error for the following program:

```
C:> type test4_4.cpp

#include <iostream.h>     // necessary for cout

int i;                    // external declaration

main()
{
    i = 5;
    cout << " i is " << i << "\n";
    cout << " j is " << j << "\n";
}
```

```
int j;              // variable declared after being referenced

Error:    Undefined symbol 'j' in function main()
```

This problem can be fixed by simply moving the declaration of j next to i. Another fix would be to leave the code the way it was in the original program, and add an extern declaration for both i and j inside main():

```
      .
      .
int i;              // external declaration
      .
      .
main()
{
      extern int i;  // declare i and j as extern within main()
      extern int j;
      .
      .
}


int j;              // external declaration
```

Compiling and running this program would produce the following output:

```
i is 5
j is 0
```

And now, a word of advice. C++ capitalizes on the concept of privacy of data, and you will learn how in subsequent chapters. We recommend that you use external variables only when absolutely necessary, since privacy of data is lost, and they take up storage space throughout the duration of the program because they are global in scope. In a program of any fair length, it may be hard to keep track of what value is stored in them in different functions at different times.

4.5   REGISTER DECLARATIONS

Register variables behave like automatic variables in that they are local in their scope. However, when a variable declaration is preceded with the keyword *register,* it means that a request has been made to the compiler to store that variable in a register, if one is available. This can significantly reduce the size of a program, and improve its performance, since operations on registers are faster than those performed for variables stored in memory. The keywords auto and register cannot appear in an external declaration. Following are valid register declarations:

```
register int    a;    // register declaration
register char   b;    // register declaration
```

4.6   DURATION OF VARIABLES

The duration of a variable is the period of time that a variable is assigned memory.

As indicated previously, static and external storage class variables are assigned memory for the complete duration of the program. Auto and register variables are assigned memory while they are within their enclosing block or function.

In C, dynamic duration occurs via calls to the functions `malloc()` and `free()`. In C++, dynamic duration occurs when variables are created or destroyed via the operators *new* and *delete*. These will be discussed next.

4.6.1   Free store objects—the operators new and delete

The operator *new* is used to dynamically allocate storage to different data types from the "free store" or heap. Free store is a pool of unallocated memory that is provided to the program when it is run. The variable continues to be allocated space until memory is deallocated via the operator *delete*.

Upon successful allocation, the operator `new` returns a pointer to that location in memory. A null pointer is returned upon unsuccessful allocation. The operator `delete` uses the same pointer to deallocate memory for that type, presumably when it is no longer required. A word of caution here—if for some reason the value of the pointer returned by new is changed, then `delete` will duly delete the amount of memory allocated by `new`, but at the new location being pointed to. The results could be quite disturbing. Make sure the value of the pointer does not change through the duration of the program.

The use of the `delete` operator is not mandatory, since memory will obviously be automatically deallocated upon termination of the program.

Take a look at the following program, which illustrates the use of these operators:

```
C:> type test4_5.cpp

#include <iostream.h>    // necessary for cout

main()
{
    int *ptr1;           // pointer to integer data type
    double *ptr2;        // pointer to double data type

    ptr1 = new int ;     // allocate memory for 1 object of
                         // type int
```

```
    ptr2 = new double;    // allocate memory for 1 object of
                          // type double
    *ptr1 = 5;            // store 5 in the area allocated by
                          // new, and pointed to by ptr1
    *ptr2 = 6.45;         // store 6.45 in the area allocated by
                          // new, and pointed to by ptr2

    cout << "ptr1 is " << ptr1 << "\n";
    cout << "ptr2 is " << ptr2 << "\n";
    cout << "*ptr1 is " << *ptr1 << "\n";
    cout << "*ptr2 is " << *ptr2 << "\n";

    delete ptr1;          // deallocate memory allocated by new,
                          // and pointed to by ptr1
    cout << "ptr1 is " << ptr1 << "\n";
    cout << "ptr2 is " << ptr2 << "\n";
    cout << "*ptr1 is " << *ptr1 << "\n";
    cout << "*ptr2 is " << *ptr2 << "\n";
}
```

```
C:>
```

Compiling and running this program results in the following output:

```
ptr1 is 0x8f4d11ac
ptr2 is 0x8f4d11b4
*ptr1 is 5
*ptr2 is 6.45
ptr1 is 0x8f4d11ac
ptr2 is 0x8f4d11b4
*ptr1 is 4520
*ptr2 is 6.45
```

ptr1 and ptr2 indicate the location in memory that the operator new assigned storage space for one object of type int and double, respectively. These pointers are displayed as hexadecimal values. A null pointer or 0 would have been returned if there was not enough memory to store objects of that type.

*ptr1 show us the contents of what is stored at the memory location that is pointed to by ptr1. As expected, this is the value 5. Likewise, the value 6.45 is stored in the area pointed to by ptr2, and printed via cout.

Next, the operator delete is used to delete the memory allocated by new and pointed to by ptr1. ptr1 and ptr2 still contain the same values. This is what we expected, since ptr1 and ptr2 have not been reset to point to anything else. However, the contents of what was stored in the area pointed to by `ptr1` is lost; the value 4520 (or garbage) is stored in it instead. This is because the operator `delete` has already deallocated that memory and returned it to the free store. `*ptr2` still contains the value 6.45, since we have not used delete to deallocate memory pointed to by `ptr2`.

The operators `new` and `delete` can be used to allocate memory to arrays, classes, and other data types. These operators will be discussed in greater detail when constructors and destructors are described later on in the book. For now, we just want you to understand the concept of dynamic duration as it exists in C++.

4.7 REVIEW

In this chapter, we discussed storage classes and discovered that C++ carries the same types as C, plus one additional type. Here's a table that illustrates the major concepts discussed:

TABLE 4.1   Storage Classes in C++

Storage class	Scope	Memory Allocation	Initialization by compiler
auto	Local to block, subsumed block, or function in which it is declared. Values do not persist.	While in scope	None
static	Local to block, subsumed block, or function in which it is declared. Values persist.	Duration of program	0
extern	Globally available to all functions within the same file, if declared outside and above them. Values persist.	Duration of program	0
register	Local to block, subsumed block, or function in which it is declared. Values do not persist.	While in scope	None
new, delete	Depends on type of object created.	Until delete is called, or program terminates	None

Functions in C++

5.1   INTRODUCTION

In this chapter, we will discuss how functions are put together in C++ programs. All C programs comprise one function called *main()*. In addition to this, they may have one or more functions that interact with each other to produce the output. One function can call another; it can even call itself. A function itself is a self-contained block of code, the inner workings of which are invisible to the remainder of the program. Arguments can be sent to functions. The argument itself is not sent; instead, a copy of that argument is sent. Exceptions to this comprise *arrays* and *external variables*. Inside the called function, the value of these arguments can be manipulated through pointers only (unless they happen to be arrays or externals). Hence, if the value of an argument is to be changed inside another function, then a pointer to that argument has to be sent over as well. Values can be returned from the called function. The return and argument data types must be declared in the function prototype area. The return type, function name, and number and type of arguments must correspond with the actual use of the function. In C++, the rules are the same. C++ adds quite a few nice features of its own.

5.2   main()

As noted previously, all C and C++ programs have a central entry point to the program called main(). In C, you were not required to state the return value of main(). In C++, even though you are not required to specify the return type, main() is defined to match one of the following prototypes:

```
int main();                              // prototype 1
int main(int argc, char *argv[]);        // prototype 2
```

The second prototype should be familiar to you. argc is the count of arguments that are being sent to main(). argv is a pointer to each one of those arguments.

The first prototype implies that a status is being returned to the operating system upon successful or unsuccessful execution of the program. Since C++ declares main() to return a value, it is good programming practice to actually do so, upon program termination, indicating successful or unsuccessful execution of your program. A return value of 0 indicates successful execution. Take a look at the following program:

```
C:> type test5_1.cpp


#include <iostream.h>           // necessary for cout

int main(void)
{
    cout << "This program returns a 0 \n";
    return (0);
}
```

Compiling and running this program results in the following output:

```
This program returns a 0
```

Recall that void indicates the absence of a type. If this keyword precedes the function name, it means that the function returns no value. If it is within the function parameter list, it indicates that the function takes no arguments. In C++, a function declared as follows:

```
int function_1(void);
```

is equivalent to the following declaration:

```
int function_1();
```

The compiler will ensure that no arguments are passed to function_1(). Now let's get back to our original program and modify it to return a string.

```
C:> type test5_2.cpp


#include <iostream.h>           // necessary for cout
int main(void)
{
```

```
     cout << "This program returns abc \n";
     return("abc");
}
```

Compiling and running this program results in the following output:

```
Error:    Expression type does not match the return type in
          function main()
```

This is because C++ expects `main()` to return a value of type integer only. Let's reenumerate what we have just learned:

1. C++ forces `main()` to return an integer value to the operating system.

2. It is good programming practice to return an integer value upon successful execution of a program.

3. Errors will be generated by the compiler if you try to return a value other than an integer type.

5.3   FUNCTION PROTOTYPING

The new ANSI C allows *function prototyping*. That is, the return value, function name, and number and type of arguments can be specified in the function prototype, right before `main()`. The function itself must correspond to the specifications set down in the prototype area, or errors will be generated. What you might find interesting to note here is that C borrowed the function prototype concept from C++. While ANSI C allows function prototyping, C++ requires it. Take a look at the following program:

```
C:> type test5_3.cpp

#include <iostream.h>             // necessary for cout

int main(void)
{
     int i = 1;
     function_1(i);
}

void function_1(i)
{
     cout << "i is " << i << " \n";
}
```

While C would have let you get away with the code above (replacing `cout` with `printf()`, of course), the C++ compiler will generate the following error messages:

```
Error:    Function 'function_1' should have a prototype should have
          a prototype in function main()
```

The problem can be fixed by prefixing function_1() with the keyword *void* and adding the function prototype as follows:

```
C:> type test5_4.cpp

#include <iostream.h>              // necessary for cout

void function_1(int i);           // notice function prototype

int main(void)
{
    int i = 1;
    function_1(i);
}

void function_1(int i)
{
    cout << "i is " << i << " \n";
}
```

Compiling and running this program results in the following output:

```
i is 1
```

Now let's modify the program again to illustrate what happens if the return value, number or arguments, or argument types do not correspond with the actual function definition:

```
C:> type test5_5.cpp

#include <iostream.h>              // necessary for cout

void function_1(int i);           // function prototype

int main(void)
{
    int i, j;
    i = j = 1;
    function_1(i, j);             // illegal number of arguments
}

void function_1(int i)
```

```
{
    cout << "i is " << i << " \n";
}
```

Compiling this program will result in the following error message:

```
Error:    Extra parameter to call in function_1(int) in function
          main()
```

This error is generated because the function call itself

```
function_1(i, j);
```

does not correspond with the function prototype:

```
void function_1(int i);
```

Some C compilers might have let you get away with the above code. However, the problem would have surfaced when the program would be run. The C++ compiler would catch the discrepancy at compilation time, thereby prompting the programmer to fix the problem before the program is run.

Just like C, it is not necessary to specify the variable name in the function prototype. However, you are still required to specify the variable name in the function definition. (A function definition contains the body of the function.) The compiler will accept the following modification to the program:

```
C:> type test5_6.cpp

#include <iostream.h>         // necessary for cout

void function_1(int);         // notice missing parameter name

int main(void)
{
    int i = 1;
    function_1(i);
}

void function_1(int i)
{
    cout << "i is " << i << " \n";
}
```

Compiling and executing this program results in this output:

```
i is 1
```

But this won't work:

```
C:> type test5_7.cpp

#include <iostream.h>          // necessary for cout

void function_1(int)          // notice missing parameter name

int main(void)
{
    int i = 1;
    function_1(i);
}

void function_1(int)          // notice missing parameter name
{
    cout << "i is " << i << " \n";
}
```

The compiler generates the following message:

```
Error:    Undefined symbol i in function function_1(int)
```

If you modify the definition of function_1() as follows:

```
    .

    .
void function_1(int i)
{

    cout << "i is " << i << " \n";
}
```

then the program will compile correctly. When this program is run, the output looks as follows:

```
i is 1
```

Another variant that is acceptable to the compiler is as follows:

```
C:> type test5_8.cpp

#include <iostream.h>          // necessary for cout
void function_1(int x);       // notice use of variable x

int main(void)
```

```
{
    int i = 1;

    function_1(i);
}

void function_1(int x)         // notice use of variable x
{
    cout << "i is " << x << " \n";
}
```

In `test5_8.cpp`, the name of the actual argument (that which is passed from the calling function to the called function) is `i`. The name of the formal argument (that which is declared within the parentheses at the time that the function is defined) is `x`. Compiling and running this program results in the same output:

```
i is 1
```

Note, however, that the value of `x` is output to `cout`. We would have received the Undefined Symbol error message again if the value of `i` would have been output. `x` is used as a mask name for any argument that is passed to this function. `x` is the only variable name that `function_1()` understands.

The strong type checking, regardless of the style used, ensures that illegal values are not passed to functions. Thus,

1. C++ programs require function prototyping.
2. The function prototype must agree with its corresponding function call and definition.

5.4 FUNCTION DEFINITION

A *function definition* is the actual body of the function itself. It comprises the following components:

return type of the function

name

argument list

code

Each will be discussed, and illustrated via small C++ programs.

5.4.1 Return type

As stated previously, the return type of the function in the function definition must correspond with its corresponding prototype. If a return type is not specified explicitly in the function prototype, then a default return type of int is assumed by the compiler. It is necessary that you insert a return statement in the called function, and return an int, or an error message will be generated. Take a look at the following program:

```
C:> type test5_9.cpp

#include <iostream.h>          // necessary for cout

function_1(int i);            // function prototype
int main(void)
{
     int i = 1;
     function_1(i);
}
function_1(int i)
{
     cout << "i is " << i << " \n";
     return(0)
}
```

Compiling and running this program gives the expected output:

```
i is 1
```

Let's see what happens if a character instead of an integer is returned:

```
function_1(int i)
{
     .
     .
     return('c');
}
```

The program compiles and executes as before. This is because the compiler performs type conversions when it can. The character is converted to int, and therefore there are no problems. Let's try to return a string next:

```
function_1(int i)
{
     .
     .
     return("abc");
}
```

This version of the program generates an error because the compiler is unable to convert data type of string to integer. This problem was encountered when compiling `test5_2.cpp` as well. We recommend that you always indicate the return type in the function prototype and leave nothing to chance.

A summary of features of return types follows:

1. The return type in a function definition must agree with its corresponding prototype.
2. If it does not, then the compiler will perform some type conversions and try to find a correspondence. If it fails in its efforts, then it will generate error messages.
3. A default type of int is assumed for those functions in which the return type is not specified.

5.4.2 Function names

In C, you were required to assign a different function name to each function in your program. In C++, two or more distinct functions can have the same name. This is called function overloading. You encountered this feature in Chap. 1. This is a powerful new capability that will be discussed at length in this chapter.

Take a look at this C program:

```
C:> type test5_10.c

void sum_integer(int i);        // function prototype
void sum_float(float j);

main()
{
    int i = 5;                  // initialize variables
    float j = 5.5;

    sum_integer(i);
    sum_float(j);
}

void sum_integer(int i)
{
    i += 5;
    printf (" i is %d \n", i);
}

void sum_float(float j)
{
    j += 5;
    printf (" j is %f \n", j);
}
```

Compiling and running this program gives us the following output:

```
i is 10
j is 10.500000
```

What we want you to notice here is that sum_integer() and sum_float() do exactly the same thing; they add a value of 5 to the argument passed to them, and then display that value via the printf() statement.

Now take a look at an equivalent C++ program:

```
C:> type test5_11.cpp

#include <iostream.h>      // necessary for cout

void sum(int i);           // function prototype area
void sum(float j);         // notice use of same name

main(void)
{
     int i = 5;
     float j = 5.5;

     sum(i);               // call sum() to add integer
     sum(j);               // call sum() to add float
}

void sum(int i)
{
     i += 5;
     cout << "i is " << i << " \n";
}

void sum(float j)
{
     j += 5;
     cout << "j is " << j << " \n";
}
```

Compiling and running the program above results in the following output:

```
i is 10
j is 10.5
```

What you see here is a very simple case of function overloading. The function name sum() is "overloaded" to mean that the same function name has more than one implementation. The execution of the correct implementation is performed by the compiler, not the programmer. The compiler matches up the type of the arguments in the function call with the types in the function definition, and executes the one which matches the type of the argument in the function call. That's all there is to it.

Now let's modify the program and see what happens if different data types are sent to the two functions:

```
C:> type test5_12.cpp

#include <iostream.h>          // necessary for cout

void sum(char i);             // function prototype
void sum(float j);

main(void)
{
    char i = 'c';
    float j = 5.6;
    sum(i);               // send ASCII c to sum()
    sum(j);               // send floating point to sum()
}

void sum(char i)
{
    cout << "Inside sum(char) \n";
}

void sum(float j)
{
    cout << "Inside sum(float) \n";
}
```

This program compiles properly. The output looks as follows:

```
Inside sum(char) c
Inside sum(float) 6.5
```

Now how did the C++ compiler figure out which function to invoke each time? The process is really very simple. First, it checks for the implementation of an overloaded function with identical parameter types, so that they match the type of the argument in the called function. If one is found, then that function is implemented. If one is not found, then C++ performs type conversions and implements the function which allows the easiest type conversion.

In our example, sum(int) was called the first time around because the ASCII character c was converted to integer, and thereby matched the function definition of sum(int).

The second time around, the value 3.14323 matched the data type of `float`, and `sum(float)` was called.

Now let's modify the program again and see what happens if an integer is sent to a function that expects a character:

```
C:> type test5_13.cpp

#include <iostream.h>          // necessary for cout

void sum(char);               // sum expects char as argument
void sum(float);              // sum expects float as argument

main(void)
{
    int i = 65;
    float j = 6.5;
    sum(i);                   // send integer value to sum()
    sum(j);                   // send float to sum()
}

void sum(char i)
{
    cout << "Inside sum(char) - i is " << i << " \n";
}

void sum(float j)
{
    cout << "Inside sum(float) - j is " << j << " \n";
}
```

Compiling this program results in the following error message:

```
Error:    Ambiguity between 'sum(float)' and 'sum(char)' in
          function main()
```

This message is generated because the compiler expected to find a character sent to `sum(char i)` instead of an `int`, and it was unable to perform the necessary type conversions the other way round. Function overloading will be rediscussed in later chapters. For now, we just want you to understand the concept behind it, how it works in its simplest application, and what advantages it offers over rules for function names as they exist in C. A summary follows:

1. In C++, more than one function can have the same name.

2. The data types of the arguments in the function call must match the data types in the function prototype and definition.

3. If they don't, the compiler will perform type conversions. It will generate error messages if it is unable to match data types.

5.4.3   Argument list

As stated previously, the number of arguments and argument types in a function definition must correspond to their corresponding function proto-type. If there is no exact correspondence, then the C++ compiler will attempt to convert the type of the actual arguments so that they can match the for-mal arguments in the called functions. The const and volatile modifiers can precede the types of the formal arguments to indicate specific instructions to the compiler. Let's discuss these modifiers next.

5.4.3.1   The const modifier

You can precede an argument type with the modifier *const* to indicate that this argument cannot be changed. The object to which it applies cannot be assigned a value, or changed in any way.

The following program illustrates its use:

```
C:> type test5_14.cpp

#include <iostream.h>                // necessary for cout

void function_1(const int i);       // notice use of const modifier

main(void)
{
     int i = 1;
     function_1(i);        // pass i as an actual argument
}

void function_1(const int i)        // notice use of const modifier
{
     cout << " i is " << i << " \n";
}
```

Compiling and running this program gives the following output:

```
i is 1
```

So far, so good.
Now let's modify the program and change the value of i.

```
C:> type test5_15.cpp

#include <iostream.h>                // necessary for cout
```

```
void function_1(const int i); // argument is type const

main(void)
{
    int i = 1;
    function_1(i);            // pass i as actual argument
}

void function_1(const int i)  // formal argument is type const
{
    i++;
    cout << "i is " << i << " \n";
}
```

Compiling this program results in an error:

```
Error:   Cannot modify a const object in function_1(const int)
```

This is because an attempt is being made to change the value of the argument i that was specified as type const.

5.4.3.2   The volatile modifier

The *volatile modifier* is the flip side of const. This keyword can be used to precede formal arguments to indicate that they are liable to be changed during the course of the normal execution of the program. Declaring arguments as such also prevents the compiler from storing them in registers. Let's modify test5_13.cpp to use the keyword volatile instead of const:

```
C:> type test5_16.cpp

#include <iostream.h>              // necessary for cout

void function_1(volatile int i);   // notice use of volatile

main(void)
{
    int i = 1;
    function_1(i);                 // pass i an an actual argument
}

void function_1(volatile int i)    // notice use of volatile
{
    i++;
    cout << "i is " << i << " \n";
}
```

This program gives the following output:

```
i is 2
```

5.4.3.3 Default initializers

In C++, you can have arguments default to values that you specify at the time that the function is declared in the function prototype. Take a look at the following program:

```
C:> type test5_17.cpp

#include <iostream.h>          // necessary for cout

void function_1(int i, int j = 2); // notice initialization

main(void)
{
     int i = 1;
     int j;

     function_1(i, j);
}
void function_1(int i, int j)
{
     cout << "i is " << i << "\n";
     cout << "j is " << j << "\n";
}
```

Compiling and running this program gives the following output:

```
i is 1
j is 8689
```

The argument j is initialized to garbage; initialization simply in the prototype does not have the required effect.

Now let's modify the program to see what happens if the parameter j is initialized inside main().

```
C:> type test5_18.cpp

#include <iostream.h>          // necessary for cout

void function_1(int i, int j = 2);

main(void)
{
```

```
        int i = 1;
        int j = 5;              // set j to 5
        function_1(i, j);       // send j as well
}

void function_1(int i, int j)
{
        cout << "i is " << i << " \n";
        cout << "j is " << j << " \n";
}
```

The output for this program looks like this:

```
i is 1
j is 5
```

The value of j is output as 5, instead of 2. The default value of 2 assigned in the function prototype area is overridden by the value that is explicitly assigned to j within main().

Now let's modify the program again to see what happens if j is initialized at the time that the function is called.

```
C:> type test5_19.cpp

#include <iostream.h>                // necessary for cout

void function_1(int i, int j = 2); // function prototype

main(void)
{
        int i = 1;
        int j;

        function_1(i, j = 8);
}
void function_1(int i, int j)
{
        cout << "i is " << i << " \n";
        cout << "j is " << j << " \n";
}
```

Compiling this version results in the output:

```
i i 1
j is 8
```

OK. Now let's see what happens if a value is assigned to an argument at the time that the function is defined.

```
C:> type test5_20.cpp

#include <iostream.h>          // necessary for cout

void function_1(int i, int j = 2);

main(void)
{
    int i;

    function_1(i);      // trying to initialize actual
                              // argument
}
void function_1(int i, int j = 8)
{
    cout << "i is " << i << " \n";
    cout << "j is " << j << " \n";
}
```

Compiling this program gives an error:

```
Error:    Previously specified default argument value cannot be
          changed.
```

OK. Now let's try something else. Let's try to initialize more than one argument:

```
C:> type test5_21.cpp

#include <iostream.h>                    // necessary for cout

void function_1(int i = 1, int j, int k = 2);

main(void)
{
    int i, k;       // not initialized
    int j = 2;

    function_1(i, j, k);
}

void function_1(int i, int j, int k)
{
```

```
        cout << "i is " << i << " \n";
        cout << "j is " << j << " \n";
        cout << "k is " << k << " \n";
}
```

Compiling this program results in the following error:

```
Error:    Default value missing
```

This is because C++ has another rule about default arguments. This rule states that only the last arguments in a parameter list can be initialized; the variable i is not one of the last. OK. Let's modify test5_18.cpp to initialize the variables j and k only, and see what happens:

```
C:> type test5_22.cpp

#include <iostream.h>              // necessary for cout

void function_1(int i, int j = 2, int k = 3); // function prototype

main(void)
{
    int i = 1;
    int j, k;

    function_1(i);
}
void function_1(int i, int j; int k)
{
    cout << "i is " << i << " \n";
    cout << "j is " << j << " \n";
    cout << "k is " << k << " \n";
}
```

This program compiles properly. Here's the output:

```
i is 1
j is 2
k is 3
```

The output is as we expected.

Now we can summarize the rules which apply to default arguments in parameter lists.

1. Arguments can be assigned default values only in the function prototype.

2. Only the last arguments in the list can be assigned values.

3. If a default argument is reassigned, it must be passed as an argument to the calling function.

5.4.3.4   Ellipses

In C++ you can enter ellipses in the formal parameter declaration of a function to indicate that the function will be called with different sets of arguments on different occasions. Type checking is not performed for the variable arguments. You have encountered this feature in C as well, perhaps without even knowing about it. The function printf() is nothing but a function that takes a variable number of arguments. If you do not specify the correct argument data types in the format specification, then the results can be erratic, since there is no type checking. Implementation of variable number of arguments is a little bit complicated. The header file stdarg.h has to be included, and use is made of macros defined in this header file to obtain the necessary output. Since this is only a primer, therefore, we will leave a detailed explanation of the implementation of these functions to your reference manual. For now, we just want you to be aware of this capability.

5.4.3.5   Reference arguments

A *reference* is simply another name for a variable. Take a look at the following code:

```
C:> type test5_23.cpp

#include <iostream.h>          // necessary for cout

main(void)
{
    int devil = 666;    // simple assignment
    int &satan = devil; // satan is another name for devil
    cout << "devil is " << devil << " \n";
    cout << "satan is " << satan << " \n";
}
```

The program's output looks like this:

```
devil is 666
satan is 666
```

The variable devil, which is of type integer, is initialized to 666. Then, the reference type satan is set equal to devil. Or, to say it in simpler words, satan is simply another name for devil. devil was initialized to 666. After setting the reference type satan equal to devil, satan also contains the value 666. Notice that the value of satan is output, and not &satan. &satan would give the address of where this reference type is stored in memory.

Let's change the value of the reference type, and see what happens:

```
C:> type test5_24.cpp

#include <iostream.h>            // necessary for cout

main(void)
{
    int devil = 666;     // simple assignment
    int &satan = devil; // satan is another name for devil

    cout << "devil is " << devil << " \n";
    cout << "satan is " << satan << " \n";
    satan = 999;         // changed value of reference
    cout << "devil is " << devil << " \n";
    cout << "satan is " << satan << " \n";
}
```

The output for this program follows:

```
devil is 666
satan is 666
devil is 999
satan is 999
```

As you can see, changing the value of the reference type satan resulted in changing the value of the variable that it was assigned to, i.e., devil. This makes sense. After all, it's just another name for it!

Now that you understand what a reference is, let's see how it can be used as an argument in functions.

Recall that in C language, arguments are passed to functions by value. In other words, the variable itself is not passed to the function, but a copy of that variable. What this meant for you as a programmer was, that if you wanted to change the value of that variable in the called function, you had to pass a pointer to it, and then manipulate its contents via that pointer. Here's a simple C program that illustrates this feature.

```
C:> type test5_25.c

int function_1(int *j);  /* function prototype */

main()
{
    int i;
    int *j;        /* j is pointer to integer */
    i = 1;         /* initialize i */
    j = &i;        /* set j to contain address of i */
```

```
    printf ("i is %d \n", i);
    function_1(j);
    printf ("i is %d \n", i);
}

void function_1(int *j)
{
    *j += 1;  /* increment contents of what j is pointing to */
}
```

Compiling and running this program results in the following output:

```
i is 1
i is 2
```

In C++, you can pass arguments by value and by reference. Take a look at the program below, which is the C++ equivalent of test5_25.c. The only difference is that it uses a reference instead of a pointer to change the contents of i in the called function.

```
C:> type test5_26.cpp

#include <iostream.h>          // necessary for cout

int function_1(int j);         // notice reference type j

main(void)
{
    int i = 66;
    int &j = i;                // j is reference to integer type

    cout << "j is " << j << " i is " << i << " \n";
    i = function_1(j);             // send reference to i
    cout << "j is " << j << " i is " << i << " \n";
}
int function_1(j)
{
    j = 3;
    return j;
}
```

Compiling and running this program results in the following output:

```
j is 66 i is 66
j is 3 i is 3
```

The argument j is passed by reference, not value. Therefore, this argument provides direct access to the object that it was made to reference to (i.e., *i*), and its contents are modified without the use of pointers in the called function.

Let's review what has been learned:

1. References are just another name for the object that they are assigned to. A reference is suffixed with an & sign on the left side of the assignment operator.

2. References provide a convenient way of passing arguments to functions by reference, instead of value, as was the case in C.

5.5   INLINE FUNCTIONS

When a function is called, there is a certain amount of processing overhead that goes along with it. In C++, you can reduce this overhead by preceding a function name at the time that it is defined with the keyword *inline*. The compiler compiles the code for the function when it encounters this keyword. Then, it simply substitutes this code for that function each time it is called within the program. This is called *inline expansion*. Since the function has already been compiled, the usual overhead incurred in a function call is avoided. Take a look at this program:

```
C:> type test5_27.cpp

#include <iostream.h>            // necessary for cout
int increment(int i);           // function prototype

inline increment(int i)      // notice keyword inline
    {
    i++;
    return i;
    }

main(void)
{
    int i = 0;
    while (i < 3)
        {
        i = increment(i);
        cout << "i is " << i << " \n";
        }
}
```

The output for this program looks like this:

```
i is 1
i is 2
i is 3
```

OK. Now let's modify the program to move the inline function below main().

```
C:> type test5_28.cpp

#include <iostream.h>              // necessary for cout

main(void)
{
    int i = 0;
    while (i != 3)
        {
        increment(i);
        cout << "i is " << i << " \n";
        }
}
inline increment(int i)       // notice keyword inline
    {
    i++;
    return i;
    }
```

Compiling this program gives an error:

```
Error:        Function increment should have a prototype in
              function main().
```

This is because inline functions must be defined before they are called. The compiler does not consider the inline function definition of increment() to the same function that is being called inside main().

Therefore, inline functions:

1. Reduce function overhead
2. Must not be defined before they are called

5.6   RECURSIVE FUNCTIONS

In C++, *recursive functions* exist as they do in C. In recursion, a function calls itself. Take a look at this program:

```
C:> type test5_29.cpp

#include <iostream.h>          // necessary for cout

void decrement(int i);        // function prototype

main(void)
{
    int i = 2;
    i = decrement(i);
    cout << "i is " << i << "\n";
}
int decrement(i)
{
    cout << "Inside decrement() \n";
    i-;
    if (i > 0)
        decrement(i);         // function calls itself
    else
        return(i);
}
```

The output for this program looks like this:

```
Inside decrement()
Inside decrement()
i is 0
```

The function decrement() calls itself recursively until the test condition evaluates to TRUE (or a zero value). When i evaluates to zero, program control returns back to main().

5.7 REVIEW

In this chapter, we learned many interesting features of functions in C++.

- main() returns a value of type int to the operating system.
- Function prototypes are mandatory.
- The return type, function name, and number and type of arguments in the prototype must agree with the actual function call and definition.
- The compiler attempts to perform type conversions of arguments and return types whenever it can, to find a correspondence if one does not exist.
- Function names can be "overloaded," that is, assigned the same name. The decision of which function is executed at any time in the program is left up to the compiler, not the programmer.

- The *const* modifier notifies the compiler that the object of this type cannot be modified.

- The *volatile* modifier notifies the compiler that the object of this type can and probably will be modified.

- Default initializers can be assigned to function parameters in their prototypes.

- Functions can be called with variable number and types of parameters, via the ellipsis.

- C++ contains reference types. These are simply another name for the variables that they are assigned to.

- References provide a convenient way of passing arguments to functions by reference, rather than value.

- C++ allows the definition of inline functions, which help reduce function call overhead.

- C++ allows functions to call themselves; these are called *recursive functions*.

The Power of C++

6

Classes in C++—Fundamental Concepts

6.1 INTRODUCTION

In Chap. 1, we presented an analogy that was designed to help you understand the key concept in C++: the *class mechanism*. In this chapter this concept will be discussed at length. Not only will you understand how to declare, define, and use classes, but, more important, the reason for using a class as opposed to the traditional C structure, and the advantages in doing so. In the next chapter, rules specific to class member declarations and definitions will be discussed.

Most of you should be familiar with traditional C structures. These will be reviewed first. Then, we will describe structures as they exist in C++.

6.2 STRUCTURES IN C AND C++

A *structure* is a special data type that gathers together, in a fixed pattern, other valid data types. Here's a simple structure declaration:

```
struct family
    {
    char *husband;
    char *wife;
    char *son;
    char *daughter;
```

```
    };
struct family Anderson;
```

The structure family comprises four variables which are pointers to character arrays. These variables are called husband, wife, son, and daughter, respectively. Anderson is a structure of type family. The members of Anderson can also be initialized at the time it is declared, and accessed through a pointer:

```
Anderson.husband      = "John Anderson";
Anderson.wife         = "Mary Anderson";
Anderson.son          = "Joey Anderson";
Anderson.daughter     = "Marla Anderson";
```

The members of Anderson can be accessed through a pointer, as follows:

```
struct family
     {
     char *husband;
     char *wife;
     char *son;
     char *daughter;
     };
struct family Anderson = {{"John Anderson"}, {"Mary Anderson"},
                          {"Joey Anderson"}, {"Marla Anderson"}};
stuct family *ptr;     /* ptr points to structure of type family */

main()
{
     ptr = &Anderson; /* ptr points to 1st member of Anderson */
     printf ("husband is %s \n",  ptr->husband,
             "wife is    %s \n",  ptr->wife,
             "son is     %s \n",  ptr->son,
             "daughter is %s \n", ptr->daughter);
}
```

Compiling and running this program results in the following output:

```
husband is   John Anderson
wife is      Mary Anderson
son is       Joey Anderson
daughter is Marla Anderson
```

A structure with a tag name of family is declared, Anderson is defined as a structure of this type, and initialized. Next, ptr is declared as a pointer to structures of that type. Inside main(), ptr is set to point to the location in memory where the structure Anderson is stored. The structure members of

Anderson are printed through a printf() statement, using ptr to point to the correct member. Simple enough to understand. Right? OK. Now let's see how structures are handled in C++.

Well, everything that has been said about structures in C is true for C++ as well. Take a look at the following C++ program:

```
C:> type test6_1.cpp


#include  <iostream.h>          // necessary for I/O

struct family
    {
    char *husband;
    char *wife;
    char *son;
    char *daughter;
    };
// Anderson is declared as a structure of type family
// notice that keyword struct or structure is missing
family Anderson = {{"John Anderson"}, {"Mary Anderson"},
                {"Joey Anderson"}, {"Marla Anderson"}};
family *ptr;      // ptr points to structure of type family

main(void)
{
    ptr = &Anderson; // ptr points to 1st member of Anderson
    cout <<"husband is  " << ptr->husband <<"\n"
        <<"wife is     " << ptr->wife    <<"\n"
        <<"son is      " << ptr->son      <<"\n"
        <<"daughter is " << ptr->daughter<<"\n";
}
```

Running this program gives the following output:

```
husband is  John Anderson
wife is     Mary Anderson
son is      Joey Anderson
daughter is Marla Anderson
```

Notice that the keyword struct (or structure) is missing when Anderson and ptr are declared. In C++, this keyword is optional. However, it is not optional when the structure template is declared.

If you take another look at main(), you will realize that it can perhaps be logically divided into two parts. The first part initializes ptr to point to the structure Anderson. The second part simply outputs the contents of each member. Since functions are used to divide a program into its logical compo-

nents, where each function performs a coherent task on its own, let's modify
test6_1.cpp and create two functions to do the job:

```
C:> type test6_2.cpp

#include  <iostream.h>          // necessary for I/O

struct family
    {
    char *husband;
    char *wife;
    char *son;
    char *daughter;
    };
family Anderson = {{"John Anderson"}, {"Mary Anderson"},
                   {"Joey Anderson"}, {"Marla Anderson"}};
family *ptr;      // ptr points to structure of type family

family *initialize(family *ptr);  // function prototypes
void output(family *ptr);

main(void)
{
    ptr = initialize(ptr);   // set pointer in initialize()
    output(ptr);             // send ptr to output()
}
family *initialize(family *ptr)
{
    ptr = &Anderson;
    return ptr;
}
void output(family *ptr)
{
    cout <<"husband is  " << ptr->husband <<"\n"
         <<"wife is     " << ptr->wife    <<"\n"
         <<"son is      " << ptr->son     <<"\n"
         <<"daughter is " << ptr->daughter<<"\n";
}
```

The output for this program looks like this:

```
husband is  John Anderson
wife is     Mary Anderson
son is      Joey Anderson
daughter is Marla Anderson
```

Now assume that 300 lines of code, comprising, say, 15 additional functions, is added to the original program. The calls to these additional functions are made from main(). The program would look something like this:

```
C:> type test6_3.cpp

#include  <iostream.h>        // necessary for I/O

struct family
    {
    char *husband;
    char *wife;
    char *son;
    char *daughter;
    };
struct family Anderson;
family Anderson = {{"John Anderson"}, {"Mary Anderson"},
                  {"Joey Anderson"}, {"Marla Anderson"}};
family *ptr;     // ptr points to structure of type family

family  *initialize(family *ptr);  // function prototypes
void output(family *ptr);
// function prototypes for the 15 additional functions is
// added  here.

main(void)
{
    ptr = initialize(ptr);   // receive pointer to Anderson
    // Calls to the 15 additional functions are made here
    output(ptr);                // send ptr to output
}

// The code for function initialize() is stil the same
family *initialize(family *ptr)
{
    ptr = &Anderson;
    return ptr;
}

// Code for 15 additional functions is over here

// The code for function output() is still the same
void output(family *ptr)
{
    cout <<"husband is  " << ptr->husband <<"\n"
```

```
            <<"wife is      " << ptr->wife     <<"\n"
            <<"son is       " << ptr->son      <<"\n"
            <<"daughter is " << ptr->daughter<<"\n";
}
```

Suppose this program produces the following output:

```
husband is  Mark Davis
wife is     Jennifer Davis
son is      Michael Davis
daughter is Maria Davis
```

Upon verification of the output, it appears that somewhere through the course of the program, ptr has been erroneously made to point to some other structure of type family (perhaps called Davis), and its structure members have been initialized to the member names of the Davis family.

What this means for you as a programmer is many hours of headache and wasted time, tracing through the 300 line program, trying to locate the function in which ptr was reset to point to the location in memory of the Davis family, instead of Anderson. This is where C++ comes to the rescue.

6.3   THE CLASS MECHANISM IN C++

C++ has a class mechanism which allows you to specify a unique set of objects which comprises that class, and the operations allowed on these objects. Let's modify the original version of the program (test6_2.cpp) to use a class instead of a structure, and see how classes work.

```
//    test6_4.cpp
#include <iostream.h>          // necessary for I/O
class family
    {
    private:                   // notice use of keyword private
    char *husband;             // member list follows
    char *wife;
    char *son;
    char *daughter;
    family *ptr;               // ptr declaration inside family
    public:                    // notice use of keyword public
    void initialize(void);     // member functions follow
    void output(family *ptr);
    };
family Anderson;               // Anderson is object of type family

main(void)
```

```
{
    // initialize() is qualified by class object name.
    // notice the dot operator.
    Anderson.initialize();
}
// initialize() is qualified by class name
void family::initialize(void)  // notice scope resolution operator
{
    // initializing member list of object Anderson
    // class members are qualified by class object name
    Anderson.ptr = &Anderson;
    Anderson.ptr->husband = "John Anderson";
    Anderson.ptr->wife = "Mary Anderson";
    Anderson.ptr->son = "Joey Anderson";
    Anderson.ptr->daughter = "Marla Anderson";
    Anderson.output(Anderson.ptr);
}
// output() is qualified by class name
void family::output(family *ptr)
{
    cout <<"husband is  " << ptr->husband   <<"\n"
         <<"wife is     " << ptr->wife      <<"\n"
         <<"son is      " << ptr->son       <<"\n"
         <<"daughter is " << ptr->daughter  <<"\n";
}
```

This program produces the following output:

```
husband is   John Anderson
wife is      Mary Anderson
son is       Joey Anderson
daughter is  Marla Anderson
```

Now let's step through this program and understand why a class was used instead of a struct, and it was declared as it is.

The keyword class is followed by the class tag name, called family (just like a structure tag name in C), and then an opening curly brace (once again, like C structure declarations). What this does is create a unique type, or a class type, called family.

Next is the keyword private, followed by a colon, and then a list of declarations. The list of declarations that are enclosed within the opening and closing curly braces within a class declaration are known as the *member list*. The keyword private is an access specifier, which indicates access privileges for the declarations that follow it. This keyword specifies that the variables that follow can be used only by the member functions that exist within that class (or its friends, but we will postpone discussion of the friend mechanism to a later chapter). But what are member functions? Let's continue to analyze the declaration, before we answer that question.

Following the keyword `private` are the declarations for `husband`, `wife`, `son`, `daughter`, and then one for `family`, `*ptr`. `husband`, `wife`, `son`, and `daughter` are known as *class members* (just like structure members). `ptr` is declared to be a pointer to a class of type `family`. Notice that the keyword class does not precede the class tag name `family`, just like `struct` is not required to precede the declaration of a structure of that type. The compiler understands that `family` is a class name, because it was specified as such at the beginning of the class declaration.

Next is the keyword `public`, followed by a list of function declarations. These functions are called *member functions*, or *methods*. Since these functions are declared as `public`, they can be accessed by members of their class, as well as nonmembers. They can be passed arguments and accessed from anywhere within program scope.

Inside `main()`, there is a function call to the class member function `initialize()`. Notice that this function is prefixed with `Anderson`, and a dot, ".". Recall how structure members are accessed in C. A code fragment from `test6_1.c` is redisplayed for your convenience:

```
struct family
    {
    char *husband;
    char *wife;
    char *son;
    char *daughter;
    };
struct family Anderson;

Anderson.husband    = "John Anderson";
Anderson.wife       = "Mary Anderson";
Anderson.son        = "Joey Anderson";
Anderson.daughter   = "Marla Anderson";
```

The structure members are prefixed with the name given to structures of that type, and the dot operator.

In C++, class (or structure members) are referenced the same way. `initialize()` is a member function of the class `family`, `Anderson` is an object of that type, and, therefore, a function call to `initialize()` is as follows:

```
Anderson.initialize();
```

Next, the function definition of `initialize()`:

```
void family::initialize(void)
```

{

Notice that the function name is preceded by the class name and scope resolution operator ::. Recall from Part 1 of the book how C++ allows different functions to have the same name. It is possible that there may be other functions in our program that have the name initialize(). However, the compiler understands this to be a member function of the class family simply because it is preceded with the class name! To say it a little bit differently, this function is qualified by a class name. Now you should be able to understand why :: is called the scope resolution operator—it resolves the scope of the function name that it precedes and allows the compiler to understand whether the function definition that follows belongs to a class or structure, or is simply an independent entity. Let's continue with the code:

```
Anderson.ptr = &Anderson;
Anderson.ptr->husband = "John Anderson";
Anderson.ptr->wife = "Mary Anderson";
Anderson.ptr->son = "Joey Anderson";
Anderson.ptr->daughter = "Marla Anderson";
Anderson.output(Anderson.ptr);
```

The class member ptr is assigned the location in memory of the object Anderson. Then, the remaining members are initialized. Finally, the function member output() is called, and this call is also qualified by the class name.

The program ends with a definition of the function output(). This function is also qualified by class name. The return value, type, and number of arguments agree with the class declaration.

Summarizing,

1. Classes are declared via the keyword class.

2. Classes have tag names, like structures. The tag name family is assigned to the class in the sample program.

3. A class comprises a list of declarations of variables and/or functions. Our class member list comprises the pointers to character arrays called husband, wife, son, and daughter, respectively. In addition to this, ptr is declared as a pointer to a class of type family. The functions initialize() and output() are the member functions in the class member list.

4. The keyword *class* does not have to precede the declaration of variables that are objects or instances of that type. In the sample program, Anderson is an object or an instance of a class of type family.

5. Access specifiers, such as *private* and *public*, are used to specify access privileges of the member list within the class. In the program, the class members husband, wife, son, daughter, and ptr are private. The member

functions `initialize()` and `output()` are public. What this means is that any valid argument can be passed to `initialize()` and `output()` from anywhere within the program. However, the private class members can be accessed or manipulated by the functions `initialize()` and `output()` only. To reiterate, `husband`, `wife`, `son`, `daughter`, and `ptr` can be assigned values, or manipulated through the functions `initialize()` and `output()` only.

6. Member function calls are qualified by the class object name, and the dot operator.

7. Member function definitions are qualified by the class name, and the scope resolution operator.

8. The return value type, function name, and number and type of arguments of a function must agree with its corresponding declaration within the class.

So why bother with classes anyway? Well, let's go back to the scenario that was presented in `test6_3.cpp`. In that program, `ptr` had somehow been erroneously set to point to the location in memory of the `Davis` family structure. The problem was that you, as a programmer, had to sift through 300 lines of code comprising more than 15 functions to figure out where `ptr` had been reset. However, if 300 lines of code were added to `test6_4.cpp`, and something were to go wrong, you can narrow down your search to two functions only: `initialize()` and `output()`. This is because the variables which have the incorrect value in them were specified as private members of a class, resulting in their being able to be manipulated by these two functions only.

Thus, a class mechanism allows you to group together variables and functions that can be performed on these variables as a single and unique type. It also allows you to localize problems quickly, through the access privileges specified within the class declaration. In addition to this, suppose you were required to modify the program at a later date, and the modifications pertain to the members of the class `family` only? Given that these members are declared as private, all you have to do is modify the logic within the two functions which are the member functions of this class. Just think of the ease of maintenance of such programs; think of the power that is placed at your fingertips!

Now that you understand the fundamental concept of classes, a few variations will be made to `test6_4.cpp` to see how the compiler responds to these changes. `main()` will be modified to qualify `initialize()` by class name, instead of class object name. All subsequent changes to the original program will be highlighted by imbedding a double asterisk within the comment. Make sure you pay special attention to these changes.

```
C:> type test6_5.cpp

//    test6_5.cpp
#include <iostream.h>          // necessary for I/O
```

```
class family
    {
    private:                 // notice use of keyword private
    char *husband;           // member list follows
    char *wife;
    char *son;
    char *daughter;
    family *ptr;             // ptr declaration inside family
    public:                  // notice use of keyword public
    void initialize(void);   // member functions follow
    void output(family *ptr);
    };
family Anderson;             // Anderson is object of type family

main(void)
{
    // ** initialize() is qualified by class name only.
    family::initialize();
}
// initialize() is qualified by class name
void family::initialize(void) // notice scope resolution operator
{
    // initializing member list of object Anderson
    // class members are qualified by class object name
    Anderson.ptr = &Anderson;
    Anderson.ptr->husband = "John Anderson";
    Anderson.ptr->wife = "Mary Anderson";
    Anderson.ptr->son = "Joey Anderson";
    Anderson.ptr->daughter = "Marla Anderson";
    Anderson.output(Anderson.ptr);
}
// output() is qualified by class name
void family::output(family *ptr)
{
    cout <<"husband is  " << ptr->husband   <<"\n"
         <<"wife is     " << ptr->wife      <<"\n"
         <<"son is      " << ptr->son       <<"\n"
         <<"daughter is " << ptr->daughter  <<"\n";
}
```

Compiling this program results in the following unfriendly message from the compiler:

```
Error:   Use . or -> to call family::initialize() in function
         main().
```

The declaration

```
family Anderson;
```

could just as well have been a declaration such as this:

```
family Anderson, Davis, Samuel;
```

The compiler needs to know which one of these objects or instances is being operated on. That is why it is necessary to prefix the object name that is being operated in the function call in main(). Recall that initialize() is a public member of family; it is accessible from anywhere within the program. That is why the compiler did not issue any unfriendly messages with reference to the function being called from main().

OK. Now let's modify the original version (test6_4.cpp) and reference the class members without qualifying them by the class object name, in the function initialize(). Remember, the changes are highlighted by a double asterisk within the comment.

```
C:> type test6_6.cpp

//    test6_6.cpp                        .
#include <iostream.h>          // necessary for I/O
class family
    {
    private:                    // notice use of keyword private
    char *husband;              // member list follows
    char *wife;
    char *son;
    char *daughter;
    family *ptr;                // ptr declaration inside family
    public:                     // notice use of keyword public
    void initialize(void);      // member functions follow
    void output(family *ptr);
    };
family Anderson;                // Anderson is object of type family

main(void)
{
    // initialize() is qualified by class object name.
    Anderson.initialize();
}
// initialize() is qualified by class name
void family::initialize(void) // notice scope resolution operator
{
    // initializing member list of object Anderson
```

```
        // ** class members are not qualified by class object name
        ptr = &Anderson;
        ptr->husband = "John Anderson";
        ptr->wife = "Mary Anderson";
        ptr->son = "Joey Anderson";
        ptr->daughter = "Marla Anderson";
        output(ptr);
}
// output() is qualified by class name
void family::output(family *ptr)
{
        cout <<"husband is   " << ptr->husband    <<"\n"
             <<"wife is      " << ptr->wife        <<"\n"
             <<"son is       " << ptr->son         <<"\n"
             <<"daughter is  " << ptr->daughter    <<"\n";

}
```

When this program is compiled (much to our amazement), there are no errors. Let's think about this for a second.

Well, ptr is set to the location in memory of the object Anderson. Hence, each time ptr is used to initialize members of the class, the object Anderson is being operated on. That is why there is no need to qualify ptr by object name; the compiler understands.

Let's modify the original version again, and try to initialize ptr in main(). ptr will be sent as an actual argument to initialize(), and the class declaration and function definitions will be modified accordingly.

```
C:> type test6_7.cpp

//   test6_7.cpp
#include <iostream.h>           // necessary for I/O
class family
    {
    private:                    // notice use of keyword private
    char *husband;              // member list follows
    char *wife;
    char *son;
    char *daughter;
    family *ptr;                // ptr declaration inside family
    public:                     // notice use of keyword public
    void initialize(family *ptr);   // ** send ptr as argument
    void output(family *ptr);
    };
family Anderson;                // Anderson is object of type family

main(void)
```

```
{
    // ** accessing private member in main()
    Anderson.ptr = &Anderson;
    // ** Send ptr to initialize()
    Anderson.initialize(Anderson.ptr);
}
// ** initialize() receives ptr as argument
void family::initialize(family *ptr)
{
    // initializing member list of object Anderson
    // class members are not qualified by class object name
    ptr->husband = "John Anderson";
    ptr->wife = "Mary Anderson";
    ptr->son = "Joey Anderson";
    ptr->daughter = "Marla Anderson";
    output(ptr);
}
// output() is qualified by class name
void family::output(family *ptr)
{
    cout <<"husband is  " << ptr->husband   <<"\n"
         <<"wife is     " << ptr->wife      <<"\n"
         <<"son is      " << ptr->son       <<"\n"
         <<"daughter is " << ptr->daughter  <<"\n";
}
```

Compiling this program results in the following message:

```
Error:   family::ptr is not accessible in function main()
```

The reason for this message should be obvious. ptr is declared as a private member of the class family. It can be manipulated only by its class member functions. It cannot be initialized in main().

6.4   REVIEW

Let's summarize what we have learned in this chapter:

- Classes offer a mechanism for grouping together variables and functions that can be performed by those variables within a single, unique type.

- Classes allow quick localization of problems and ease of maintenance of programs.

- The member list within a class comprises variable declarations and, optionally, member functions.

- Public member function calls are prefixed with the class object name.

- Member function definitions are prefixed with the class name.

Classes in C++—Scope, Members, and Access Specifiers

7.1 INTRODUCTION

Rules specific to classes, class members, and member functions will be discussed in this chapter. If you understood the fundamental concepts described in the previous chapter, you should be able to breeze fairly quickly through this one. If you are not comfortable yet, then this chapter should help in achieving that end. Some of the information here may seem redundant, but this will help reinforce the ideas introduced in prior chapters. It is essential that you understand classes completely, in order to recognize their full potential and power.

7.2 CLASS DECLARATIONS

Classes are declared as follows:

```
class class_name
    {
    member_1;               // member list follows
    member_2;
    member_3;
    member_function_1();    // member functions are also
    member_function_2();    // known as methods.
    };
```

and objects or instances of classes are defined as follows:

```
class_name instance_1;    // instance_1 is an instance of class
                          // type class_name.
```

7.3   CLASS NAME SCOPE

Class name has to be unique within its scope. You cannot assign the same class name to two different types of classes. Take a look at the following program:

```
C:> type test7_1.cpp

//    test7_1.cpp
#include <iostream.h>      // necessary for I/O
class increment
    {
    public:                // public member list follows
    int i;
    int j;
    int add_one(int i, int j);
    };
class increment            // ERROR! SAME CLASS NAME
    {
    public:                // public member list follows
    int k;
    int sub_one(int k);
    };
increment var1;            // var1 is an instance of class increment
increment var2;            // var2 is an instance of class increment

main(void)
{
    int x, y;         // x and y are local to main()
    var1.i = 1;       // initialize class members of object var1
    var1.j = 2;
    x = var1.increment::add_one(var1.i, var1.j);
    var2.k = 5;       // initialize class members of object var2
    y = var2.increment::sub_one(var2.k);
    cout << "x is " << x << " \n"
            "y is " << y << " \n";
}
//    add_one is qualified by class name
int increment::add_one(int i, int j)
{
    int l;
    l = i + j;
    return l;
}
```

```
//   sub_one is qualified by class name
int increment::sub_one(int k)
{
    k -= 1;
    return k;
}
```

Compiling this program results in this error:

```
Error:   Multiple declaration for increment()
```

The problem can be fixed by changing one of the class names, as follows.

```
C:> type test7_2.cpp

//   test7_2.cpp
#include <iostream.h>     // necessary for I/O
class increment
    {
    public:              // public member list follows
    int i;
    int j;
    int add_one(int i, int j);
    };
class decrement          // ** Notice different class name
    {
    public:              // public member list follows
    int k;
    int sub_one(int k);
    };
increment var1;          // var1 is an instance of class increment
decrement var2;          // var2 is an instance of class decrement

main(void)
{
    int x, y;        // x and y are local to main()
    var1.i = 1;      // initialize class members of object var1
    var1.j = 2;
    x = var1.increment::add_one(var1.i, var1.j);
    var2.k = 5;      // initialize class members of object var2
    y = var2.decrement::sub_one(var2.k);
    cout << "x is " << x << " \n"
            "y is " << y << " \n";
}
//   add_one is qualified by class name
int increment::add_one(int i, int j)
```

```
{
    int l;
    l = i + j;
    return l;
}
//   sub_one is qualified by class name
int decrement::sub_one(int k)
{
    k -= 1;
    return k;
}
```

Compiling and running this program results in the following output:

```
x is 3
y is 4
```

Now take a look at this program:

```
C:> type test7_3.cpp

//   test7_3.cpp
#include <iostream.h>      // necessary for I/O
class increment
    {
    public:               // public member list follows
    int i;
    int j;
    int add_one(int i, int j);
    };
increment var1;           // var1 is an instance of class increment

int sub_one(int y);       // function prototype
main(void)
{
    int x, y;        // x and y are local to main()
    var1.i = 1;      // initialize class members of object var1
    var1.j = 2;
    x = var1.increment::add_one(var1.i, var1.j);
    y = sub_one(y);
    cout << "x is " << x << " \n"
        << "y is " << y << " \n";
}
//   add_one is qualified by class name
int increment::add_one(int i, int j)
{
    int l;
```

```
        l = i + j;
        return l;
}
int sub_one(int k)    // sub_one not qualified by any class name
{
class increment       // ** Notice same class name
    {
    public:           // public member list follows
    int k;
    };
increment var2;       // var2 is an object of type class increment
    var2.k = 5;       // initialize member of class increment
    return var2.k;
}
```

This program produces the following output:

```
x is 3
y is 5
```

This version worked, even though two class names were assigned the same name. The reason for this is because the second declaration of the class increment() is out of scope of the first declaration. So what is the scope of a class name? It starts at the point of declaration, and ends at the end of the enclosing block. Two classes of the same name will be correctly recognized by the compiler, as long as they are not within scope of each other. In the sample program, the second declaration of initialize() is within the function sub_one, which is out of scope of the first declaration of initialize().

7.4   CLASS MEMBER DATA TYPES

The class member list can comprise any valid C++ data type. It can contain the usual primary types:

```
class primary
    {
    int a;        // integer
    char b;       // character
    float c;      // float
    double d;     // double
    };
primary class_1;  // class_1 is an object of type primary.
```

It can contain structures:

```
class structure_1
```

```
     {
     struct family;   // member list contains structure of type
                       //    family.
     };
structure_1 Anderson // Anderson is object of type strucuture_1
```

It can contain pointers to any valid type:

```
class pointer_1
     {
     struct family;
     struct family *ptr; // ptr is pointer to structure of type
                         //    family.
     };
pointer_1 Anderson;      // Anderson is an object of type pointer_1
```

It can even contain classes. However, the class inside a class must have been declared elsewhere, before it can be declared within another. Take a look at the following program:

```
C:> type test7_4.cpp

//   test7_4.cpp
#include <iostream.h>    // necessary for I/O
class class_2
     {
     public:
     int i;
     };
class class_1
     {
     public:
     int j;
     class_2 variable_2; // variable_2 is a nested class
     };
class_1 variable_1;      // variable_1 is an object of type
                         //    class_1.
main(void)
{
     variable_1.variable_2.i = 12;
     cout << "i is " << variable_1.variable_2.i << "\n";
}
```

This program gives the following output:

```
i is 12
```

Notice the syntax for accessing a member of a nested class:

```
variable_1.variable_2.i
```

The rule to follow is to start with the object name of the outermost class, and then to work your way to the class that is being accessed.

Now take a look at what happens if we move the declaration of class_1 below class_2:

```
C:> type test7_5.cpp

//   test7_5.cpp
#include <iostream.h>     // necessary for I/O
class class_1
     {
     public:
     int j;
     class_2 variable_2; // variable_2 is a nested class
     };
class_1 variable_1;       // variable_1 is an object of type class_1

class class_2             // class_2 is declared after class_1
     {                    //    references it.
     public:
     int i;
     };

main(void)
{
     variable_1.variable_2.i = 12;
     cout << "i is " << variable_1.variable_2.i << "\n";
}
```

Compiling this version results in the following message:

```
Error:    Type name expected
```

This is because the class class_2 is declared inside class_1, but class_2 has not been declared yet.

7.5   CLASS MEMBER STORAGE SPECIFIERS

The class member list declarations can be preceded with any storage class specifier except auto, extern, and register. A class declared as follows:

```
class invalid_1
```

```
    {
    auto int a;          // invalid storage class specifier
    extern char b;       // invalid storage class specifier
    register int c;      // invalid storage class specifier
    };
invalid_1 variable;      // variable is object of type invalid_1
```

will generate the following messages from the compiler:

```
Error:    Storage class 'auto' not allowed for a field
Error:    Storage class 'extern' not allowed for a field
Error:    Storage class 'register' not allowed for a field
```

7.5.1   Static class members

Take a look at the following class declaration:

```
class add_1
    {
    int counter;
    int i;
    int add_number(int);
    };
```

The declaration above declares a class add_1, which contains declarations for two integers, and one function. Now when several variables of that class type are declared:

```
add_1 variable_1, variable_2, variable_3;
```

copies of the data members of add_1 are assigned to each.

Now suppose that the value of counter is the same for all variables. (Perhaps counter counts the number of times a loop is entered.) For the duration of the program, three copies of this value will be floating around, when, in fact, it would be more efficient to have just one. C++ allows us to get around situations such as these by allowing the keyword *static* to precede the declaration of any type within a class.

Static implies that there will be only one copy of the type declared as such, and it will be shared by all data objects or instances of that type. Now take a look at the following declaration:

```
class add_1
    {
    private:
    static int counter;            // notice keyword static
    public:
```

```
int i;
int add_number(int);
};
```

The keyword `static` precedes the declaration of `counter`. When objects of this class are declared:

```
add_1 variable_1, variable_2, variable_3;
```

the location in memory for their static member `counter` will be the same. This is more efficient, since there is only one copy of the member, and its contents will not vary for each instance of that type.

The advantages offered by static members can now be summarized:

1. They reduce the need for global variables.

2. They make obvious the data which can be logically shared within a class.

7.6   CLASS MEMBER ACCESS SPECIFIERS

You should be able to breeze through this section rapidly, since it mainly reinforces concepts that you have already read about and seen used extensively in prior programs.

Class members can be made `public`, `private`, or `protected`. Within a class declaration, each one of these keywords can be used to precede one or more class member declarations. The class members acquire special characteristics, based on their access specifier.

7.6.1   Public access

In C++, all members of a structure are `public` by default. In the declaration below:

```
struct familiy
    {
    char *husband;
    char *wife;
    char *son;
    char *daughter;
    };
family Anderson;    // Anderson is structure of type family
```

the structure members `husband`, `wife`, `son`, and `daughter` can be accessed from anywhere within the program. However, *class members* are `private` by default. Hence, all public members must be specified as such:

```
class family
```

```
     {
     public:          // class members that follow are public
     char *husband;
     char *wife;
     char *son;
     char *daughter;
     };
family Anderson;      // Anderson is class of type family
```

The modifier remains effective for all declarations that follow it, until a different access modifier is encountered. The modifier can be reinserted more than once. The following declaration is valid:

```
class family
     {
     public:          // class members that follow are public
     char *husband;
     char *wife;
     private:         // class members that follow are private
     char *son;
     char *daughter;
     public:          // class members that follow are public again
     char *niece;
     };
```

Here's a short program that uses public class members:

```
C:> type test7_6.cpp
//   test7_6.cpp

#include <iostream.h>     // necessary for I/O
void function_1(int i);
class add_numbers
     {
     public:              // public class members follow
     int i;
     int add_sum(int);
     };
add_numbers one;          // one is an object of type add_numbers
main(void)
{
     one.i = 1;
     function_1(one.i);
}
void function_1(int i)
{
     i += 5;
```

```
        cout << "i is " << i << "\n";
}
```

The output looks like this:

```
i is 6
```

Notice that `function_1()` is not a member function of the class `add_numbers`. Yet the compiler allowed it to take `i` as an argument, and change its value. This is because `i` was declared as public, and therefore there are no access restrictions on it.

7.6.2 Private access

In C++, all member declarations are private by default. Thus, the following declaration:

```
class family
    {
    char *husband;
    char *wife;
    char *son;
    char *daughter;
    };
```

is equivalent to

```
class family
    {
    private:
    char *husband;
    char *wife;
    char *son;
    char *daughter;
    };
```

Private members can be assessed only by their class member functions (and friends of a class, a topic that we will discuss later on in this chapter). Here's another version of `test7_6.cpp`, that specifies its class members as private instead of public:

```
C:> type test7_7.cpp

//   test7_7.cpp
#include <iostream.h>    // necessary for I/O

void function_1(int i);
```

```
class add_numbers
    {
    int i;              // class members private by default
    int add_sum(int);
    };
add_numbers one;        // one is an object of type add_numbers

main(void)
{
    one.i = 1;
    function_1(one.i);
}
void function_1(int i)
{
    i += 5;
    cout << "i is " << i << "\n";
}
```

Compiling this version gives an error:

```
Error:   add_numbers::i is not accessible in function main()
```

This is because there is a call to function_1() inside main(), in which an argument of type integer is being sent. However, the integer that is being sent happens to be a private member of the class add_numbers, and function_1() does not have access privileges to it because it is not a member (or friend) function.

Let's modify test7_7.cpp to see what would happen if some other variable is sent to function_1():

```
C:> type test7_8.cpp

//    test7_8.cpp
#include <iostream.h>    // necessary for I/O
void function_1(int i);

class add_numbers
    {
    int i;              // class members private by default
    int add_num(int);
    };
add_numbers one;        // one is an object of type add_numbers

main(void)
{
    int k = 10;         // k is local to main()
```

```
        function_1(k);        // send k as argument to function_1()
}
void function_1(int k)
{
    k += 5;
    cout << "k is " << k << "\n";
}
```

This program compiles correctly, and results in the following output:

```
k is 15
```

The reason for this is simple. The variable k is declared within main(), it is not a class member, and therefore has no access restrictions. Hence, it can be sent as an argument to function_1(), which is also not a class member.

OK. Now let's try to send the class member i to its class member function add_num():

```
C:> type test7_9.cpp

//    test7_9.cpp
#include <iostream.h>    // necessary for I/O
void function_1(int i);

class add_numbers
    {
    int i;              // class members private by default
    void add_num(void);
    };
add_numbers one;        // one is an object of type add_numbers

main(void)
{
    int k = 10;         // k is local to main()
    function_1(k);      // send k as argument to function_1()
    one.add_num();      // call add_num()

}
void function_1(int k)
{
    k += 5;
    cout << "k is " << k << "\n";
}
void add_numbers::add_num(void)
{
    one.i = 5;
```

```
    cout << "i is " << one.i << "\n";
}
```

Compiling this program results in the following message:

```
Error:    add_numbers::add_num is not accessible in function main()
```

The reason for this message is obvious. add_num is a private member of its class, and therefore not accessible from main(). So how can add_num() be accessed? Well, it is common (and logical) to declare data members of a class as private, and member functions as public. Doing so to test 7_9.cpp will fix the problem:

```
class add_numbers
    {
    int i;              // class members private by default
    public:             // function declaration is public
    void add_num(void);
    };
```

The output looks as follows:

```
k is 15
i is 5
```

7.6.3   Protected access

Protected access has to do with member access by a derived class. But since derived classes have not been discussed just yet, a discussion on this topic will be deferred until then.

7.7   CLASS MEMBER FUNCTIONS

All functions that are declared within a class are called *member functions,* or *methods.* Member function scope and access rules are the same as regular class members.

7.8   FRIEND FUNCTIONS

A class member function name can be prefixed with the keyword friend. This is a *friend function.* Take a look at the following declaration:

```
class family
    {
    private:                        // private members follow
    char *husband;
    char *wife;
    char *son;
```

```
    char *daughter;
    family *ptr;
    public:                              // public members follow
    void initialize(void);
    friend void output(family *ptr);   // notice friend function
    };
```

A class of type family is declared, with private members husband, wife, son, daughter, and ptr, and public function member initialize(). The function output() is prefixed with the keyword friend; thus, this is a *friend function*. A friend function is not a member of that class. However, it has full access to the private and protected members of a class. Now take a look at this program that uses this class.

```
C:> type test7_11.cpp

//   test7_11.cpp
#include <iostream.h>;                  // necessary for I/O
class family
    {
    private:
    char *husband;
    char *wife;
    char *son;
    char *daughter;
    family *ptr;
    public:
    void initialize(void);
    friend void output(family *ptr);   // notice friend function
    };
family Anderson;            // Anderson is object of type family
void output(family *ptr); // notice function prototype for output()

main(void)
{
    Anderson.initialize();
}
void family::initialize(void) // notice class name and :: operator
{
    Anderson.ptr = &Anderson;
    ptr->husband =  "John Anderson";
    ptr->wife    =  "Mary Anderson";
    ptr->son     =  "Joey Anderson";
    ptr->daughter = "Marla Anderson";
    output(ptr);
}
```

```
void output(family *ptr)     // notice no class name
{
     cout << "husband is  "    << ptr->husband  << "\n"
          << "wife is     "    << ptr->wife     << "\n"
          << "son is      "    << ptr->son      << "\n"
          << "daughter is "    << ptr->daughter << "\n";
}
```

In the declaration of class `family`, we find that `output()` is declared as a `friend` function. This means that it is not a member function of the class family. However, it can access its private members `husband`, `wife`, `son`, `daughter`, and `ptr`, since it is a `friend`. The output for this program follows:

```
husband is     John Anderson
wife is        Mary Anderson
son is         Joey Anderson
daughter is    Marla Anderson
```

Friend functions are not affected by access specifiers. If the declaration of `output()` within class `family` was moved as follows:

```
class family
    {
    private:                      // private members follow
    char *husband[25];
    char *wife[25];
    char *son[25];
    char *daughter[25];
    friend void output(family *ptr);   // friend inside
                                       //   private list.
    family *ptr;
    public:                       // public members follow
    void initialize(void);
    };
```

it would not mean that the friend function is private. That's the whole point of friend functions anyway. They are "outside" functions which can access private and protected members of the class that they are friends of. Also, their function prototype need not necessarily exist. We included it to illustrate that no error messages are generated during compilation, as they would have if it were a class member.

All members of one class can become friends of another class via a single statement. Take a look at this program:

```
C:> type test7_12.cpp
```

```
//   test7_12.cpp
#include <iostream.h>    // necessary for I/O
class neighbor;          // notice incomplete class declaration

class family
     {
     friend neighbor;    // all functions of class neighbor
                         //   are friends of class family.

     char *husband;      // private members follow
     char *wife;
     family *ptr;
     public:
     void initialize(void);
     };
family Anderson;          // Anderson is object of type family

class neighbor
     {
     public:
     void output(family *ptr);
     };
neighbor Davis;           // Davis is object of type neighbor

main (void)
{
     Anderson.initialize();
}
void family::initialize(void)
{
     Anderson.ptr = &Anderson;
     ptr->husband = "John Anderson";
     ptr->wife    = "Mary Anderson";
     // send ptr to freind function output()
     Davis.output(Anderson.ptr);
}
void neighbor::output(family *ptr)
{
     cout << "husband is " << ptr->husband << " \n"
          << "wife is    " << ptr->wife    << " \n";
}
```

Compiling and running this program gives the desired result:

```
husband is John Anderson
wife is    Mary Anderson
```

Notice the incomplete declaration of class `neighbor`. It was necessary for us to do so, since reference is made to the class `neighbor` before it is declared. Remember, however, that objects of type `neighbor` cannot be declared unless the class declaration is complete.

The function `output()` is declared as a member function of class `neighbor`. The class `neighbor` is declared a friend of the class `family`. Hence, all functions of the class `neighbor` become friends of the class `family`, even without this keyword having to prefix their individual declarations. This is why the friend function `output()` was able to access the private member `ptr` of `family`.

7.9   INLINE FUNCTIONS

There is one more subject to be discussed before this chapter is concluded, and that is *inline functions*. A member function can be defined within a class declaration, as follows:

```
C:> type test7_13.cpp


//   test7_13.cpp
#include <iostream.h>     // necessary for I/O
class display
    {
    int i;
    public:
    void output(void)   // output() is an inline function
        { cout << "i is " << i << "\n"; }
    };
display object_1;        // object_1 is an object of type display

main(void)
{
    object_1.output();
}
```

In the class declaration of `display`, the function `output()` is defined within the class itself. This is an example of an implicit inline definition.

Inline function declarations, as mentioned in prior chapters, reduce function call overhead. Small functions are best suited to be inline within class declarations. This is because the code of an inline function will become a part of each instance of that class, and thereby waste a lot of memory if there is a lot of code. Inline functions can also be declared explicitly. Following is an example of an explicit declaration:

```
C:> type test7_14.cpp


//   test7_14.cpp
#include <iostream.h>     // necessary for I/O
```

```
class display
    {
    int i;
    public:
    void output(void);   // output() is defined inline elsewhere
    };
display object_1;          // object_1 is an object of type display

// display is defined inline explicitly
inline void display::output(void)
{
    cout << "i is " << i << " \n";
}

main(void)
{
    object_1.output();
}
```

The explicit declaration of the inline function `output()` is outside the class declaration, and is preceded by the keyword `inline`. This results in inline expansion of the code for the function `output()`, each time this function is called. Remember that inline functions must be defined before they can be referenced. Our program would not have compiled properly if its definition existed below `main()`.

7.10   REVIEW

In this chapter, features specific to class member declarations and definitions were described.

- Class names must be unique within their scope.
- Class member lists can comprise any valid C++ data type.
- Static class members allow multiple objects of a class type to share a location in memory. This reduces the need for global variables.
- Structure members are public by default.
- Class members are private by default.
- Class members can have public, private, and protected access.
- Class member functions follow the same scope and access rules as regular class members.
- Friend functions have access to the private and protected members of a class.
- Inline functions reduce function call overhead. Small functions are best declared inline within a class.

Chapter

8

Derived Classes—Fundamental Concepts

8.1 INTRODUCTION

When a child is born, he or she inherits certain characteristics from the mother, and some from the father. With the passage of time, this child develops traits which uniquely identify him or her from the rest. This child is a combination of characteristics inherited from the parents, and those derived from the environment that he or she grows up in.

As we grow older, our outlook of life changes. Our dreams, goals, and ambitions are derived from what we are taught, and what we experience in the circle in which we grow up and interact. And then, we pass on what we have learned and achieved to those who are near and dear to us, and give them the opportunity to build on what we built ourselves.

If you think of your life in a nutshell, you will realize just how much of it has been derived from what you inherited from your parents, what you learned from the social structure that you grew up in, and what your own ambition drives you to achieve. If features inherited from your parents could be grouped together as one class, and features derived from your social structure as another, then you are analogous to a "derived" class; you have inherited features from your base classes (your parents, education, and social structure), and you have added a few unique characteristics of your own (your ambitions, achievements, and more!).

Derived classes, as they exist in C++, are analogous to the simple life story presented above. A derived class inherits characteristics from one or more base classes. Then, it adds a few unique features of its own. This class can then be used as a base class for some other derived class, and so on. This is how a hierarchy of classes is created. This is how one object is built from another. This is what makes C++ the powerful language that it is.

8.2   A SIMPLE C APPLICATION

We will deviate from the main subject of this chapter for a moment. But trust us—we have a good reason for doing so, and this reason will become apparent as you conclude this section.

A simple C application will be developed that will add, find, modify, and delete records from a file. The code for the individual functions which will perform these tasks is not important. Therefore, it will suffice to simply output a statement indicating which function is being executed at the time. What we want you to understand is how a C program handles a certain situation, and how C++ improves on it. Here's the code.

```c
C:> type test8_1.c
/* test8_1.c */

#include <stdio.h>        /* necessary for getc() */

void add(void);           /* function prototypes */
void find(void);
void modify(void);
void delete(void);

main()
{
    char string[2], option = '\0';
    while (option != 'q')
    {
    printf ("Please enter option: \n");
    printf ("<a>dd, <f>ind, <m>odify, <d>elete or <q>uit:");
    gets(string);
    option = string[0];
    switch(option)
        {        /* start switch */
        case 'a':
            add();
            break;
        case 'f':
            find();
            break;
        case 'm':
            modify();
```

```
                    break;
            case 'd':
                    delete();
                    break;
            case 'q':
                    break;
            default:
                    printf ("Invalid input! Please re-enter. \n");
            }     /* end switch */
      }     /* end while() */
      return (0);
}     /* end main() */

void add(void)
{
      printf ("Inside add() \n");
}
void find(void)
{
      printf ("Inside find() \n");
}
void modify(void)
{
      printf ("Inside modify() \n");
}
void delete(void)
{
      printf ("Inside delete() \n");
}
```

Compiling and running this program results in the following message being output on the screen:

```
Please enter option
<a>dd, <f>ind, <m>odify, <d>elete or <q>uit
```

Upon entry of a valid option, the corresponding function is executed. Otherwise, the message "Invalid option! Please reenter" is displayed.

Now let's bring a small company into the picture. This company provides consulting services to its clients. Customer information is stored inside a master file.

Mr. Edward Heath is the owner of this company. He has four employees: Mary, Joseph, Ronald, and Sandra. Mr. Heath is interested in classifying the functions that can be performed by his employees. All of them should have the capability to find records from the master file. Only Mary and Joseph are allowed to add and modify records. Only Mr. Heath is allowed to delete them.

This logic can be incorporated inside the C program by assigning pass-words to each employee. Access to various functions is allowed only upon entry of a valid password. Mary and Joseph are assigned the passwords 10 and 20. Mr. Heath is assigned the password 99. Now take a look at the modi-fied program.

```
C:> type test8_2.c

/* test8_2.c */

#include <stdio.h>        /* necessary for gets() */
#include <stdlib.h>       /* necessary for atoi() */

void add(void);           /* function prototypes */
void find(void);
void modify(void);
void delete(void);

main()
{
    char string[2], option = '\0';
    int i, *intptr;
    char *password, *charptr;
    printf ("Please enter password: ");
    charptr = gets(password);        /* get input from user */
    i = atoi(charptr);               /* convert to integer */

    while (option != 'q')
    {
    printf ("Please enter option: \n");
    printf ("<a>dd, <f>ind, <m>odify, <d>elete or <q>uit:");
    gets(string);              /* get option from user */
    option = string[0];
    switch(option)
        {        /* switch on option entered */
        case 'a':
            /* add() can be accessed by select employees */
            if (i == 10 || i == 11 || i == 99)
                add();
            else
                printf ("Permission denied!\n");
            break;
        case 'f': /* find() is accessible by all */
            find();
            break;
        case 'm':
```

```
                /* modify() is accessible by select employees */
                 if (i == 10  || i == 20 || i == 99)
                       modify();
                else
                       printf ("Permission denied! \n");
                break;
            case 'd': /* delete is accessible by 1 person only */
                if (i == 99)
                       delete();
                else
                       printf ("Permission denied! \n");
                break;
            case 'q':
                break;
            default:
                printf ("Invalid input! Please reenter. \n");
            }    /* end switch */
        }    /* end while() */
        return (0);
    }    /* end main() */

void add(void)
{
    printf ("Inside add() \n");
}
void find(void)
{
    printf ("Inside find() \n");
}
void modify(void)
{
    printf ("Inside modify() \n");
}
void delete(void)
{
    printf ("Inside delete() \n");
}
```

Notice that the header file <stdlib.h> is included. This header file contains the definition of the function atoi(), which simply converts an ASCII string to integer. In the example, input for password has to be converted to integer, in order to perform the correct checking.

Code is added inside the switch case construct to restrict access to various functions based on the password entered.

Now let's rewrite this program in C++. The functions that can be performed by various employees will be grouped together into classes. The program will be broken up into its logical fragments, and each fragment will be explained before proceeding to the next. First, take a look at the class declarations:

```
C:> type test8_1.cpp


//    test8_1.cpp


#include <iostream.h>    // necessary for I/O
#include <stdio.h>       // necessary for getch()
#include <stdlib.h>      // necessary for atoi()

class group_1
    {
    public:
    void find(void);
    };
group_1 everyone;    // everyone is an object of type group_1

class group_2
    {
    public:
    void add(void);
    void modify(void);
    };
group_2 select_few; // select_few is an object of type group_2

class group_3
    {
    public:
    void add(void);
    void modify(void);
    void remove(void);  // notice function name remove()
                        // delete is a reserved word in C++
    };
group_3 heath;      // heath is an object of type group_3
```

Three classes are declared. These are group_1, group_2, and group_3. Notice that group_2 and group_3 have two sets of functions which are exactly the same in name. These functions are add() and modify(). It is necessary for us to do so, since we are interested in grouping together the set of functions which can be performed by one group as a separate entity. C++ allows us to do so through the use of classes. The function called delete() in the C program is called remove() in the C++ program. This is because delete is a reserved word in C++ (it is an operator that will be discussed in later chapters).

Here's the main processing loop:

```
main(void)
{
    char string[2], option = '\0';
    int i, *intptr;
    char *password, *charptr;
    cout << "Please enter password: ";
    charptr = gets(password);       // get input from user
    i = atoi(charptr);              // convert to integer

    while (option != 'q')
    {   /* begin while() */
    cout << "Please enter option \n"
        << "<a>dd, <f>ind, <m>odify, <d>elete or <q>uit: ";
    cin  >> option;
    switch(option)
        {     // switch on option entered
        case 'a':
            // select employees can access add()
          if (i == 10 || i == 20)
          {
            select_few.add();
          }
          else if (i == 99)
          {
            heath.add();
          }
          else
            cout << "Permission denied \n";
          break;
      case 'f':
          everyone.find();
          break;
      case 'm':
          // select few can access modify()
          if (i == 10 || i == 20)
          {
            select_few.modify();
          }
          else if (i == 99)
          {
            heath.modify();
          }
          else
            cout << "Permission denied!";
```

```
            break;
      case 'd':
            if (i == 99)
            {
               heath.remove();
            }
            else
               cout << "Permission denied! \n";
            break;
      case 'q':
         break;
      default:
            cout << "Invalid option entered! \n";
      }     /* end switch */
   }     /* end while() */
}     /* end main() */
```

In main(), the inherent logic is the same as we saw in test8_2.c. However, we invoke member functions of different classes, based on the password entered, instead of the same copy of the appropriate function as we did in the C program. Take a look at the function definitions next:

```
//    function definitions follow

void group_1::find(void)
{
     cout << "Inside group1 find() \n";
}


void group_2::add(void)
{
     cout << "Inside group2 add() \n";
}


void group_2::modify(void)
{
     cout << "Inside group3 modify() \n";
}


void group_3::add(void)        // add() function for group_3
{
     cout << "Inside group3 add() \n";
}


void group_3::modify(void)     // modify() function for group_3
```

```
{
    cout << "Inside group3 modify() \n";
}

void group_3::remove(void)
{
    cout << "Inside group3 remove() \n";
}
```

Notice that there are two versions of add() and modify(), which are member functions of classes of type group_2 and group_3, respectively. There is only one version of remove(), which is a member function of the class group_3. The output statement has been modified, in order to qualify exactly which function is being executed at any time.

Now, if you take a look at the code for each version of these functions, you will realize that it is exactly the same. So how can multiple versions of the same code be eliminated, without loss of the reasons for having them grouped together in the same class? The answer is through the use of derived classes.

8.3 DERIVED CLASSES IN C++

C++ allows you to derive a class from one or more base classes. A *derived class* inherits all members of its base class. Access privileges of inherited members can be changed by the derived class through access specifiers that prefix the declaration of the base class. Valid access specifiers are public and private. Take a look at this fragment of code:

```
class group_1
    {
    public:
    void find(void);
    };
group_1 everyone;    // everyone is an object of type group_1
```

This is a declaration of a base class. Nothing unusual here. Now let's derive the class group_2 from it:

```
//   notice declaration of class group_2
class group_2:public group_1
    {
    public:          // notice missing declaration of find()
    void add(void);
    void modify(void);
    };
group_2 select_few; // select_few is an object of type group_2
```

OK. Now it's time to understand what happened. The class group_2 is derived from the class group_1, via the statement:

```
class group_2:public group_1
```

The name of the first class in the list is that of the derived class. The name of the class that follows the colon (:) is that of the base class. The class group_2 inherits all members of its base class group_1. These members now belong to the member list of the class group_2. However, only the public and protected members of the base class can be used. (Protected members will be discussed in detail in the next chapter.) The private members of the base class are not accessible to the derived class.

The access specifier public, which precedes the name of the base class:

```
class group_2:public group_1
```

is used to specify access privileges of the inherited member list as they relate to the derived class. This keyword indicates that the public members of the base class will also be public members inside the derived class. Along the same lines, protected members of the base class will be protected members inside the derived class. In other words, the keyword public indicates that the access privileges of the inherited members in the derived class will be the same as they exist in the base class.

Remember, however, that the private members of the base class continue to remain private for it, they cannot be accessed by the derived class. This makes sense. The very idea behind private members of a class is to limit their access privileges. The whole point would be lost if derived classes were to inherit access to these members. A derived class is often used as a building block for some other object. If a hierarchy of ten derived classes were created, then the private members of each class would be accessible to the next. The advantages derived from the restriction of class members would be lost completely.

We could also have derived the class as follows:

```
class group_2:private group_1        // notice keyword private
    {
    public:          // notice missing declaration of find()
    void add(void);
    void modify(void);
    };
group_2 select_few; // select_few is an object of type group_2
```

This declaration is synonymous to the following:

```
class group_2:group_1
```

```
    {
    public:           // notice missing declaration of find()
    void add(void);
    void modify(void);
    };
group_2 select_few; // select_few is an object of type group_2
```

This is because the default is private for a derived class. If this keyword prefixes the name of the base class, then both the public and protected members of the base class become private members of the derived class.

Now test8_1.cpp will be modified to use derived classes. The code will once again be presented in fragments, and each will be explained before proceeding to the next. First, the class declarations:

```
C:> type test8_2.cpp

//   test8_2.cpp

#include <iostream.h>   // necessary for I/O
#include <stdio.h>      // necessary for getch()
#include <stdlib.h>     // necessary for atoi()

class group_1
    {
    public:
    void find(void);
    };
group_1 everyone;   // everyone is an object of type group_1

class group_2
    {
    public:
    void add(void);
    void modify(void);
    };
group_2 select_few; // select_few is an object of type group_2

class group_3:public group_2  // notice derived class
    {
    public:
    void remove(void);
    };
group_3 heath;       // heath is an object of type group_3
```

The class group_3 is derived from the class group_2. The base class group_2 is specified as public. This results in the functions add() and modify() also

being public members for the class group_3. Now take a look at the code for
main().

```
main(void)
{
    char string[2], option = '\0';
    int i, *intptr;
    char *password, *charptr;
    cout << "Please enter password: ";
    charptr = gets(password);
    i = atoi(charptr);

    while (option != 'q')
    {    /* begin while() */
    cout << "Please enter option \n"
        << "<a>dd, <f>ind, <m>odify, <d>elete or <q>uit: ";
    cin  >> option;
    switch(option)
        {    // start switch
        case 'a':
            // select employees can access add()
          if (i == 10 || i == 20)
          {
            select_few.add();
          }
          else if (i == 99)
          {
            heath.add();
          }
          else
            cout << "Permission denied \n";
          break;
        case 'f':
            everyone.find();
            break;
        case 'm':
            // select few can access modify()
            if (i == 10 || i == 20)
            {
              select_few.modify();
            }
            else if (i == 99)
            {
              heath.modify();
            }
            else
```

```
            cout << "Permission denied!";
          break;
    case 'd':
          if (i == 99)
          {
            heath.remove();
          }
          else
            cout << "Permission denied! \n";
          break;
    case 'q':
        break;
    default:
          cout << "Invalid option entered! \n";
    }    /* end switch */
  }    /* end while() */
}    /* end main() */
```

The code is the same as test8_1.cpp. Now take a look at the function definitions.

```
//    function definitions follow

void group_1::find(void)
{
    cout << "Inside group1 find() \n";
}
void group_2::add(void)
{
    cout << "Inside group2 add() \n";
}
void group_2::modify(void)
{
    cout << "Inside group3 modify() \n";
}
void group_3::remove(void)
{
    cout << "Inside group3 remove() \n";
}
```

Notice that only one version of each function is defined. Compiling and running this program results in the following message being displayed on the screen:

```
Please enter password
```

Let's pretend that we are the designated employee-of-the-month who has the privilege of deleting records from the master file (and the burden of living with the knowledge that a valid record might have been deleted!!).

We enter the password 99. Let's enter option *f* to find a record.

The following message displays on the screen:

```
Inside group1 find()
Please enter option
<a>dd  <f>ind  <m>odify  <d>elete, or <q>uit
```

Entering option a results in the following message being displayed:

```
Inside group2 add
Please enter option
<a>dd  <f>ind  <m>odify  <d>elete, or <q>uit
```

Entering d results in this message:

```
Inside group3 remove()
Please enter option
<a>dd  <f>ind  <m>odify  <d>elete, or <q>uit
```

and entering q allows exit from the program.

Now take a look at this fragment of code again:

```
case 'a':
    // select employees can access add()
    if (i == 10 || i == 20)
    {
      select_few.add();
    }
    else if (i == 99)
    {
      heath.add();
    }
```

As you can see, heath.add() is supposed to execute if the password is 99. However, there is no definition for heath.add()! The compiler accepted this because heath is an instance of class group_3, and group_3 is derived from the class group_2. Hence, it inherits all public members of its base class. If functions are inherited by one class, then there is no need to re-define them; the compiler understands.

Take a look at Fig. 8.1 for a picture of the logic that is being implemented by the code.

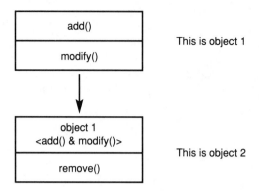

If the class group_2 can be considered an object, then the class group_3 contains that object, plus a unique function that differentiates it from group_2. group_3 cannot be group_3 without group_2. Thus, one object is used as a building block for another. The concept of derived classes should be clear to you now.

8.4   REVIEW

In this chapter, we learned the reasons for deriving a class from a base class, and how to do so. You already understand the reason for using a class instead of a structure. Derived classes offer the advantages offered by classes, in addition to the capability of building a hierarchical structure of objects. The object at the top of the hierarchy is the most generalized object of the set. Each object derived from it contains features of the object that it is derived from, along with a few characteristics that make it unique.

You should now be thinking in terms of building objects, instead of writing procedural loops, as you are used to doing when you code in C. The possibilities that can be derived from derived classes should now be beginning to emerge.

Access Privileges of Members of Derived Classes

9.1 INTRODUCTION

In this chapter, access privileges of inherited members of classes derived from public and private base classes will be explained. But first, here's a discussion on *protected members*.

9.2 PROTECTED MEMBERS IN A CLASS

Consider the following class declaration:

```
class group_1
    {
    int a;    // a is private by default;
    protected:
    int b;    // b is protected
    public:
    void output1(void);
    }
group_1 everyone;
```

group_1 is a class in which a is a private member, b is a protected member, and the function output1() is public. Now take a look at the complete program.

```
C:> type test9_1.cpp

//    test9_1.cpp    12/29/90 9:30 pm

#include <iostream.h>      // necessary for I/O

class group_1
     {
     int a;     // a is private by default;
     protected:
     int b;     // b is protected
     public:
     void output1(void);
     };
group_1 everyone;

class group_2:public group_1   // group_2 derived from group_1
     {
     int c;     // c is private by default
     public:
     void output2(void);
     };
group_2 a_few;

void main(void)
{
     everyone.output1();
}

void group_1::output1(void)
{
     a = 5;
     b = 10;
     cout << "a is " << a << " b is " << b << "\n";
     a_few.output2();
}
void group_2::output2(void)
{
     c = 15;
     b += 10;
     cout << "c is " << c << " b is " << b << "\n";
}
```

Compiling and running this program yields the following output:

```
a is 5 b is 10
c is 15 b is 10
```

Class members a and b are public and private members of the class group_1. Hence, there are no suprises when the compiler allows access to these members from the function output1(), since it is a member function of group_1. The protected member b is also being accessed from the function output2(), which is a public member of the class group_2. What you should note here is that group_2 is derived from group_1; therefore, it inherits all members of group_1. Hence, the compiler does not issue any error messages when a class member of group_1 is accessed by a class member function of group_2.

Let's modify the program and try to access the private member a from output2().

```
C:> type test9_2.cpp

//    test9_2.cpp    12/30/90 8:30 pm

#include <iostream.h>    // necessary for I/O

class group_1
    {
    int a;    // a is private by default;
    protected:
    int b;    // b is protected
    public:
    void output1(void);
    };
group_1 everyone;

class group_2:public group_1  // group_2 derived from group_1
    {
    int c;    // c is private by default
    public:
    void output2(void);
    };
group_2 a_few;

void main(void)
{
    everyone.output1();
}

void group_1::output1(void)
{
    a = 5;
    b = 10;
    cout << "a is " << a << " b is " << b << "\n";
```

```
        a_few.output2();
}
void group_2::output2(void)
{
        c = 15;
        b += 10;
        cout << "a is " << a << "\n"; //* access private member a
        cout << "c is " << c << " b is " << b << "\n";
}
```

Compiling and running this program results in the following error message:

```
Error:    'group_1::a' is not accessible in function
          group_2::output2()
```

This program illustrates that private members of a base class are not accessible to members of the derived class. (Recall that we had stated as such in the prior chapter.) Note that no error message is generated for when a is accessed inside group_1::output1(). Test9_1.cpp illustrated that protected members of a base class are accessible by members of the derived class. Now let's modify this program one more time and see if private and protected members of a base class are accessible to the public at large. You should already know the answer to this one, but we will present the code to reinforce what you may already know.

```
C:> type test9_3.cpp

//    test9_3.cpp    12/30/90 9:06 pm

#include <iostream.h>    // necessary for I/O

class group_1
    {
    int a;    // a is private by default;
    protected:
    int b;    // b is protected
    public:
    void output1(void);
    };
group_1 everyone;

class group_2:public group_1  // group_2 derived from group_1
    {
    int c;    // c is private by default
```

```
      public:
      void output2(void);
      };
group_2 a_few;

void main(void)
{
    cout << "a is " << a " b is " << b << "\n";
    everyone.output1();
}

void group_1::output1(void)
{
    a = 5;
    b = 10;
    cout << "a is " << a << " b is " << b << "\n";
    a_few.output2();
}
void group_2::output2(void)
{
    c = 15;
    b += 10;
    cout << "c is " << c << " b is " << b << "\n";
}
```

Compiling this program results in the following error messages:

```
Error:    Undefined symbol 'a' in function main()
          Undefined symbol 'b' in function main()
```

It would be safe to conclude that private and protected members of a base class can be accessed only by members of that class, and members of classes derived from it.

9.3 ACCESS PRIVILEGES OF PUBLICLY DERIVED CLASSES

The following short program illustrates access rules of members of base classes in derived classes.

```
C:> type test9_4.cpp

//   test9_4.cpp    12/30/90 9:45 pm

#include <iostream.h>    // necessary for I/O

class group_1
```

```
     {
     int a;     // a is private by default;
     protected:
     int b;     // b is protected
     public:
     void output1(void);
     };
group_1 class1;

class group_2:public group_1   // group_2 derived from group_1
     {
     public:
     void output2(void);
     };
group_2 class2;

class group_3:public group_2   // group_3 derived from group_2
     {
     public:
     void output3(void);
     };
group_3 class3;


void main(void)
{
     class1.output1();
     class2.output2();
     class3.output3();
}

void group_1::output1(void)
{
     a = 5;
     b = 10;
     cout << "a is " << a << " b is " << b << "\n";
}
void group_2::output2(void)
{
     cout << "a is " << a << " b is " << b << "\n";
}
void group_3::output3(void)
{
     cout << "a is " << a << " b is " << b << "\n";
}
```

Compiling this program results in the following error messages:

```
Error:    group_1::a is not accessible in function
          group_2::output2()
          group_1::a is not accessible in function
          group_3::output3()
```

Notice that no error messages were issued for accessing b from either one of the member functions of the derived classes group_2 and group_3. In conclusion, we can say that:

1. Public members of a base class continue to remain public for the derived class, and therefore, are accessible to the public at large. The functions output2() and output3() were declared as public members of the derived classes group_2 and group_3. Hence, they could be called from main().

2. Protected members of a base class continue to remain protected for the derived classes. b is a protected member inside the base class group_1. Yet the compiler does not issue any error messages for this variable when it is accessed from member functions of the derived classes. The compiler would issue an error message if this variable were accessed from a non-member function.

3. Private members of a base class continue to remain private to it. They cannot be accessed by member functions of derived classes.

9.4   ACCESS PRIVILEGES OF PRIVATELY DERIVED CLASSES

Test9_4.cpp will now be modified to prefix the base class with the keyword private instead of public. Here's the code.

```
C:> type test9_5.cpp

//    test9_5.cpp    12/30/90 10:22 pm

#include <iostream.h>    // necessary for I/O

class group_1
    {
    int a;    // a is private by default;
    protected:
    int b;    // b is protected
    public:
    void output1(void);
    };
group_1 class1;

class group_2:private group_1 // * notice private derivation
```

```
        {
        public:
        void output2(void);
        };
    group_2 class2;

    class group_3:private group_2  // * notice private derivation
        {
        public:
        void output3(void);
        };
    group_3 class3;


    void main(void)
    {
        class1.output1();
        class2.output2();
        class3.output3();
    }

    void group_1::output1(void)
    {
        a = 5;
        b = 10;
        cout << "a is " << a << " b is " << b << "\n";
    }
    void group_2::output2(void)
    {
        cout << "a is " << a << " b is " << b << "\n";
    }
    void group_3::output3(void)
    {
        cout << "a is " << a << " b is " << b << "\n";
    }
```

Compiling this program results in the following set of rather interesting error messages:

```
Error:   group_1::a is not accessible in function
         group_2::output2()
         group_1::a is not accessible in function
         group_3::output3()
         group_1::b is not accessible in function
         group_3::output3()
```

Take a moment to analyze these error messages.

The first one states that `group_1::a` is not accessible in function `group_2::output2()`. This is understandable. `a` is a private member of the class `group_1`, and continues to remain private to its class. It cannot be accessed by members of derived classes.

The second message states that `group_1::a` is not accessible in function `group_3::output3()`. This makes sense, for the same reason as the first error message.

The third message states that `group_1::b` is not accessible in function `group_3::output3()`. This one should have gotten you thinking a bit. Well, the reason this message was generated is because `b` is a protected member inside its base class. `group_2` is privately derived from `group_1`. This private derivation results in protected members of the base class becoming private members inside the derived class. Hence, `b` is now a private member for the derived class `group_2`. Therefore, `b` is inaccessible from a member function of `group_3`, since it is private for its base class, which is `group_2`. So how come we didn't get this message when `b` was accessed from `group_2::output2()`? Because, `b` is a protected member inside `group_1`, and therefore accessible by members of the derived class `group_2`. However, since `group_2` is privately derived, `b` becomes a private member for `group_2`, and therefore inaccessible to any subsequent derived classes.

So much for access of private base members inside privately derived classes. Let's modify `test9_5.cpp` to see how access privileges of public base members are affected by private derivation.

```
C:> type test9_6.cpp

//   test9_6.cpp     12/30/90 11:04 pm

#include <iostream.h>    // necessary for I/O

class group_1
    {
    int a;     // a is private by default;
    protected:
    int b;     // b is protected
    public:
    void output1(void);
    };
group_1 class1;

class group_2:private group_1 // * notice private derivation
    {
    public:
    void output2(void);
    };
group_2 class2;
```

```
class group_3:private group_2 // * notice private derivation
     {
     public:
     void output3(void);
     };
group_3 class3;


void main(void)
{
     class1.output1();
     class2.output2();
     class3.output3();
     class2.output1();    // * access of public member output1()
     class3.output1();    // * access of public member output1()
}

void group_1::output1(void)
{
     a = 5;
     b = 10;
     cout << "a is " << a << " b is " << b << "\n";
}
void group_2::output2(void)
{
     cout << "a is " << a << " b is " << b << "\n";
}
void group_3::output3(void)
{
     cout << "a is " << a << " b is " << b << "\n";
}
```

Compiling this program results in the set of three error messages that the compiler issued in the previous program, in addition to these two:

```
Error:   group_1::output1() is not accessible in function main()
         group_1::output1() is not accessible in function main()
```

These messages are generated for the following statements:

```
     class2.output1();   // * access of public member output1()
     class3.output1();   // * access of public member output1()
```

The reason for these messages is that public members of privately derived classes become private for the derived class. output1() is a public member of the class group_1. group_2 is privately derived from group_1. Hence, output1()

becomes a private member of group_1. class2 is an instance of the class group_2. The statement class2.output1() is invoked from main(). But since output1() is now a private member of group_2, it can be accessed only by its class member list, and main() does not fall inside that category. This problem could be fixed by invoking class2.output1() inside the function group_2::output2() instead of main().

```
void group_2::output2(void)
{
    class2.output1();
    cout << "a is " << a << " b is " << b << "\n";
}
```

However, the following code would still present a problem:

```
void group_3::output3(void)
{
    class3.output1();
    cout << "a is " << a << " b is " << b << "\n";
}
```

The first invocation would be acceptable, since output1() is being accessed from output2(), which is a member function of the class group_2, and group_2 is derived from group_1. The second invocation would be unacceptable, since group_2 is privately derived from group_1; hence, the public member output1() becomes private to it, and therefore inaccessible to group_3. Here is the complete program that would work. Code for the output of the variables a and b inside output2() and output3() have been taken out, as they are inapplicable to what is being currently explained.

```
C:> type test9_7.cpp

//    test9_7.cpp    12/31/90 12:01 am

#include <iostream.h>    // necessary for I/O

class group_1
    {
    int a;    // a is private by default;
    protected:
    int b;    // b is protected
    public:
    void output1(void);
    };
group_1 class1;

class group_2:private group_1 // * notice private derivation
```

```
    {
    public:
    void output2(void);
    };
group_2 class2;

class group_3:private group_2 // * notice private derivation
    {
    public:
    void output3(void);
    };
group_3 class3;


void main(void)
{
    class1.output1();
    class2.output2();
    class3.output3();
}

void group_1::output1(void)
{
    a = 5;
    b = 10;
    cout << "a is " << a << " b is " << b << "\n";
}
void group_2::output2(void)
{
    cout << "Inside output2() \n";
    class2.output1();   // * access output1() from output2()
}
void group_3::output3(void)
{
    cout << "Inside output3() \n";
}
```

Another solution would have been simply to derive group_2 and group_3 publicly instead of privately. Which alternative you choose depends on how you want the visibility of these variables and functions to be affected.

The important point to note here is that data hiding, such as can be achieved via access specifiers for class member lists and base classes, is the key to designing "modular" programs. Your program will be composed of stand-alone sections that are easily identifiable, and therefore that much more flexible and modifiable. This is because you understand the scope of each variable, based upon the use of access specifiers. What is required is that you take the time to plan a hierachy of classes, and determine access privileges of members of base classes inside derived classes, and understand exactly why you did what you did!

9.5   REVIEW

In this chapter, we described access privileges of base class members inside derived classes. Here's a table that summarizes the major concepts presented.

TABLE 9.1   Access Privileges of Base Class Members Inside Derived Classes

Base class specifer	Access inside base class	Access inside derived class
public	public	public
	private	nonaccessible
	protected	protected
private	public	private
	private	nonaccessible
	protected	private

Class Initialization and Deactivation—Constructors and Destructors

10.1 INTRODUCTION

In this chapter, we will discuss how C++ offers a mechanism for initializing classes, when they are created, and a corresponding mechanism for destroying objects when they are no longer in scope, or needed. C++ allows automatic initialization of objects when they are created through constructors. Destructors are the opposite of constructors. They provide a way to deallocate memory that may have been allocated to objects through constructors. The discussion will begin with constructors.

10.2 CONSTRUCTORS—AN INTRODUCTION

Consider the following sample program:

```
C:> type test10_1.cpp

// test10_1.cpp  01/12/91 3:32 pm

#include <iostream.h>    // necessary for I/O

class sum
```

```
    {
    public:
    int sum_1;
    int sum_2;
    };
sum object_1, object_2;

void main(void)
{
    cout << "Inside main() \n";
    cout << "object_1.sum_1 is "<< object_1.sum_1 << "\n";
    cout << "object_1.sum_2 is "<< object_1.sum_2 << "\n";
    cout << "object_2.sum_1 is "<< object_2.sum_1 << "\n";
    cout << "object_2.sum_2 is "<< object_2.sum_2 << "\n";
}
```

Compiling and executing this simple program results in the following output:

```
Inside main()
object_1.sum_1 is 0
object_1.sum_2 is 0
object_2.sum_1 is 0
object_2.sum_2 is 0
```

sum_1 and sum_2 are automatically initialized to zeroes, since they are declared outside of main(), and never set to any other value. But suppose these class members were to contain some other values. Let's try to initialize these members inside the class declaration:

```
C:> type test10_2.cpp

// test10_2.cpp  01/12/91 3:32 pm

#include <iostream.h>     // necessary for I/O

class sum
    {
    public:
    int sum_1 = 1; // ** we try to initialize class members
    int sum_2 = 2;
    };
sum object_1, object_2;

void main(void)
```

```
{
    cout << "Inside main() \n";
    cout << "object_1.sum_1 is "<< object_1.sum_1 << "\n";
    cout << "object_1.sum_2 is "<< object_1.sum_2 << "\n";
    cout << "object_2.sum_1 is "<< object_2.sum_1 << "\n";
    cout << "object_2.sum_2 is "<< object_2.sum_2 << "\n";
}
```

Compiling this program results in the following error message:

```
Error:    Cannot initialize a field
```

Obviously, class members cannot be initialized at the time that they are declared. Instead, C++ allows objects to be initialized at the time that they are created through constructors.

10.3 DEFAULT CONSTRUCTORS

A *constructor* is a function that has the same name as the class that it initializes. It can be defined inline, or outside the class declaration. However, it has no return value, like ordinary function prototypes and definitions, and it is called automatically by the compiler, if you fail to call it explicitly! Take a look at test10_3.cpp.

```
C:> type test10_3.cpp
// test10_3.cpp  01/12/91 3:24 pm

#include <iostream.h>    // necessary for I/O

class sum
    {
    public:
    int sum_1;
    int sum_2;
    sum();           // ** notice function with same name as class

    };
sum object_1, object_2;

void main(void)
{
    cout << "Inside main() \n";
    cout << "object_1.sum_1 is "<< object_1.sum_1 << "\n";
    cout << "object_1.sum_2 is "<< object_1.sum_2 << "\n";
    cout << "object_2.sum_1 is "<< object_2.sum_1 << "\n";
    cout << "object_2.sum_2 is "<< object_2.sum_2 << "\n";
}
```

```
sum::sum()      // ** this is the constructor function
{
    cout << "Inside sum() \n";
}
```

Compiling and executing this program results in the following output:

```
Inside sum()
Inside sum()
Inside main()
object_1.sum_1 is 0
object_1.sum_2 is 0
object_2.sum_1 is 0
object_2.sum_2 is 0
```

As you look at the declaration of class sum, you see that it has a class member also called sum(). This is a *default constructor*, and it is called such because it has no arguments. (Constructors with arguments will be discussed later on in the chapter.) What is important to note is that it *has the same name as the class for which it is a member, and it has no return type*. The output of this program demonstrates an interesting feature about constructors. You were perhaps surprised to see that the print statement "Inside sum()" output before "Inside main()". The reason for this is because the sum() constructor is called at the time that objects of type sum are created. Or, constructors for objects are called at the time that objects of that type are declared. If you take a look at the test10_3.cpp, you will see that object_1 and object_2 are created outside of main(). Hence, "Inside sum()" is output before "Inside main()". Also, "Inside sum()" outputs twice, since two objects of type sum are created. sum() would have been called three times if three objects of that type had been created, and so on.

Another interesting feature (which, regretfully, we cannot figure out how to illustrate to you), is that a default constructor is called implicitly by the compiler each time an object is declared, if one is not specified inside the class declaration. Just think back to all of the programs in the prior chapters. Default constructors were being generated each time an object was declared, and you never even knew about it!

The values of sum_1 and sum_2 continue to be zero, because the class objects are declared outside main(), and they are not set to anything else. Let's see what happens if object_1 and object_2 are declared inside main().

```
C:> type test10_4.cpp

// test10_4.cpp  01/12/91 3:45 pm

#include <iostream.h>    // necessary for I/O
```

```
class sum
     {
     public:
     int sum_1;
     int sum_2;
     sum();          // ** notice function with same name as class

     };

void main(void)
{
     cout << "Inside main() \n";

     sum object_1, object_2;  // ** declare objects inside main()

     cout << "object_1.sum_1 is "<< object_1.sum_1 << "\n";
     cout << "object_1.sum_2 is "<< object_1.sum_2 << "\n";
     cout << "object_2.sum_1 is "<< object_2.sum_1 << "\n";
     cout << "object_2.sum_2 is "<< object_2.sum_2 << "\n";
}
sum::sum()      // ** this is the constructor function
{
     cout << "Inside sum() \n";
}
```

Compiling and executing this program gives us the following results:

```
Inside main()
Inside sum()
Inside sum()
object_1.sum_1 is 0
object_1.sum_2 is 8815
object_1.sum_1 is 1
object_1.sum_2 is 0
```

This time the class members display garbage values. This is because objects of type sum are created inside main(), they are not global in scope, and hence, not initialized to zero. So how can class members be initialized to specific values? The answer is through the use of *parameters,* or *default arguments.* Parameters will be discussed next.

10.4 CONSTRUCTORS WITH PARAMETERS

Take a look at test10_5.cpp.

```
C:> type test10_5.cpp
```

```
// test10_5.cpp  01/12/91 4:00 pm

#include <iostream.h>     // necessary for I/O

class sum
     {
     int sum_1;      // ** notice sum_1 and sum_2 are now private
     int sum_2;
     public:
     sum(int i, int j);  // ** notice no return type, & arguments

     };

void main(void)
{
     // ** object_1 and object_2 are created with parameters
     sum object_1(10,20), object_2(20,30);
     cout << "Inside main() \n";
}

sum::sum(int i, int j)
{
     sum_1 = i;      // ** notice initialization to parameters
     sum_2 = j;
     cout << "sum_1 is " << sum_1 <<
          " sum_2 is " << sum_2 << "\n";
}
```

sum_1 and sum_2 are declared as private, since we are interested in utilizing the data hiding features that are offered by C++. Next, the constructor sum() is declared with arguments:

```
     sum(int i, int j);
```

Inside main(), object_1 and object_2 are declared with values substituted for the arguments:

```
     sum object_1(10,20), object_2(20,30)
```

Inside sum(), the two private class members sum_1 and sum_2 are initialized to the corresponding arguments i and j:

```
     sum_1 = i;
     sum_2 = j;
```

Compiling and executing this program gives the following output:

```
sum_1 is 10 sum_2 is 20
sum_1 is 20 sum_2 is 30
Inside main()
```

A couple of warnings are also issued in this (and subsequent programs), that object_1 and object_2 are never used inside main(). But these warnings will be overlooked, since these programs are meant to demonstrate specific features that relate to constructors, and the code does just that.

Notice that the class members of each object are initialized in the same order in which they are declared. Class members sum_1 and sum_2 of object_1 are created first, and initialized to 10 and 20, respectively. Next, class members sum_1 and sum_2 of object_2 are created, and initialized to 20 and 30.

10.5   CONSTRUCTORS WITH DEFAULT ARGUMENTS

Class members can be initialized in a variety of ways. Default arguments can be specified in the constructor declaration. Class members will be initialized to these default values, if none other are specified, as is demonstrated by the following program:

```
C:> type test10_6.cpp

// test10_6.cpp  01/12/91 5:00 pm

#include <iostream.h>    // necessary for I/O

class sum
    {
    int sum_1;     // ** notice sum_1 and sum_2 are now private
    int sum_2;
    public:
    sum(int i, int j = 5);   // ** notice default arguments
    };
// ** object_1 is created with only 1 argument
sum object_1(10), object_2(20,30);

void main(void)
{
    cout << "Inside main() \n";
}

sum::sum(int i, int j)
```

```
    {
        sum_1 = i;
        sum_2 = j;
        cout << "sum_1 is " << sum_1 <<
            " sum_2 is " << sum_2 << "\n";
    }
```

The output for this program looks as follows:

```
sum_1 is 10 sum_2 is 5
sum_1 is 20 sum_2 is 30
Inside main()
```

The declaration of the constructor sum looks like this:

```
sum(int i, int j = 5);
```

The second parameter is initialized to a default value. Now notice the way object_1 and object_2 are created:

```
sum object_1(10), object_2(20,30);
```

Class member sum_1 for object_1 is initialized to 10, and sum_2 defaults to 5. The values for class members sum_1 and sum_2 for object_2 are self-explanatory.

10.6   OVERLOADING CONSTRUCTORS

Constructors can be overloaded, that is, a constructor can have the same name, but different data types for arguments. The correct constructor will be invoked by the compiler, based on the data type of its argument. Take a look at test10_7.cpp

```
C:> type test10_7.cpp

// test10_7.cpp  01/12/91  5:40 pm

#include <iostream.h>     // necessary for I/O

class sum
    {
    int sum_1;
    double sum_2;
    public:
    sum(int i);    // ** notice function name is overloaded
    sum(double k);
    };
```

```
void main(void)
{
     sum object_1(10);   // ** sum(int) is called
     sum object_2(10.5);    // ** sum(double) is called
     cout << "Inside main() \n";
}
sum::sum(int i)
{
     sum_1 = i;
     cout << "Inside sum(int) \n";
}
sum::sum(double k)
{
     sum_2 = k;
     cout << "Inside sum(double) \n";
}
```

Compiling and executing this program produces the following output:

```
Inside sum(int)
Inside sum(double)
Inside main()
```

When `object_1` is declared, the constructor `sum(int)` is invoked, since the parameter 10 is of type `int`. When `object_2` is declared, the constructor `sum(double)` is invoked.

10.7 ORDER OF CALLING CONSTRUCTORS

The following program demonstrates the order in which constructors are called when dealing with base and derived classes:

```
C:> type test10_8.cpp

// test10_8.cpp          01/13/91 2:20 pm

#include <iostream.h>    // necessary for I/O

class one
     {
     public:
     one();
     };

class two : public one    // ** two is derived from one
     {
     int b;
```

```
    public:
    two(int j);
    };

main(void)
{
    one object_1();
    two object_2(20);
    cout << "Inside main() \n";
}
one::one()
{
    cout << "Inside one \n";
}
two::two(int j)
{
    b = j;
    cout << "Inside two  b is " << b << "\n";
}
```

The class two is derived from one. Inside main, an object of type one is declared, and then an object of type two. The constructor one is a default constructor; it takes no arguments. The constructor two is passed an argument. Compiling and executing this program results in the following output:

```
Inside one
Inside two b is 20
Inside main()
```

The order in which the constructors are called is self-explanatory. But what would happen if an object of the type of the derived class only is created, and an object for the base class is not? Take a look at test10_9.cpp.

```
C:> type test10_9.cpp

// test10_9.cpp          01/13/91 2:30 pm

#include <iostream.h>    // necessary for I/O

class one
    {
    public:
    one();
    };

class two : public one    // ** two is derived from one
```

```
        {
        int b;
        public:
        two(int j);
        };
main(void)
{
// ** We do not create object of type base class first
        two object_2(20);
        cout << "Inside main() \n";
}
one::one()
{
        cout << "Inside one \n";
}
two::two(int j)
{
        b = j;
        cout << "Inside two  b is " << b << "\n";
}
```

Compiling and executing this program produces the following output:

```
Inside one
Inside two b is 20
Inside main()
```

As you can see, the base class constructor is still called. This is necessary (and makes sense). Since two is derived from one, one must be constructed first. (How can you derive something from something that does not exist? It must be created first.) The base class constructor is constructed first, and then the derived class constructor.

Now take a look at the following program which illustrates the order of calling constructors from multiple base classes. (By the way, we are obliged to shorten our program names to tst10_10.cpp instead of the usual test10_10.cpp, since DOS does not understand file names longer than 12 characters. This naming convention will be adhered to for all subsequent programs whose names are longer than 12 characters.)

```
C:> type tst10_10.cpp

// test10_10.cpp        01/13/91 2:34 pm

#include <iostream.h>    // necessary for I/O

class one
```

```
        {
        public:
        one();
        };
class three
        {
        public:
        three();
        };

class two : public one, public three
// ** notice multiple base classes
        {
        int b;
        public:
        two(int j);
        };
main(void)
{
// ** We do not create object of type base class first
        two object_2(20);
        cout << "Inside main() \n";
}
one::one()
{
        cout << "Inside one \n";
}
two::two(int j)
{
        b = j;
        cout << "Inside two  b is " << b << "\n";
}
three::three()
{
        cout << "Inside three \n";
}
```

Compiling and executing this program produces the following output:

```
Inside one
Inside three
Inside two b is 20
Inside main()
```

As you can see, the base class constructors are called in the same order in which they are declared:

```
class two : public one, public three
```

10.8   BASE CLASS CONSTRUCTORS WITH PARAMETERS

So far, so good. But what happens if you wish to create an object of a derived class, whose base class requires parameters? Take a look at the following code, and you will understand what we mean:

```
C:> type tst10_11.cpp

// test10_11.cpp          01/13/91 9:40 pm

#include <iostream.h>     // necessary for I/O

class one
    {
    int a;
    public:
    one(int i);
    };

class two : public one    // ** two is derived from one
    {
    int b;
    public:
    two(int j);
    };

main(void)
{
// ** We do not create object of type base class first
    two object_2(20);
    cout << "Inside main() \n";
}
one::one(int i)
{
    a = i;
    cout << "Inside one a is " << a << "\n";
}
two::two(int j) : one(j)
{
    b = j;
    cout << "Inside two  b is " << b << "\n";
}
```

As you can see, the constructor for the base class one requires a parameter:

```
    one(int i);
```

The object two is derived from one:

```
class two : public one
```

and an object of type two is created with the required parameter:

```
    two object_2(20);
```

Then, there is an interesting definition for the constructor for the derived class:

```
two::two(int j) : one(j)
{          .
           .
           .
}
```

This is one of the ways in which parameters can be sent to the base class. The definition of the constructor of the derived class follows the usual syntax. However, it is appended with a colon (indicating derivation), the name of the base class, and the parameter list. Compiling and executing this program results in the following output:

```
Inside one a is 20
Inside two b is 20
Inside main()
```

The order of calling the constructors (base class, then derived class) remains the same.

Parameters can be passed to base classes in a variety of other ways as well. You can place a constant in the parameter list, as follows:

```
C:> type tst10_12.cpp

// test10_12.cpp          01/13/91 9:45 pm

#include <iostream.h>     // necessary for I/O

class one
    {
    int a;
    public:
    one(int i);
    };
```

```
class two : public one    // ** two is derived from one
     {
     int b;
     public:
     two(int j);
     };
main(void)
{
// ** We do not create object of type base class first
     two object_2(20);
     cout << "Inside main() \n";
}
one::one(int i)
{
     a = i;
     cout << "Inside one a is " << a << "\n";
}
two::two(int j) : one(10)   // ** notice constant argument for one()

{
     b = j;
     cout << "Inside two  b is " << b << "\n";
}
```

As you take a look at the definition of the constructor for two:

```
two::two(int j) : one(10)
```

you find a constant being sent as a parameter to one. Compiling and executing this program results in the following output:

```
Inside one a is 10
Inside two b is 20
Inside main()
```

The output should be self-explanatory.

Global parameters can also be passed to the base class constructor, as is illustrated by tst10_13.cpp:

```
C:> type tst10_13.cpp

// test10_13.cpp          01/13/91 9:45 pm

#include <iostream.h>    // necessary for I/O

class one
```

```
    {
    int a;
    public:
    one(int i);
    };

class two : public one
    {
    int b;
    public:
    two(int j);
    };
int k;    // ** notice external variable declaration

main(void)
{
    k = 5;    // ** external variable is initialized
// ** We do not create object of type base class first
    two object_2(20);
    cout << "Inside main() \n";
}
one::one(int i)
{
    a = i;
    cout << "Inside one a is " << a << "\n";
}
two::two(int j) : one(k)
{
    b = j;
    cout << "Inside two  b is " << b << "\n";
}
```

k is declared as a global variable, outside of main(), and initialized inside
main() to 5. Then, it is passed as a parameter to the base class constructor:

```
two::two(int j) : one(k)
```

Compiling and executing this program results in the following output:

```
Inside one a is 5
Inside two b is 20
Inside main()
```

The output should be self-explanatory.

10.9 DESTRUCTORS

The complement to constructors are *destructors*. Destructors are used to
deactivate the storage allocated to classes when they are created.
Destructors have the same name as constructors, except that they are preceded by a tilde (~). Take a look at the following simple program which illustrates the use of a constructor and a destructor:

```
C:> type tst10_14.cpp

//    test10_14.cpp  01/13/90 10:00 pm

#include <iostream.h>     // necessary for I/O

class one
     {
     public:
     one();          // ** this is the constructor
     ~one();          // ** this is the destructor
     };
main(void)
{
     cout << "Inside main() \n";
     one object_1;
     cout << "Inside main() - after creating object_1 \n";
}
one::one()     // ** this is the constructor function
{
     cout << "Inside one \n";
}
one::~one()     // ** this is the destructor function
{
     cout << "Inside ~one \n";
}
```

There are two member functions for the class one: These are one() and
~one(). one() is the default constructor, and ~one() is the destructor.
Compiling and executing this program gives the following output:

```
Inside main()
Inside one
Inside main() - after constructing object_1
Inside ~one
```

As you can see, the destructor ~one is called automatically upon exit from main(). Just like a constructor, it would have been called even if it had not explicitly defined.

A destructor does not have a return type or value, like a constructor. But unlike constructors, it accepts no parameters. It is called implicitly when a variable goes out of scope (as it did in the sample program). For local variables, this occurs when they are no longer within block scope. For global variables, this occurs upon termination of the program.

10.10   ORDER OF CALLING DESTRUCTORS

Destructors are called in the exact opposite order as constructors. Take a look at the following program:

```
C:> type tst10_15.cpp

//    test10_15.cpp  01/13/90 10:10 pm

#include <iostream.h>     // necessary for I/O

class one
    {
    public:
    one();
    ~one();
    };
class two : public one   // ** two is derived from one
    {
    public:
    two();
    ~two();
    };
main(void)
{
    cout << "Inside main() \n";
    two object_1;
    cout << "Inside main() - after creating object_1 \n";
}
one::one()     // ** this is the base class constructor
{
    cout << "Inside one \n";
}
one::~one()     // ** this is the base class destructor
{
    cout << "Inside ~one \n";
}
two::two()     // ** this is the derived class constructor
```

```
{
    cout << "Inside two \n";
}
two::~two()     // ** this is the derived class destructor
{
    cout << "Inside ~two \n";
}
```

Here the class two is derived from one. Compiling and executing this program results in the following output:

```
Inside main()
Inside one
Inside two
Inside main() - after creating object_1
Inside ~two
Inside ~one
```

Inside main(), an object of type two is created. However, two is derived from one. Therefore, one is constructed first, and then two. Next, the program is exited. Here we see that first the destructor for the derived class is called (~two), and then the destructor for the base class (~one). Destruction follows the opposite order of construction, as it would only be logical to do so.

10.11 REVIEW

In this chapter, we learned a lot of interesting things about constructors and destructors.

- Constructors are functions that have the same name as their classes. They initialize objects when they are created.

- They are called automatically by the compiler, if they are not explicitly called within the program, at the time that objects of their class type are declared.

- Default arguments can be supplied to constructors.

- Constructors can be overloaded; the correct version will be automatically invoked by the compiler.

- They are called in the logical order that is followed by base and derived classes, i.e., base class constructors will precede derived class constructors.

- Destructors are the complement to constructors. They have the same name as constructors, except they are preceded by a tilde(~).

- Destructors deallocate memory allocated to objects created through constructors.

- They are called automatically upon exit from `main()`, if they are not explicitly called.

- They accept no parameters.

- Destructors are called in the opposite order as constructors, i.e., derived class destructors are called before base class destructors.

Virtual Functions and Polymorphism—Fundamental Concepts

11.1 INTRODUCTION

You have come a long way since you first started reading Chap. 1 of this book (and it has been a fairly smooth journey, we hope). In Chap. 1, we introduced you to the concept of a virtual function. At the time, you probably did not understand the full power of this feature of C++. In this chapter, this concept will be reintroduced, and illustrated in detail. You will be introduced to words such as "polymorphism," and expressions such as "early binding" and "run-time binding." By the time you conclude this chapter, you will feel comfortable with these little catch words that C++ programmers and books freely use, and realize that these concepts are really not as difficult to understand as you originally thought.

11.2 BACK TO POINTERS

Before we begin our discussion of virtual functions, here is a short refresher on pointers. (Pointers will be discussed in detail in Chap. 12.) This discussion is necessary, since it is through pointers to base and derived classes that run-time polymorphism is achieved in C++.

A pointer, as you already know, contains the location in memory of a data type. The concept, syntax, and use of pointers is the same for C++ (save for a few enhancements), as it is in C. For example, if you declare an integer variable in your program, like so:

```
int a;    // a is an integer data type
```

then, a pointer to this variable would be declared, as follows:

```
int *ptr; // ptr is a pointer to an integer
```

Next, `ptr` would be set to the address or location in memory of a:

```
ptr = &a; // ptr is set to the address of a
```

Once this is done, the contents of the variable a can be accessed indirectly through `ptr`. The following two statements result in the same output:

```
*ptr = 5; // access contents of a through ptr, set a to 5
a = 5;    // access contents of a directly, set a to 5
```

If `ptr` was output without the * operator, the location in memory of a would be obtained. The following statement illustrates what has just been said:

```
cout << "At location " << ptr << "is stored " << *ptr
```

The statement above would result in the following output on your computer:

```
At location xxxxxx is stored 5
```

where 'xxxxxx' is the address of a.

The first invocation of `ptr` results in the address of a being output. The second invocation of `ptr` results in the output of what is stored at that address, or the contents of a.

11.3 POINTERS TO CLASSES

C++, just like C, has pointers to characters, floats, doubles, arrays, etc. You can also have pointers to structures, and, in C++, you also have pointers to classes. The syntax for accessing class members via pointers is the same as accessing structure members in C. Take a look at the following program:

```
C:> type test11_1.cpp

// test11_1.cpp          01/14/91 7:52 pm

#include <iostream.h>    // necessary for I/O
```

```
class one
    {
    public:
    void output(void)
        {
        cout << "Inside output \n";
        }
    };

main(void)
{
    one object_1;   // declare object of type one
    one *pointer;   // declare pointer to object of type one

    pointer = &object_1;      // set pointer to address of object_1

    pointer->output();   // execute output()

    return(0);
}
```

Compiling and executing this program results in the following output:

```
Inside output
```

First, the class `one` is declared. The function `output()` is inline. Inside `main()`, `object_1` is an object of type `one`. Then, `pointer` is declared as a pointer to objects of type `one`. `pointer` is set equal to the address of `object_1`. Next, the class member `output()` of the class `one` is executed via the statement:

```
pointer->output();
```

The -> operator is one way to access a class member through a pointer. The following statement would have given the same result:

```
pointer.output();
```

We will use the -> operator in our programs, since the arrow intuitively symbolizes that something is being pointed to, which is exactly what is being implemented in the program.

11.4 POINTERS TO DERIVED CLASSES

In C++, you can have pointers to base classes, and pointers to derived classes. You can access a member of a derived class via a pointer to the base class, as long as the member being accessed in the derived class has been inherited

from the base class. What we just said will become clear to you as you read
the next program:

```
C:> type test11_2.cpp

// test11_2.cpp          01/14/91 8:00 pm

#include <iostream.h>    // necessary for I/O

class one
    {
    public:
    void output(void)
        {
        cout << "Inside output \n";
        }
    };

class two : public one    // two is derived from one
    {
    public:
    void output2(void)
        {
        cout << "Inside output2 \n";
        }
    };

main(void)
{
    one object_1;  // declare object of type one
    two object_2;  // declare object for the derived class
    one *pointer;  // declare pointer to base class

    pointer = &object_1;     // set pointer to address of object_1

    pointer->output();       // execute object_1::output()
    // now set pointer to address of derived class
    pointer = &object_2;
    pointer->output();       // execute object_2::output()
    return(0);
}
```

Compiling and running this program results in the following output:

```
Inside output
Inside output
```

Here you see the original definition of class one. Then, class two is publicly derived from one. Thus, the class one has one class member: output(). However, the class two has two class members: output(), which it inherits from class one, and output2(), which is unique to it.

Inside main(), a pointer is declared to the base class one. Next, it is set to the address of object_1, which is an object of type one. The function output() is executed as follows:

```
pointer->output();
```

Next, pointer is set to the address of an object of type two, which is the derived class:

```
pointer = &object_two;
```

and output() is executed again:

```
pointer->output();
```

The compiler did not voice any complaints, since the function output() for object_two is inherited from the base class one. The following modification to test11_2.cpp would result in errors:

```
C:> type test11_3.cpp

// test11_3.cpp          01/14/91 8:20 pm

#include <iostream.h>     // necessary for I/O

class one
    {
    public:
    void output(void)
        {
        cout << "Inside output \n";
        }
    };

class two : public one    // two is derived from one
    {
    public:
    void output2(void)
        {
        cout << "Inside output2 \n";
        }
    };
```

```
main(void)
{
    one object_1;  // declare object of type one
    two object_2;  // declare object for the derived class
    one *pointer;  // declare pointer to base class

    pointer = &object_1;       // set pointer to address of object_1
    pointer->output();         // execute object_1::output()

    // now set pointer to address of derived class
    pointer = &object_2;
    pointer->output2();        // execute object_2::output2()
    return(0);
}
```

Compiling and executing this program results in the following message:

```
Error:    output2 is not a member of one in function main()
```

The compiler issues this complaint in response to the following statement:

```
    pointer->output2();
```

This is because pointer is declared as a pointer to the base class one, and output2() is specific to the class two; it is not inherited from one.*

However, elements of the derived class which are not inherited from the base class can be accessed conveniently through a pointer to the derived class. Take a look at this version of the program:

```
C:> type test11_4.cpp

// test11_4.cpp          01/14/91 8:20 pm

#include <iostream.h>    // necessary for I/O

class one
    {
    public:
    void output(void)
```

---

*Incidentally, you can typecast the base class pointer to a pointer to the derived class, and succeed in executing output2 through pointer as follows:

```
    ((two *)pointer)->output2();
```

but we don't want to get into too many messy details about statements that look like the one above (confusing, to say the least), and hence won't elaborate on it further in this chapter.

```
        {
        cout << "Inside output \n";
        }
    };

class two : public one    // two is derived from one
    {
    public:
    void output2(void)
        {
        cout << "Inside output2 \n";
        }
    };

main(void)
{
    one object_1;  // declare object of type one
    two object_2;  // declare object for the derived class
    one *pointer;  // declare pointer to base class
    two *pointer2; // declare pointer to derived class

    pointer = &object_1;     // set pointer to address of object_1
    pointer->output();       // execute object_1::output()

    // now set pointer to address of derived class
    pointer2 = &object_2;
    pointer2->output2();     // execute object_2::output2()
    return(0);
}
```

Compiling and running this program results in the following output:

```
Inside output
Inside output2
```

11.5   VIRTUAL FUNCTIONS REVISITED

With this introduction to pointers to base and derived classes, we return to our discussion on virtual functions. It was necessary for you to understand how class members are accessed through pointers, since this is the fundamental mechanism by which virtual functions are executed.

So exactly what does the word *polymorphism* mean? We refer to our handy *Webster's Encyclopedic Unabridged Dictionary,* and narrow in on the following explanations:

   . . . existence of an animal or plant in several form or color varieties . . .

... state or condition of being polymorphous ...

Meanwhile, polymorphous means

... having, assuming or passing through many or various forms ...

Think about the first definition for a minute. Think of a rose. A rose is a rose, but some roses are red, and some are white, and some are pink, and maybe one day someone will somehow create a rose that is black or some other peculiar color.

Now think of a rose as an object. We know that a rose is a rose because it is of a certain shape, its petals are soft, it has a distinct bouquet, and it has thorns on its stems. Now we are not quite sure of how a rose came into existence, or who created it, but let's attribute its existence to nature. Nature created a flower of this specific shape, and gave it the remaining attributes that made it a rose. And when everything was ready, suppose it left the implementation of the color to a different entity. It would send a rose with no color, or a default color (say red), to the entity and allow it to determine the exact method in which a specific color would be assigned to that particular rose. This entity would determine the color of the rose in its own distinct way, and pass the color back to nature. Each time a new color would have to be assigned to the rose, nature would send the default rose to the entity, and, after the color is assigned, the rose would be sent back to nature.

The interface or interconnection is the same each time a rose is sent—a rose with no or default color. The object returned from the entity is also always the same—a rose with a color. However, the way the color is determined, or the method in which it is assigned, is different for each color. If a green rose is to be created, then the colors yellow and blue would have to be mixed. If a purple rose is to be created, then the colors red and blue would have to be mixed, and so on. There is only one interface, but there are multiple implementations. Based on the definition from the dictionary, believe it or not, a rose is polymorphous; it can exist in several color varieties. Furthermore, believe it or not, the one-interface–multiple-implementations concept is the key to understanding polymorphism in C++.

We will now build upon the one-interface–multiple-implementations concept, using a different example and sample programs, to help you further understand this powerful object-oriented mechanism.

We know of a little travel agency that specializes in Caribbean vacation packages. When this agency first started out, they decided to design a program in C++ that would list the salient attractions of the Caribbean resorts that are included in each package. The astute programmer who was assigned this task understood the advantages of using classes instead of structures, and so he decided to build a class hierarchy where the base class will describe those features which are common to all Caribbean islands. Each island will then be derived from the base class, and contain descriptions of the attractions that are specific to the island.

This program was designed to be as flexible as possible, so that changes could be easily incorporated into it. What if a hurricane struck one island, or local tensions broke out in another? Obviously, these islands would have to be taken off the list of available packages. At the same time, new packages may be added as the company grows. What was needed was a program that could add and delete functions that were inherently the same (i.e., they listed attractions) but are implemented differently (a different set of attractions would be listed for each island). Based upon these needs, it was apparent that virtual functions were the answer. Here's the result:

```
C:> type test11_5.cpp

// test11_5.cpp          01/14/91 7:22 PM

#include <iostream.h>

class caribbean_isles    // this will be the main base class
    {
    public:
    // ** notice keyword virtual
    virtual void other_attractions(void)
        {
        cout << "!!COME VISIT THE CARIBBEAN ISLANDS!! \n";
        cout << "White sand beaches \n";
        cout << "Crystal-clear water \n";
        cout << "No hassles - No worries - No cares \n\n";
        }
    };
```

The code is broken up into logical fragments, since it is longer than most of the other programs. The program starts off by declaring a base class called caribbean_isles. This class contains one public function called other_attractions(). The definition of this function is preceded by the keyword *virtual*. It is inline (it does not have to be), and it outputs those features which are common to all Caribbean islands in the list of available packages: white sand beaches, crystal-clear water, no hassles, worries, or cares. Let's continue with the code.

```
// bahamas, grand_cayman and st_thomas are derived from
// caribbean_isles.

class bahamas : public caribbean_isles
    {
    public:
    // ** notice same function name, no keyword virtual
    void other_attractions(void)
        {
        cout << "!!BAHAMAS!! \n";
```

```
            cout << "Fun-filled casinos \n";
            cout << "Action-packed water sports \n";
            cout << "Great rum punches \n\n";
            }
        };

class grand_cayman : public caribbean_isles
    {
    public:
    // ** notice same function name, no keyword virtual
    void other_attractions(void)
        {
        cout << "!!GRAND CAYMAN!! \n";
        cout << "Incredible scuba diving \n";
        cout << "Big time game fishing \n";
        cout << "Duty free shopping \n\n";
        }
    };

class st_thomas : public caribbean_isles
    {
    public:
    // ** notice same function name, no keyword virtual
    void other_attractions(void)
        {
        cout << "!!ST THOMAS!! \n";
        cout << "Excellent shopping \n\n";
        }
    };
```

Next, the `bahamas`, `grand_cayman` and `st_thomas` are derived from the `caribbean_isles`. These islands inherit all features of the `caribbean_isles`, and then add a few features of their own. The thing to notice here is that each of these classes contains a member function whose name is common to the virtual function in the base class (`other_attractions()`). In addition to this, the return type is the same (`void`), and so are the parameters (`void` again). However, the implementation of each function is different (a different set of attractions is listed for each method). Now take a look at the code for `main()`.

```
main(void)
{
    // ** declare object and ptr to caribbean_isles class
    caribbean_isles islands, *ptr;

    // declare objects for derived classes
    bahamas package_1;
```

```
    grand_cayman package_2;
    st_thomas package_3;

    // set ptr to address of base class object
    ptr = &islands;
    // execute virtual function
    // the compiler will know which version to execute!!
    ptr->other_attractions();
    // now set ptr to address of derived class objects
    ptr = &package_1;
    ptr->other_attractions();
    ptr = &package_2;
    ptr->other_attractions();
    ptr = &package_3;
    ptr->other_attractions();

    return(0);
}
```

Inside `main()`, objects of the base and derived classes, and a pointer to the base class, are declared. Next, `ptr` is set to the address of the base class, and the function `other_attractions()` is implemented. But which version of the function will be implemented? Well, C++ determines the answer to this question at run time, as opposed to compile time, based upon the type of object that is being pointed to. This is called *late binding,* and *run-time polymorphism.* These little catch words should now be starting to make sense.

Compiling and executing this program results in the following output:

```
!!COME VISIT THE CARIBBEAN ISLANDS!!
White sand beaches
Crystal-clear water
No hassles - No worries - No cares

!!BAHAMAS!!
Fun-filled casinos
Action-packed water sports
Great rum punches

!!GRAND CAYMAN!!
Incredible scuba diving
Big time game fishing
Duty free shopping

!!ST THOMAS!!
Excellent shopping
```

Initially, ptr is set to point to the islands, which is an object of type caribbean_isles. Hence, the statement:

```
ptr->other_attractions();
```

results in the execution of the version of other_attractions() which belongs to the base class.

Next, ptr is set to point to the object package_1, which is an object of type bahamas. Hence, the statement:

```
ptr->other_attractions();
```

results in the execution of the version of other_attractions() which belongs to the derived class bahamas.

Step through the remainder of the program yourself, and you should be able to understand which version is being implemented, and why.

11.6   SO WHAT'S A VIRTUAL FUNCTION?

A *virtual function* is one that is declared as such in the base class. Then, it is redefined (although it does not have to be, as you will see shortly), in one or more classes derived from the base class. The correct implementation of the function is selected at *run time*, as *opposed* to *compile time*, based upon the kind of object that is being pointed to.

A virtual function is preceded with the keyword virtual inside the base class. Then, this function is redefined inside the derived classes. The name, return type, and parameters for the function must be exactly the same as the original prototype in the base class; otherwise, the virtual nature of these functions is lost. For this reason, we do not use the term "overloaded" to describe these special functions. (Recall that overloaded functions have the same name, but different parameters.) Instead, the function is "overridden" inside the derived class.

Run-time polymorphism is achieved by accessing these functions through a pointer to the base class. The base class specifies the functions which will be common to all classes which will be derived from it. It provides the uniform interface to these functions inside the derived classes. However, the derived class defines the actual method in which this function will be implemented.

11.7   AND WHAT'S EARLY BINDING AND LATE BINDING?

Early binding indicates the occurrence of the determination of events that are to take place at the time that a program is compiled. Examples of early binding are standard and overloaded function calls. Information required to implement standard and overloaded functions is known at the time that a program is compiled.

Late binding indicates the occurrence of the determination of events that are to take place at the time that a program is run. Examples of late binding include virtual functions. Information required to implement a virtual function is known at the time that a program is run, not when it is compiled. Let's explain this a little bit further.

Take a look at this very simple program:

```
C:> type test11_6.cpp

main(void)
{
    int a = 5;      // 1st statement
    a += 2;         // 2nd statement
}
```

Compiling and executing this program generates no errors and produces no output; we have deliberately kept it this simple. However, this program illustrates two major points.

The first statement is executed at compile time. When test11_6.cpp is compiled, the compiler assigns storage for an integer to the variable a, and stores the value of 5 in it.

The second statement is executed at run time. When test11_6.cpp is run, 2 is added to whatever is stored in a. This event occurs at run time.

So why are virtual functions a run-time phenomenon? Well, you already know that the function that is to execute is determined by which object is being pointed to at the time. The value of ptr is modified at run time. Hence, the related version of the function that is to execute is also determined at run time.

11.8   REVIEW

In this chapter, we learned the how and why of virtual functions. We learned:

- How pointers to base and derived classes are used to invoke function class members.

- That a pointer to a base class can be used to access a member of the derived class, as long as that class member has been inherited from the base.

- How virtual functions can be invoked using pointers to base classes to access objects of different types. Terms such as "late binding" and "run-time polymorphism" were used to describe this phenomenon.

12

Virtual Functions and Abstract Classes

12.1 INTRODUCTION

In the previous chapter, we reintroduced and explained how virtual functions are invoked, and why. In this chapter, we will build upon this concept further, and introduce you to pure virtual functions and abstract classes.

12.2 FLEXIBILITY OF VIRTUAL FUNCTIONS

In Chap. 11, a C++ program was designed that listed the main attractions of the vacation packages offered by our travel agency. This program was designed in such a way that it would be flexible enough to handle deletion and addition of islands to the packages, without major redesign of the main code. This objective was achieved by utilizing virtual functions. It is presented all in one place for your convenience.

```
C:> type test11_5.cpp˜

// test11_5.cpp        01/14/91 7:22 PM

#include <iostream.h>

class caribbean_isles    // this will be the main base class
```

```
    {
    public:
    virtual void other_attractions(void)
    // ** notice keyword virtual
        {
        cout << "!!COME VISIT THE CARIBBEAN ISLANDS!! \n";
        cout << "White sand beaches \n";
        cout << "Crystal-clear water \n";
        cout << "No hassles - No worries - No cares \n\n";
        }
    };


// bahamas, grand_cayman and st_thomas are derived from
// caribbean_isles
class bahamas : public caribbean_isles
    {
    public:
    // ** notice same function name, no keyword virtual
    void other_attractions(void)
        {
        cout << "!!BAHAMAS!! \n";
        cout << "Fun-filled casinos \n";
        cout << "Action-packed water sports \n";
        cout << "Great rum punches \n\n";
        }
    };


class grand_cayman : public caribbean_isles
    {
    public:
    // ** notice same function name, no keyword virtual
    void other_attractions(void)
        {
        cout << "!!GRAND CAYMAN!! \n";
        cout << "Incredible scuba diving \n";
        cout << "Big time game fishing \n";
        cout << "Duty free shopping \n\n";
        }
    };


class st_thomas : public caribbean_isles
    {
    public:
    // ** notice same function name, no keyword virtual
    void other_attractions(void)
```

```
            {
            cout << "!!ST THOMAS!! \n";
            cout << "Excellent shopping \n\n";
            }
      };

main(void)
{
      // ** declare object and ptr to caribbean_isles class
      caribbean_isles islands, *ptr;

      // declare objects for derived classes
      bahamas package_1;
      grand_cayman package_2;
      st_thomas package_3;

      // set ptr to address of base class object
      ptr = &islands;
      // execute virtual function
      // the compiler will know which version to execute!!
      ptr->other_attractions();
      // now set ptr to address of derived class objects
      ptr = &package_1;
      ptr->other_attractions();
      ptr = &package_2;
      ptr->other_attractions();
      ptr = &package_3;
      ptr->other_attractions();

      return(0);
}
```

Now suppose a fourth hot spot package comes into the picture. The code of the original program would be modified as follows:

```
C:> type test12_1.cpp

// test12_1.cpp          01/14/91 8:40 PM

#include <iostream.h>

class caribbean_isles     // this will be the main base class
      {
      public:
      virtual void other_attractions(void)
```

```
           {
           cout << "!!COME VISIT THE CARIBBEAN ISLANDS!! \n";
           cout << "White sand beaches \n";
           cout << "Crystal-clear water \n";
           cout << "No hassles - No worries - No cares \n\n";
           }
     };


// bahamas, grand_cayman and st_thomas are derived from
// caribbean_isles
class bahamas : public caribbean_isles
     {
     public:
     // ** notice same function name, no keyword virtual
     void other_attractions(void)
           {
           cout << "!!BAHAMAS!! \n";
           cout << "Fun-filled casinos \n";
           cout << "Action-packed water sports \n";
           cout << "Great rum punches \n\n";
           }
     };


class grand_cayman : public caribbean_isles
     {
     public:
     // ** notice same function name, no keyword virtual
     void other_attractions(void)
           {
           cout << "!!GRAND CAYMAN!! \n";
           cout << "Incredible scuba diving \n";
           cout << "Big time game fishing \n";
           cout << "Duty free shopping \n\n";
           }
     };


class st_thomas : public caribbean_isles
     {
     public:
     // ** notice same function name, no keyword virtual
     void other_attractions(void)
           {
           cout << "!!ST THOMAS!! \n";
           cout << "Excellent shopping \n\n";
           }
     };
```

```
class st_lucia : public caribbean_isles
     {
     public:
     void other_attractions(void)
          {
          cout << "!!ST. LUCIA!! \n";
          }
     };
```

As you can see, a new class, st.lucia, has been added. This is the latest hot spot package, with its own implementation of other_attractions(). Now take a look at the code for main().

```
main(void)
{
     // ** declare object and ptr to caribbean_isles class
     caribbean_isles islands, *ptr;

     // declare objects for derived classes
     bahamas package_1;
     grand_cayman package_2;
     st_thomas package_3;
     st_lucia package_4;

     // set ptr to address of base class object
     ptr = &islands;
     // execute virtual function
     // the compiler will know which version to execute!!
     ptr->other_attractions();
     // now set ptr to address of derived class objects
     ptr = &package_1;
     ptr->other_attractions();
     ptr = &package_2;
     ptr->other_attractions();
     ptr = &package_3;
     ptr->other_attractions();
     ptr = &package_4;
     ptr->other_attractions();

     return(0);
}
```

The following lines of code are the only changes required inside main() to implement the function for the new derived class:

```
st_lucia package_4;
        .
        .
        .
ptr->&package_4;
ptr->other_attractions();
```

This program illustrates the ease with which new functions can be integrated into the program. Removal of assignment of a pointer to a derived class would result in the corresponding ease with which virtual functions can be removed from the main logic.

12.3   DEVIATIONS FROM THE NORM

There is a small island in the heart of the Caribbean. Not many know about it, but this quaint little haunt has majestic mountains, white sandy beaches, and breathtaking undersea cliffs. This island's name is Saba.

Suppose this island was to be included as one of the prime attractions, called the "mystery package." However, at the moment, no one is quite sure as to how to classify its attractions. So how would this situation be handled? Well, we forgot to tell you. If a virtual function is not defined inside the derived class, then the base virtual function is automatically executed instead. Or, to say it a different way, if a derived class does not provide a function to override the base virtual function, then the base virtual function will execute when an object of the type of the new class is pointed to. Take a look at this version of the original program:

```
C:> type test12_2.cpp

// test12_2.cpp        01/14/91 9:15 PM

#include <iostream.h>

class caribbean_isles    // this will be the main base class
    {
    public:
    // ** we will output the header separately
    void header(void)
        { cout << "!!COME VISIT THE CARIBBEAN ISLANDS!! \n";}
    virtual void other_attractions(void)
        {
        cout << "White sand beaches \n";
        cout << "Crystal-clear water \n";
        cout << "No hassles - No worries - No cares \n\n";
        }
    };
```

As you can see, this is a modified definition of the base class. It was modified by outputting the header line separate from the remainder of the original function. The new header function is not declared as virtual; there is no need to do so.

```
// bahamas, grand_cayman and st_thomas are derived from
// caribbean_isles.
// ** so is saba
class bahamas : public caribbean_isles
      {
      public:
      // ** notice same function name, no keyword virtual
      void other_attractions(void)
            {
            cout << "!!BAHAMAS!! \n";
            cout << "Fun-filled casinos \n";
            cout << "Action-packed water sports \n";
            cout << "Great rum punches \n\n";
            }
      };


class grand_cayman : public caribbean_isles
      {
      public:
      // ** notice same function name, no keyword virtual
      void other_attractions(void)
            {
            cout << "!!GRAND CAYMAN!! \n";
            cout << "Incredible scuba diving \n";
            cout << "Big time game fishing \n";
            cout << "Duty free shopping \n\n";
            }
      };


class st_thomas : public caribbean_isles
      {
      public:
      // ** notice same function name, no keyword virtual
      void other_attractions(void)
            {
            cout << "!!ST THOMAS!! \n";
            cout << "Excellent shopping \n\n";
            }
      };


class saba : public caribbean_isles
```

```
{
public:
void name(void) { cout << "!!MYSTERY ISLAND SABA!! \n"; };
// ** attributes of other_attractions() not defined yet
};
```

The class saba is defined just like the rest. However, the attributes of its
function other_attractions() has not been determined yet. These attributes
are expected to be known some time in the future. For now, the mystery
island simply inherits attributes from its base class. Let's continue with
main().

```
main(void)
{
    // ** declare object and ptr to caribbean_isles class
    caribbean_isles islands, *ptr;

    // declare objects for derived classes
    bahamas package_1;
    grand_cayman package_2;
    st_thomas package_3;
    saba mystery_package;

    // output header
    islands.header();

    // set ptr to address of base class object
    ptr = &islands;
    // execute virtual function
    // the compiler will know which version to execute!!
    ptr->other_attractions();

    // now set ptr to address of derived class objects
    ptr = &package_1;
    ptr->other_attractions();
    ptr = &package_2;
    ptr->other_attractions();
    ptr = &package_3;
    ptr->other_attractions();

    mystery_package.name(); // ** output name of mystery island

    ptr = &mystery_package;  // ** set ptr to address of package_4

    // ** caribbean_isles::other_attractions executes
    ptr->other_attractions();
```

```
        return(0);
}
```

An obect of type `saba` is given the name `mystery_package`. After the attractions of the other islands have been listed, the name of the mystery package island is output, `ptr` is set to point to an object of that type, and the function `other_attractions()` is executed. Here's the output of this program:

```
!!COME VISIT THE CARIBBEAN ISLANDS!!
White sand beaches
Crystal-clear water
No hassles - No worries - No cares

!!BAHAMAS!!
Fun-filled casinos
Action-packed water sports
Great rum punches

!!GRAND CAYMAN!!
Incredible scuba diving
Big time game fishing
Duty free shopping

!!ST THOMAS!!
Excellent shopping

!!MYSTERY ISLAND SABA!!
White sand beaches
Crystal-clear water
No hassles - No worries - No cares
```

As you can see, the base virtual function turns out to be the default function which executes in the absence of an overridding function in the derived class. At a future date, the `other_attractions()` function can be defined for the new derived class. Then, when the statement

```
ptr->other_attractions()
```

is executed

```
saba::other_attractions()
```

will be implemented instead of

```
caribbean_isles::other_attractions().
```

12.4 PURE VIRTUAL FUNCTIONS AND ABSTRACT CLASSES

Pure virtual functions exist for scenarios which are the flip side of the coin of the prior section. There are circumstances in which the attributes of the virtual function in the base class are undefined. It is simply a placeholder for events that are expected to be derived from it in future derived classes. In these cases, we have what is called a *pure virtual function*. It has no definition in the base class. For this reason, any class derived from it will be required to provide its own implementation. A pure virtual function is defined as follows:

```
C:> type test12_3.cpp

// test12_3.cpp          01/14/91 8:40 PM

#include <iostream.h>

class caribbean_isles     // this will be the main base class
    {
    public:
    void header(void) // ** we output the header separately
        {cout << "!!COME VISIT THE CARIBBEAN ISLANDS!! \n\n";}

    // attributes of other_attractions either do not exist,
    // or are simply a place holder
    // therefore, we define it as a pure virtual function
    virtual void other_attractions(void) = 0;
    };
```

As you can see, the virtual function other_attractions() in the base class is initialized to 0. This is a pure virtual function. Declaring a pure virtual function results in each derived class being forced to provide its own implementation.

```
// bahamas, grand_cayman and st_thomas are derived from
// caribbean_isles.
class bahamas : public caribbean_isles
    {
    public:
    // ** notice same function name, no keyword virtual
    void other_attractions(void)
        {
        cout << "!!BAHAMAS!! \n";
        cout << "Fun-filled casinos \n";
        cout << "Action-packed water sports \n";
        cout << "Great rum punches \n\n";
        }
    };
```

```
class grand_cayman : public caribbean_isles
    {
    public:
    // ** notice same function name, no keyword virtual
    void other_attractions(void)
        {
        cout << "!!GRAND CAYMAN!! \n";
        cout << "Incredible scuba diving \n";
        cout << "Big time game fishing \n";
        cout << "Duty free shopping \n\n";
        }
    };

class st_thomas : public caribbean_isles
    {
    public:
    // ** notice same function name, no keyword virtual
    void other_attractions(void)
        {
        cout << "!!ST THOMAS!! \n";
        cout << "Excellent shopping \n\n";
        }
    };
```

Now take a look at the first few lines inside main().

```
main(void)
{
    // ** declare ptr only to caribbean_isles class
    // ** we can not create an object of a class type that has
    // ** a pure virtual function.
    caribbean_isles *ptr;
```

As you can see, an object for the base class is not declared. This is because a base class which has a pure virtual function is said to be *abstract*. Abstract classes can be used only as a base class that will be inherited by subsequent classes. You cannot declare objects for abstract classes. However, also note that it is OK to declare pointers to this special type of class. This is necessary, in order to implement run-time polymorphism. Let's continue with the code:

```
    // declare objects for derived classes
    bahamas package_1;
    grand_cayman package_2;
    st_thomas package_3;

    // ** we output header() function of the base class,
```

```
    // ** but as an element of the derived class.

    package_1.header();

    // ** set ptr to object of derived class
    ptr = &package_1;
    // execute virtual function
    // the compiler will know which version to execute!!
    ptr->other_attractions();
    ptr = &package_2;
    ptr->other_attractions();
    ptr = &package_3;
    ptr->other_attractions();

    return(0);
}
```

There are no further changes to the remainder of the code.

If we forget to provide an implementation for the virtual function inside one of the derived classes, say, st_thomas, the compiler issues the following error message:

```
Error:   Pure function 'caribbean_isles::other_attractions()' not
         overridden in 'st_thomas'
```

Therefore, pure virtual functions can be used as a safety mechanism inside programs where it is necessary for derived classes to provide their own version of the base virtual function.

12.5 REVIEW

In this chapter, we wrapped up our discussion on virtual functions. We learned:

• Just how easy it is to incorporate new virtual functions into a program, or delete outdated ones, based upon current needs.

• A base virtual function is invoked in those instances where a derived class fails to provide an implementation for it.

• Pure virtual functions force the programmer to provide an implementation of the virtual function inside the derived class.

• Classes which contain pure virtual functions are called abstract classes. Objects of this type cannot be declared, only pointers to it. The virtual function inside an abstract class is used as a placeholder for classes that will be derived from it.

13

Some Familiar Pointer Types and Pointer Arithmetic

13.1 INTRODUCTION

If you are a C programmer, then pointers should be no mystery to you. A brief introduction to pointers was presented in Chap. 11. In this chapter, and the next, pointers will be discussed in detail. Section 11.2 is now redisplayed. It served as a brief introduction to pointers and pointer syntax.

13.2 POINTER SYNTAX

A pointer contains the location in memory of a data type. The concept, syntax, and use of pointers is the same for C++ (save for a few enhancements), as it is in C. For example, if you declare an integer variable in your program, like so:

```
int a;    // a is an integer data type
```

then, you would declare a pointer to this variable as follows:

```
int *ptr; // ptr is a pointer to an integer
```

Next, you would set ptr to the address or location in memory of a:

```
ptr = &a; // ptr is set to the address of a
```

Once this is done, you can access the contents of the variable a indirectly through ptr. The following two statements result in the same output:

```
*ptr = 5; // access contents of a through ptr, set a to 5
a = 5;    // access contents of a directly, set a to 5
```

If you were to output ptr without the * operator, you would get the location in memory of where a is stored. The following statement illustrates what has just been said:

```
cout < "At location " < ptr < "is stored " < *ptr
```

The statement above would result in the following output on your computer:

```
At location 0xxxxxxxx is stored 5
```

where 0xxxxxxx is the address of a in hexadecimal.

The first invocation of ptr results in the address of a being output. The second invocation of ptr results in the output of what is stored at that address, or the contents of a. To summarize, the & symbol is the address of operator, and gives us the location in memory of a data type. The indirection operator * allows us to access the contents of what is stored at that address. A pointer must be initialized to point to something, or it will contain garbage.

13.3   POINTERS TO INTEGER, FLOAT, AND DOUBLE-DATA TYPES

Based on this short discussion on pointers, here's a small program that illustrates the syntax and use of pointers to integer, float, and double-data types. Tabs (\t) have been added so the columns line up.

```
C:> type test13_1.cpp

// test13_1.cpp          01/22/91 8:40 pm

#include     // necessary for I/O

main(void)
{
    int a, *ptr_int;    // delcare variables and ptr to data
types
    float b, *ptr_float;
    double c, *ptr_double;

    a = 5;              // initialize and point to their addresses
    ptr_int = &a;
    b = 10.3;
```

```
    ptr_float = &b;
    c = 50.5;
    ptr_double = &c;

    cout < "a is \t" < a
        <   "\t ptr_int is \t" < ptr_int
        < "\t *ptr_int is    " < *ptr_int < "\n";
    cout < "b is \t" < b
        < "\t ptr_float is \t" < ptr_float
        < "\t *ptr_float is  " < *ptr_float < "\n";
    cout < "c is \t" < c
        < "\t ptr_double is \t" < ptr_double
        < "\t *ptr_double is " < *ptr_double < "\n";
}
```

Compiling and running this program gives us the following output:

```
a is     5    ptr_int is 0x8f51ffe6    *ptr_int is 5
b is     10.3 ptr_float is 0x8f51ffee  *ptr_float is 10.3
c is     50.5 ptr_double is 0x8f51ffe6 *ptr_float is 50.5
```

The output statements first display the contents of what is stored in a, b, and c. Then, they display the contents of the pointers to these data types. As you can see, these pointers contain the location in memory where these variables are stored. Next, the contents of what is stored at these memory locations is obtained.

Now take a look at this version of test13_1.cpp.

```
C:> type test13_2.cpp

// test13_2.cpp          01/21/91 8:15 pm

#include     // necessary for I/O

main(void)
{
    int a, *ptr_int;
    float b, *ptr_float;
    double c, *ptr_double;

    a = 5;
    ptr_int = &a;
    b = 10.3;
    ptr_float = &b;
    c = 50.5;
    ptr_double = &c;
```

```
    // ** output addresses of pointers in the 3rd column
    cout < "a is \t" < a
        <   "\t ptr_int is \t" < ptr_int
        < "\t &ptr_int is    " < &ptr_int < "\n";
    cout < "b is \t" < b
        < "\t ptr_float is \t" < ptr_float
        < "\t &ptr_float is  " < &ptr_float < "\n";
    cout < "c is \t" < c
        < "\t ptr_double is \t" < ptr_double
        < "\t &ptr_double is " < &ptr_double < "\n";
}
```

The program output on our computer looks like this:

```
a is      5    ptr_int is    0x8f51fff4 &ptr_int is    0x8f51fff2
b is      10.3 ptr_float is  0x8f51ffee &ptr_float is  0x8f51ffec
c is      50.5 ptr_double is 0x8f51ffe4 &ptr_double is 0x8f51ffe2
```

As you can see, the third column outputs the location in memory that the pointers are stored, or the addresses of ptr_int, ptr_float, and ptr_double. Notice that the contents of the pointers are two bytes greater than the addresses of the pointers themselves.

The following chart illustrates where each variable is stored, and what is stored in it:

Variable	Address	Contents
ptr_int	0x8f51fff2	0x8f51fff4
a	0x8f51fff2	5
ptr_float	0x8f51ffec	0x8f51ffee
b	0x8f51ffec	10.3
ptr_double	0x8f51ffe2	0x8f51ffe4
c	0x8f51ffe2	50.5

Now we are going to change the syntax of the output statement. Take a look at this variation of test13_2.cpp:

```
C:> type test13_3.cpp

// test13_3.cpp          01/21/91 8:30 pm

#include <iostream.h>    // necessary for I/O

main(void)
{
    int a, *ptr_int;
```

```
        float b, *ptr_float;
        double c, *ptr_double;

        a = 5;
        ptr_int = &a;
        b = 10.3;
        ptr_float = &b;
        c = 50.5;
        ptr_double = &c;

        // ** display contents of what is stored at addresses of
        // ** pointers.
        cout << "a is \t" << a
             <<    "\t ptr_int is \t" << ptr_int
             << "\t *(&ptr_int) is    " << *(&ptr_int) << "\n";
        cout << "b is \t" << b
             << "\t ptr_float is \t" << ptr_float
             << "\t *(&ptr_float) is  " << *(&ptr_float) << "\n";
        cout << "c is \t" << c
             << "\t ptr_double is \t" << ptr_double
             << "\t *(&ptr_double) is " << *(&ptr_double) << "\n";
}
```

On our computer, the output for this program looks as follows:

```
a is      5    ptr_int is    0x8f51fff4 *(&ptr_int) is    5
b is      10.3 ptr_float is  0x8f51ffee *(&ptr_float) is  10.3
c is      50.5 ptr_double is 0x8f51ffe4 *(&ptr_double) is 50.5
```

The output for the last two columns has already been explained. Notice the syntax for the output of the first column:

```
... *(&ptr_int) is 5
```

Based upon the rules of precedence, this expression will be broken down as follows. First, the expression inside the braces will be evaluated:

```
....(&ptr_int)...
```

This will obtain the location in memory that ptr_int is stored. Next, the indirection operator (*) is used to obtain the contents of what is stored at that address:

```
....*(&ptr_int)...
```

a is stored at this location, and that is why 5 is output.

13.4   POINTERS TO ARRAYS

Arrays can be accessed through indices, as follows:

```
int array[5];
array[3] = 5;
```

The above statement declares an array of five integers. Then, the fourth element of the array is set to 5. The reason why the fourth element is set to 5, and not the third, is because indexing starts at 0, not 1.

Arrays can also be accessed through pointers. Take a look at the following extension to the fragment of code above.

```
int array[5];   // declare array containing 5 elements
int *ptr;       // declare pointer to integer

ptr = array;    // set pointer to 1st element of array[]
ptr += 3;       // add 3 to ptr - ptr now points to 4th element
*ptr = 5;       // set 4th element of array to 5
```

An array of five elements, and a pointer to integer data types, is declared. Next, ptr is set to the address of the first element of the array via the statement:

```
ptr = array;
```

Notice that there is no index to the array, only its name. This form of syntax returns the first element of the array.

Next, 3 is added to ptr. Originally, the first element was being pointed to. Now the index in incremented by 3, which is equal to the array[3], which is the fourth element of the array. The statement

```
*ptr = 5;
```

sets the contents of what is being pointed to by ptr to 5. Hence, the fourth element of array[] is set to 5.

Here's a short program that summarizes most of what has been said:

```
C:> type test13_4.cpp

// test13_4.cpp        01/21/91 8:32 pm

#include <iostream.h>    // necessary for I/O

main(void)
```

```
{
     char name[20] = "Jay Ranade";
     char *ptr;

     // set ptr to address of name[0];
     ptr = name;
     cout << "ptr is \t" << ptr << "\t name[0] is "
                         << name[0] << "\n";
     ptr++;
     cout << "ptr is \t" << ptr << "\t name is " << name << "\n";

     // access contents of what is stored at name[0] + 1
     cout << "*(name + 1) is \t" << *(name + 1) << "\n";
}
```

The output for this program looks as follows:

```
ptr is Jay Ranade name[0] is J
ptr is ay Ranade name is Jay Ranade
*(name + 1) is a
```

Here we see a 20-element character array is declared and initialized to "Jay Ranade." (Does the name ring a bell?) ptr is declared as a pointer to character data types. ptr is initialized to the first element of name[].

The first time around, the complete string is output, and the compiler knows when to stop when it encounters the terminating (and invisible to the human eye!) null at the end of the array. name[0], as expected, contains the letter *J*.

Next, ptr is incremented. It now points to the second element of the array, which is a, and hence "ay Ranade" is output. The name of the array without an index will always point to the first element of the array, and the complete array is output for "name." If "name" points to the first element of the array, then (name + 1) points to the second element. The contents of what is stored at that location is obtained via the expression:

```
*(name + 1)
```

and the second element of the array (a) is output.

13.5 POINTERS TO STRUCTURES

Pointers to structures are similar in syntax and function as pointers to any other data type. Take a look at the following program:

```
C:> type test13_5.cpp
```

```
// test13_5.cpp            01/21/91 10:30 pm

main(void)
{
struct family
    {
    char *husband;
    char *wife;
    char *son;
    };
    family anderson; // anderson is a structure of type family
    family *ptr;  // ptr is a pointer to family

    ptr = &anderson; // ptr now contains address of anderson

    // point to structure members and initialize them
    ptr->husband = "John Anderson";
    ptr->wife = "Mary Anderson";
    ptr->son = "Joey Anderson";
}
```

A structure of type family is declared. This structure contains three elements which are pointers to characters. anderson is declared as a structure of type family, and ptr is declared as a pointer to a structure of type family. Next, ptr is set to the address of anderson, and then structure members are accessed and initialized via the -> operator.

13.6   POINTER ARITHMETIC

Only three types of operations are permitted on pointers: addition, subtraction, and comparison. Take a look at the following progam which illustrates how pointers are incremented:

```
C:> type test13_6.cpp

// test13_6.cpp            01/21/91 11:34 pm

#include <iostream.h>      // necessary for I/O

main(void)
{
    int *ptr;
    int a[2] = {10, 20};      // a[] is an array of integers

    ptr = a;  // ptr contains address of 1st element of array
    cout << "ptr is " << ptr << " *ptr is " << *ptr << "\n";
```

```
    ptr += 1;
    cout << "ptr is " << ptr << " *ptr is " << *ptr << "\n";
}
```

The output for this program looks as follows:

```
ptr is 0x8f93fff2 *ptr is 10
ptr is 0x8f94fff4 *ptr is 20
```

`ptr` is declared as a pointer to integer data types. Next, an integer array is declared and initialized. `ptr` is set to the first element of array, and 10 is output. 1 is added to `ptr`. It now points to the second element of the array, and 20 is output. Notice that `ptr` is incremented by two bytes, even though only one is added to it. This is because our computer stores an integer in two bytes, and a pointer is automatically incremented by the correct number of bytes in order to access subsequent elements. Your computer may take more or less bytes to store an integer; refer to your system documentation for further details.

The following progam illustrates how pointers are decremented:

```
C:> type test13_7.cpp

// test13_7.cpp          01/21/91 11:34 pm

#include <iostream.h>    // necessary for I/O

main(void)
{
    int *ptr;
    int a[2] = {10, 20};    // a[] is an array of integers

    ptr = a;  // ptr contains address of 1st element of array
    cout << "ptr is " << ptr << " *ptr is " << *ptr << "\n";
    ptr += 1;
    cout << "ptr is " << ptr << " *ptr is " << *ptr << "\n";
    ptr-;
    cout << "ptr is " << ptr << " *ptr is " << *ptr << "\n";
}
```

The output for this program is as follows:

```
ptr is 0x8f97fff2 *ptr is 10
ptr is 0x8f97fff4 *ptr is 20
ptr is 0x8f97fff2 *ptr is 10
```

Notice that decrementing the pointer also results in a difference of two bytes in the address, not one. This is once again because our computer stores an integer in two bytes. The correct offset is automatically calculated.

Pointers can also be compared. Here's a short program that does just that:

```
C:> type test13_8.cpp

// test13_8.cpp          01/21/91 11:52 pm

#include <iostream.h>     // necessary for I/O

main(void)
{
    int *ptr1, *ptr2;
    int a[2] = {10, 10};      // a[] is an array of integers

    ptr1 = a; // ptr contains address of 1st element of array
    cout << "ptr1 is " << ptr1 << " *ptr1 is " << *ptr1 << "\n";

    ptr2 = ptr1 + 1;
    cout << "ptr2 is " << ptr2 << " *ptr2 is " << *ptr2 << "\n";

    // compare 2 pointers
    if (ptr1 ==  ptr2)
        cout << "ptr1 is equal to ptr2 \n";
    else
        cout << "ptr1 is not equal to ptr2 \n";

    if (*ptr1 == *ptr2)
        cout << "*ptr1 equals *ptr2 \n";
    else
        cout << "*ptr1 does not equal *ptr2 \n";
}
```

Compiling and executing this program results in the following output:

```
ptr1 is 0x8f78fff2 *ptr1 is 10
ptr2 is 0x8f78fff4 *ptr2 is 10
ptr1 is not equal to ptr2
*ptr1 equals *ptr2
```

The output should be self-explanatory.

And now here's a program that illustrates what you cannot do with pointers:

```
C:> type test13_9.cpp

// test13_9.cpp          01/21/91 12:00 am
```

```
main(void)
{
    int a = 5, b = 10, *ptr, *ptr2;

    ptr = &a;
    ptr2 = &b;

    // lines 10 thru 14 follow
    ptr *= 4;        // multiply pointer by constant
    ptr /= 2;        // divide pointer by constant
    ptr %= 3;        // obtain remainder by dividing pointer
    ptr *= ptr2;     // multiply 2 pointers
    ptr /= ptr2;     // divide 1 pointer into another

    // lines 18 and 19 follow
    ptr += ptr2;     // add 2 pointers
    ptr -= ptr2;     // subtract 1 pointer from another
}
```

Compiling this program results in the following error message being output for lines 10 through 14:

```
Error:    Illegal use of pointer in function main()
```

and the following messages are output for lines 18 and 19:

```
Error:    Invalid pointer addition in function main()
Error:    Invalid pointer subtraction in function main()
```

The error messages are self-explanatory. You simply cannot perform any other function with pointers but add, subtract, and compare.

13.7   REVIEW

In this chapter, we discussed pointer syntax and use. This chapter should have served as a review for seasoned (and, for that matter, nonseasoned) C programmers. We will present the operations that can and cannot be performed in table format. But before you look at the table, take a look at this fragment of code. The results in the table indicate the values that will be obtained by manipulating the following variables.

```
main()
{
    int *ptr1, *ptr2;   // pointers to integer values
    int a[2], b;        // a and b are integer data types
```

```
      ptr1 = &(a[0]);      // ptr1 contains address of a[0]
      ptr2 = &(a[1]);      // ptr2 contains address of a[1]

// Assume a[0] is stored at memory location 8000
// Therefore, a[1] is stored at address 8002

      .
      .
      .
      .
}
```

The "Result" column in Table 13.1 displays the value of the variable or the expression after the evaluation of the condition. All results are based on the initial values of the pointers. Remember that the contents of ptr1 are equal to 8000, and ptr2 are 8002.

TABLE 13.1 Operations on Pointers

Operation	Permitted	Pointer syntax	Result
Increment	Yes	++ptr1; ptr1++; ++ptr2; ptr2++;	ptr1 = 8002 ptr2 = 8004
Decrement	Yes	--ptr1; ptr1--; --ptr2; ptr2--;	ptr1 = 7998 ptr2 = 8000
Compare	Yes	if (ptr1 < ptr2). while (ptr2 < ptr1)	TRUE FALSE
Subtract a pointer from a constant	No	z = 8 - ptr1; z = 14 - ptr2;	Error
Add 2 pointers	No	z = ptr1 + ptr2;	Error
Multiply pointer by a value	No	z = ptr1 * 9; z = ptr2 * 6;	Error
Divide pointer by a value	No	z = ptr1 / 8; z = ptr2 / 60;	Error
Multiply 2 pointers	No	z = ptr1 * ptr2	Error
Divide 1 pointer by another	No	z = ptr2 / ptr1	Error

Chapter 4

Operator Overloading—Fundamental Concept

14.1   INTRODUCTION

In this chapter, we will describe an unusual and interesting feature of C++ which is called *operator overloading*. This feature allows you to change the meaning of operators such as +, −, *, /, and more. If you take the time to think through the reasons that you want to overload operators, then this can be a very powerful tool. On the other hand, indiscriminate use of overloaded operators can result in a debugging nightmare. Keep this in mind as you proceed to read the remainder of the chapter.

14.2   OPERATOR OVERLOADING—IS NOTHING UNUSUAL?

Take a look at the following five-line program.

```
C:> type test14_1.cpp

//   test14_1.cpp   01/29/91 9:30 pm

#include <iostream.h>    // necessary for I/O

main(void)
{
    cout << "Notice the use of the << operator!! \n";
}
```

Compiling and running this program results in the following output:

```
Notice the use of the << operator!!
```

There are no mysteries here. Now take a look at test14_2.cpp.

```
C:> type test14_2.cpp

//    test14_2.cpp   01/29/91 9:32 pm

#include <iostream.h>     // necessary for I/0

main(void)
{
    int a = 50;
    cout << "a is " << a << "\n";
    a = a << 12 ;  // shift a left by 2 bits
    cout << "a is " << a << "\n";
}
```

Compiling and running this program results in the following output:

```
a is 50
a is 8192
```

What is interesting in this program is the use of the << operator. In the first instance, it is used as a "put to" operator. In the statement

```
a = a << 12;
```

it is used as the left shift operator. *a* is shifted left 12 bits, and so the value outputs as 8192, instead of 50.

What you just encountered is an example of operator overloading. Operator overloading is a feature provided by C++ which allows you to change the meaning of operators. In the first example, the operator << was used as a put to operator. In the second example, it is used as a left shift operator, as well as a "put to" operator.

Operator overloading is an interesting concept, but you will be surprised to realize that it has existed all along, without your ever perhaps really knowing about it. For example, you can add two integers using the + operator:

```
a = 5 + 2;
```

and you can add two floats using the same operator:

```
a = 5.5 + 2.8;
```

You are using the same operator to perform the same function on two different data types. The + operator is overloaded to perform addition on two integer types in the first instance, and addition of two float types in the second.

Here's another example. The * operator is used to multiply two data types:

```
a = a * b;
```

However, the * operator can also be used to specifiy a pointer type when it is declared:

```
int *ptr;
```

The above statement declares ptr as a pointer to an integer type. The * operator can also be used to dereference a pointer variable, in order to manipulate the contents of what is stored at the location in memory that ptr was made to point to:

```
*ptr = 5;
```

The above statement sets the contents of location in memory stored in ptr to 5. This is another instance of operator overloading.

14.3 OPERATOR OVERLOADING—SYNTAX

Take a look at the following short program:

```
C:> type test14_3.cpp

//    test14_3.cpp    01/30/91 12:00 am

#include <iostream.h>    // necessary for I/O

class assign
    {
    public:
    int a;
    };

assign object_1, object_2;

main(void)
{
    object_1.a = 5;

    object_2 = object_1;
```

```
            cout << "object_2.a is " << object_2.a << "\n";
    }
```

Compiling and running this program results in the following output:

```
object2.a is 5
```

This program demonstrates nothing but a simple assignment of an integer value to a class member, and then `cout` is used to display this value to your screen. Now take a look at this program:

```
C:> type test14_4.cpp

//    test14_4.cpp   01/30/91 12:05 pm

#include <iostream.h>    // necessary for I/O

class assign
    {
    public:
    int a;
    // ** notice overloaded function syntax:
    void operator=(assign var1);
    };

// overloaded operator function returns no value (type void)
// it takes an object of type assign as an argument
// it follows the usual function definition rules
void assign::operator=(assign var1)
{
    a = 2 + var1.a;
}

// object_1 and object_2 are objects of type assign
assign object_1, object_2;

main(void)
{
    // class member a of object_1 is assigned the value of 5
    object_1.a = 5;

    // object_2 is set equal to object_1
    object_2 = object_1;
    cout << "object_2.a is " << object_2.a << "\n";
}
```

Compiling and running this program results in the following output:

```
object_2.a is 7
```

Interesting output, wouldn't you say? Under normal circumstances, `object_2.a` should have been 5, not 7, since `object_2` is set equal to `object_1`, and `object_1.a` was previously set to 5. Well, the reason for this unusual output is that the operator = was overloaded to assign the operand on the left equal to the operand on the right, plus 2. That is why `object_2.a` was set equal to 7, instead of 5. Let's step through this program and understand what happened.

Take a look at the declaration of the class `assign`:

```
class assign
    {
    public:
    int a;
    // ** notice overloaded function syntax:
    void operator=(assign var1);
    };
```

Notice the syntax for the member function assign():

```
    void operator=(assign var1);
```

This statement declares the existence of an overloaded operator function, and it is a member function of the class `assign`. The operator that will be overloaded is the assignment operator =. This function will return no value, and it takes an object of type `assign` as an argument. This function could just as well have been declared as follows:

```
    assign operator=(void);
```

This would imply that it returns an object of type `assign`, and takes no arguments. Or, it could have been declared as follows:

```
    int operator=(char);
```

or with any other valid return or argument type. In our example, it is declared as follows:

```
    void operator=(assign var1);
```

The definition of the class member function `operator=()` follows:

```
void assign::operator=(assign var1)
```

```
{
    a = 2 + var1.a;
}
```

The definition of this function agrees with the function prototype in the class declaration. The function returns no value, it is a member of the class assign (as can be seen by the scope resolution operator :: which precedes the function name; assign::operator=), it overloads the operator =, and it takes an object of type assign as an argument.

The function itself is only one line. It takes the class object that it receives as a parameter and adds 2 to its a class member. It assigns the resulting value to the class member a, and returns back to main( ).

Inside main( ), object_2 is assigned to object_1. This is a valid assignment, since both objects are of the same class type. Finally, the contents of object_2.a are output.

The reason for the unusual result is that the operator = has been overloaded in the context of all objects that belong to the class that the overloaded function is a member of. Let's understand this concept in greater detail.

object_1 and object_2 are objects of type assign. The operator function = is a class member of assign. Each time the operator = will be encountered or called to perform an operation on class objects that belong to the class type for which an overloaded function definition exists, the overloaded function definition will be substituted instead of the usual operation. (Friend function definitions can also be substituted; these will be discussed later on in the chapter.)

Now take another look at the code for main( ).

```
assign object_1, object_2;

main(void)
{
    // class member a of object_1 is assigned the value of 5
    object_1.a = 5;

    // object_2 is set equal to object_1
    object_2 = object_1;
    cout << "object_2.a is " << object_2.a << "\n";
}
```

object_1 and object_2 are declared as objects of type assign. Inside main( ), class member a of assign is set to 5. Next, object_2 is assigned to object_1. However, the operator = was previously declared as a member function of the class assign. Since object_1 and object_2 are objects of the same type, the compiler implements the code for that particular overloaded function.

Before proceeding to understand what happens inside the function itself, you should note that in the first assignment statement

```
object_1.a = 5;
```

5 was, in fact, assigned to `object_1`, and 2 was not added to it. The reason for this is that both operands on the left and the right of the overloaded operator must belong to the same class that the overloaded operator (or friend function) belongs to. The operand on the right is a constant; it is not a member of the class object `assign`, hence the regular assignment operation is implemented. What this implies is that operators preserve their existing functionality, in the absence of the above-mentioned conditions. (In the case of unary operators, i.e., those that operate on one operand only, e.g., ++ and −−, the overloaded operator will always be called, given that the operand belongs to the same class. These will be discussed later on in the chapter.)

Now take another look at the code for the overloaded operator function:

```
void assign::operator=(assign var1)
{
    a = 2 + var1.a;
}
```

As you can see, an argument called `var1` is accepted by `assign`. This is the template for an object of type `assign`. 2 is added to the `a` member of this object, and the result is assigned to the `a` member of the second object. You should be wondering by now exactly which object is being added to, and which object is being assigned to. The answer is that the operand on the *right* of the operator is passed as the explicit argument to the function.

Hence, in the statement

```
object_2 = object_1;
```

the argument that is passed to the overloaded operator as the explicit argument `var1` is `object_1`. The object on the *left* of the operator is assigned to. The `a` class member inside the function itself belongs to `object_2`. (This particular mechanism will be discussed in greater detail shortly.) That is why the contents of `object_2.a` are changed from 5 to 7.

Meanwhile, the contents of `object_1.a` remain unchanged. We will modify `test14_4.cpp` to demonstrate just that.

```
C:> type test14_5.cpp

//   test14_5.cpp   01/30/91 12:05 pm

#include <iostream.h>    // necessary for I/O

class assign
    {
    public:
```

```
        int a;
        // ** notice overloaded function syntax:
        void operator=(assign var1);
        };

// overloaded operator function returns no value
// it takes an object of type assign as an argument
// it follows the usual function definition rules
void assign::operator=(assign var1)
{
    a = 2 + var1.a;
}

// object_1 and object_2 are objects of type assign
assign object_1, object_2;

main(void)
{
    // class member a of object_1 is assigned the value of 5
    object_1.a = 5;

    // object_2 is set equal to object_1
    object_2 = object_1;
    cout << "object_2.a is " << object_2.a << "\n";
    cout << "object_1.a is " << object_1.a << "\n";
}
```

Compiling and running this program results in the following output:

```
object_2.a is 7
object_1.a is 5
```

The output should make sense. The operand on the right is operated on; it remains unchanged through the whole process.

14.4   OPERATOR OVERLOADING—GETTING CARRIED AWAY

Test14_5.cpp will now be modified to demonstrate an instance where we got a little bit carried away with the concept just explained, and want to play tricks with your mind. Take a look at the following code.

```
C:> type test14_6.cpp

//    test14_6.cpp    01/30/91 12:05 pm

#include <iostream.h>    // necessary for I/O
```

```
class assign
    {
    public:
    int a;
    // ** notice operator changed from = to +:
    void operator+(assign var1);
    };

// overloaded operator function returns object of type assign
// it takes an object of type assign as an argument
// it follows the usual function definition rules
void assign::operator+(assign var1)
{
    a = 2 + var1.a;
}

// object_1 and object_2 are objects of type assign
assign object_1, object_2;

main(void)
{
    // class member a of object_1 is assigned the value of 5
    object_1.a = 5;

    // ** the '+' actually performs an '='!!!!
    object_2 + object_1;
    cout << "object_2.a is " << object_2.a << "\n";
}
```

The two lines of code that you should pay special attention to are:

```
    void operator+(assign var1);
```

and

```
    object_2 + object_1;
```

In the first statement, the operator + is overloaded. In the second statement, object_2 is added to object_1, and not assigned to anything. Compiling and running this program results in the following output:

```
object_2.a is 7
```

This is because object_2.a is *assigned* to the value contained in object_1.a, inside the overloaded operator definition of +, and 2 is added to it.

If the operator + was not overloaded, the statement

```
    object_2 + object_1;
```

would have resulted in an unfriendly compiler error message. However, no errors are generated because

```
object_2 + object_1;
```

results in exactly the same sequence of operations that occurred when the code looked like this:

```
object_2 = object_1;
```

For those of us of who inherit the code of programmers that inadvertently change the meaning of operators as they wish, statements such as

```
object_2 + object_1;
```

can result in acute cases of confusion, headache, frustration, and insomnia. Hence, a word of advice from us. Please don't overload operators to mean something that goes against the grain of their original meaning. Don't overload a + operator to mean a −, a * to mean a /, and so on. Do what you have to do, but think things through before you proceed. Don't play tricks with other people's minds; you may end up playing a trick on yourself!

14.5   OVERLOADED OPERATORS ARE SIMPLY FUNCTION CALLS

An overloaded operator function syntax is simply an alternate form of a function call. Take a look at the following code. The function name operator() has been abbreviated to op().

```
C:> type test14_7.cpp

//    test14_7.cpp    01/31/91 7:14 pm

#include <iostream.h>    // necessary for I/O

class assign
    {
    public:
    int a;
    // ** notice that op is now a regular function
    // ** and it returns an object of type assign
    assign op(assign var1);
    };

assign object_1, object_2;

// op() is a regular function
```

```
// it returns an object of type assign
// it takes an object of type assign as a parameter
assign assign::op(assign var1)
{
    a = 2 + var1.a;
    object_2 = object_1;
    cout << "object_2.a in op() function is "
        << object_2.a << "\n";
    return var1;
}


main(void)
{
    // class member a of object_1 is assigned the value of 5
    object_1.a = 5;

    // object_1.op() is executed
    // the return value is assigned to object_2
    object_2 = object_1.op(object_1);

    cout << "object_2.a is " << object_2.a << "\n";
}
```

Compiling and running this program results in the following output:

```
object_2.a in op() function is 7
object_2.a is 5
```

The function op() is now a regular member function of the class assign(). object_1 and object_2 are declared as objects of type assign. When the function object_1.op() is called, object_1 is passed as a parameter to it. Inside the function, 2 is added to a class member of object_1, and assigned to object_2. Hence, object_2.a in op() gets set to 7. However, object_1.a remains unchanged, and this is the value sent back to main(). object_2 is assigned this value, and object_2.a is now once again set to 5.

As you are aware, the contents of variables inside functions can be manipulated or changed only through pointers (unless you are passing an array to the function, or they are global in scope). This is because copies of parameters are passed to functions, not the actual values. Here's a short program that illustrates this point:

```
C:> type test14_8.cpp

//   test14_8.cpp   01/31/91 8:00 pm

#include <iostream.h>    // necessary for I/O
```

```
class assign
    {
    public:
    int a;
    // ** notice that op is now a regular function
    assign op(assign *object_1);
    };

assign object_1, object_2, *ptr;

// op() is a regular function
// it returns an object of type assign
// it takes a pointer to an object of type assign as a parameter
assign assign::op(assign *ptr)
{
    // modify contents of what ptr is pointing to, i.e. object_1.a

    ptr->a = 2 + ptr->a;
    // return object_1
    return object_1;
}

main(void)
{
    // class member a of object_1 is assigned the value of 5
    object_1.a = 5;

    // set ptr to location in memory of object_1
    ptr = &object_1;

    // object_2 is set equal to return value of op()
    // this return value is an object of type assign
    object_2 = object_1.op(ptr);

    cout << "object_2.a is " << object_2.a << "\n";
}
```

Compiling and running this program results in the following output:

```
object_2.a is 7
```

This time a pointer to object_1 is sent to the function op():

```
assign op(assign *object_1);
```

ptr is set to the location in memory of object_1, and then a call to op() is initiated.

Inside op, the actual contents of object_1 are modified, via ptr:

```
ptr->a = 2 + ptr->a;
```

Member of object_1 is accessed via the -> operator. The dot (.) operator could also have been used as follows:

```
ptr.a = 2 + ptr.a;
```

The modified contents of object_1 are sent back to main( ), and object_2 is assigned to this return value. Hence, object_2.a outputs as 7.

Now here's the trick question. Which version do you think looks cleaner and more natural? The one that uses pointers:

```
C:> type test14_8.cpp

//    test14_8.cpp    01/31/91 8:00 pm

#include <iostream.h>    // necessary for I/O

class assign
    {
    public:
    int a;
    // ** notice that op is now a regular function
    assign op(assign *object_1);
    };

assign object_1, object_2, *ptr;

// op() is a regular function
// it returns an object of type assign
// it takes a pointer to an object of type assign as a parameter

assign assign::op(assign *ptr)
{
    // modify contents of what ptr is pointing to, i.e. object_1.a

    ptr->a = 2 + ptr->a;
    // return object_1
    return object_1;
}

main(void)
{
    // class member a of object_1 is assigned the value of 5
```

```
    object_1.a = 5;

    // set ptr to location in memory of object_1
    ptr = &object_1;

    // object_2 is set equal to return value of op()
    // this return value is an object of type assign
    object_2 = object_1.op(ptr);

    cout << "object_2.a is " << object_2.a << "\n";
}
```

or the one that uses operator overloading:

```
C:> type test14_4.cpp

//    test14_4.cpp    01/30/91 12:05 pm

#include <iostream.h>     // necessary for I/O

class assign
    {
    public:
    int a;
    // ** notice overloaded function syntax:
    void operator=(assign var1);
    };

// overloaded operator function returns no value
// it takes an object of type assign as an argument
// it follows the usual function definition rules
void assign::operator=(assign var1)
{
    a = 2 + var1.a;
}

// object_1 and object_2 are objects of type assign
assign object_1, object_2;

main(void)
{
    // class member a of object_1 is assigned the value of 5
    object_1.a = 5;

    // object_2 is set equal to object_1
    object_2 = object_1;
```

```
    cout << "object_2.a is " << object_2.a << "\n";
}
```

If you prefer the first version, then you probably don't feel comfortable with the syntax of overloaded operator calls. We recommend that you refrain from using overloaded operators until you feel more comfortable with the concept and syntax.

If you prefer the second version, then you are well on your way to adopting yet another powerful feature of C++.

14.6   ADVANTAGES OF OPERATOR OVERLOADING

One of the major advantages of operator overloading is that it allows you to use the same operators on user-defined data types as the built-in data types. You are used to expressions such as

```
a = a + b;
a = a * b;
```

but without operator overloading, the statements

```
object_1 = object_1 + object_2;
object_1 = object_1 * object_2;
```

would be invalid, given that `object_1` and `object_2` are user-defined data types. Operator overloading affords a more natural way for the expression of such statements. As another example, a concatenation of two strings would be expressed intuitively as follows:

```
"This is a " + "concatenation of 2 strings.";
```

However, the above statement would not compile properly without operator overloading.

14.7   DISADVANTAGES OF OPERATOR OVERLOADING

The major disadvantage of operator overloading is when the meaning of operators becomes hidden inside obscure code, and the programmer does not understand why an operator such as + is not performing the function that he or she expects it to. The programmer is bound to experience feelings of inadequacy (since he or she does not understand the code), frustration, insomnia, and emotional distress.

14.8   REVIEW

In this chapter, we understood how operator overloading works, and why it can be a powerful or destructive tool. In particular, we learned:

- That we have been inadvertently overloading operators such as << and *
all along; it is nothing new.

- This mechanism can be used to change the meaning of most operators provided by C++.

- Overloaded operator functions must be class members or friend functions.

- Overloaded operator functions are nothing more but an alternate form of a
function call.

- The syntax for an overloaded function is as follows:

```
type operator#(argument_list);
```

where `type` is the return type of the function. This can be type `void`, or any
other valid data type;

`#` is the operator that is being overloaded

argument_list is the list of arguments, if any, which are sent to the
overloaded function.

- Overloaded operators allow a more natural way to express the relationship
between two user-defined data types.

- Overloaded operators can be a programmer's nightmare, if their use results
in obscure and impenetrable code.

15

Operator Overloading, this Pointer, and Friend Functions

15.1 INTRODUCTION

In this chapter, we will introduce a pointer which is called *this* (yes, it really is called this!). This pointer (no pun intended) is an integral part of the mechanism that allows operator overloading. Use of friend functions will also be illustrated. Friends can be used to overload operators, instead of class members.

15.2 BINARY AND UNARY OVERLOADED OPERATORS

A binary operator is one that works on two objects. For example, the + is a binary operator; you have to add something to something in order for this operator to work. A unary operator is one that works on one object only. For example, ++ is a unary operator, `something++` results in `something` being incremented by one. C++ allows you to overload the following operators:

Operator	Function
++	increment
−−	decrement
!	not
−	complement
+	add
-	minus
*	multiply

/	divide
%	modulus
()	function call
[]	array subscript
new	free store allocator
delete	free store deallocator
=	assign
+=	add and assign
−=	subtract and assign
*=	multiply and assign
/=	divide and assign
&	bitwise and
		bitwise or
^	bitwise exclusive-or
||	logical or
&&	logical and
<	less than
<=	less than or equal to
>	greater than
>=	greater than or equal to
<<	left shift
>>	right shift
|=	or and assign
^=	exclusive-or and assign
&=	and and assign
<<=	left shift and assign
>>=	right shift and assign
==	logical equal
!=	not equal

The following operators cannot be overloaded:

,	comma
.	member
->	class or structure pointer
?:	ternary
sizeof	obtains size in bytes

15.3 RESTRICTIONS ON OVERLOADED OPERATORS

1. You cannot make up your own operator. You can overload existing operators only.

2. Operator overloading works when applied to class objects only.

3. You cannot change the precedence or associativity of the original operators.

4. You cannot change a binary operator to work with a single object.

5. You cannot change a unary operator to work with two objects.

6. Prefix and postfix application of the operators ++ and −− cannot be distinguished.

7. You cannot overload an operator that works exclusively with pointers.

15.4   EXPRESSION SYNTAX OF OVERLOADED OPERATORS

We would like to bring your attention to restriction numbers 4 and 5 from the prior section. These restrictions state that you must respect the general form of syntax that is associated with a particular operator; you cannot change its basic template. Take a look at the following program.

```
C:> type test15_1.cpp

//   test15_1.cpp   01/31/91 8:35 pm

#include <iostream.h>    // necessary for I/O

class assign
    {
    public:
    int a;
    // ** notice overloaded function syntax:
    void operator/(assign var1);
    };

// overloaded operator function returns type void (i.e. nothing)
// it takes an object of type assign as an argument
// it follows the usual function definition rules
void assign::operator/(assign var1)
{
    a = var1.a / 5;
}

// object_1 and object_2 are objects of type assign
assign object_1, object_2;

main(void)
{
    // class member a of object_1 is assigned the value of 5
    object_1.a = 15;
    object_2.a = 10;

    // The divide operator is treated as a unary operator
```

```
    object_2 / ;

    cout << "object_1.a is " << object_1.a << "\n";
    cout << "object_2.a is " << object_2.a << "\n";
}
```

Notice the statement:

```
    object_2 / ;
```

As you can see, an attempt is made to use the division operator, which is binary, on a single object. Compiling this program results in the following error message:

```
Error:   Operand expected in function main()
```

Now take a look at this program, which also overloads the divide operator, but it uses two objects instead of one.

```
C:> type test15_2.cpp

//    test15_2.cpp   01/31/91 8:35 pm

#include <iostream.h>     // necessary for I/O

class assign
    {
    public:
    int a;
    // ** notice overloaded function syntax:
    void operator/(assign var1);
    };

// overloaded operator function returns type void
// it takes an object of type assign as an argument
// it follows the usual function definition rules
void assign::operator/(assign var1)
{
    a = var1.a / 5;
}

// object_1 and object_2 are objects of type assign
assign object_1, object_2;

main(void)
```

```
{
    object_1.a = 15;
    object_2.a = 10;

    cout << "object_2.a is " << object_2.a << "\n";

    // object_2 is divided by object_1
    object_2 / object_1;

    cout << "object_1.a is " << object_1.a << "\n";
    cout << "object_2.a is " << object_2.a << "\n";
}
```

Compiling and running this program results in the following output:

```
object_2.a is 10
object_1.a is 15
object_2.a is 3
```

object_1.a and object_2.a are initially set to 15 and 10, respectively. The division (/) operator is overloaded. object_2 is divided by object_1. The statement

```
a = var1.a / 5;
```

can be decoded as follows:

```
object_2.a = object_1.a / 5;
```

which is equal to

```
object_2.a = 15 / 5;
```

and so object_2.a is equal to 3. The output statements should now make sense. The contents of object_1.a remain unchanged. The contents of object_2.a are set to 3.

In the prior chapter, we had mentioned that the operator on the right of the operand is sent as an explicit argument to the calling overloaded operator function. The operand on the left is implicitly sent to the calling function. In this chapter, this concept will be elaborated on, so that you understand how this mechanism works. Take another look at the function definition:

```
void assign::operator/(assign var1)
{
    a = var1.a / 5;
}
```

Based upon what has just been said, var1 will contain the value assigned to object_1, since object_1 is to the right of the overloaded operator. This is the explicit argument sent to the calling function.

A pointer to the left operand is implicitly passed to operator/(). Hence, the variable a in the statement

```
a = var1.a / 5;
```

belongs to object_2, a pointer to object_2 is implicitly passed to the overloaded function. But exactly how does this occur? The answer is through a pointer that Mr. Stroustrup chose to call the *this* pointer.

15.5   THE this POINTER

Each time a member function is invoked, it is passed a pointer to the object that invoked it. The name of this pointer is *this*. This pointer is invisible to us; it is passed automatically, or implicitly. The syntax of this pointer is similar to other pointer syntax. The only difference is that it is never declared; its existence is automatic, based upon the criteria just mentioned. And now, just to prove that a pointer to the operand on the left side of the overloaded operator is implicitly passed to the calling function through the *this* pointer, here's a modified version of test15_2.cpp.

```
C:> type test15_3.cpp

//    test15_3.cpp    01/31/91 9:35 pm

#include <iostream.h>     // necessary for I/O

class assign
    {
    public:
    int a;
    // ** notice overloaded function syntax:
    void operator/(assign var1);
    };

// overloaded operator function returns no value
// it takes an object of type assign as an argument
// it follows the usual function definition rules
void assign::operator/(assign var1)
{
    cout << "this->a is " << this->a << "\n";
    a = var1.a / 5;
}
```

```
// object_1 and object_2 are objects of type assign
assign object_1, object_2;

main(void)
{
    object_1.a = 15;
    object_2.a = 10;

    // ** object_2 is divided by object_1
    object_2 / object_1;

    cout << "object_1.a is " << object_1.a << "\n";
    cout << "object_2.a is " << object_2.a << "\n";
}
```

Compiling and running this program gives the following output:

```
this->a is 10
object_1.a is 15
object_2.a is 3
```

As you can see, this->a contains the value 10, which was assigned to object_2.a in main(). The statement

```
a = var1.a / 5;
```

can be decoded as follows:

```
object_2.a = object_1.a / 5;
```

which is equal to

```
object_2.a = 15 / 5;
```

and so object_2.a is set equal to 3. The output statements should now be clear.

Let's switch the values of object_1 and object_2 inside main(), and see how the value of the this pointer is affected. Here's the code:

```
C:> type test15_4.cpp

//   test15_4.cpp   01/31/91 9:35 pm

#include <iostream.h>   // necessary for I/O

class assign
```

```
    {
    public:
    int a;
    // ** notice overloaded function syntax:
    void operator/(assign var1);
    };

// overloaded operator function returns object of type assign
// it takes an object of type assign as an argument
// it follows the usual function definition rules
void assign::operator/(assign var1)
{
    cout << "this->a is " << this->a << "\n";
    a = var1.a / 5;
}

// object_1 and object_2 are objects of type assign
assign object_1, object_2;

main(void)
{
    object_1.a = 15;
    object_2.a = 10;

    cout << "object_2.a is " << object_2.a << "\n";

    // object_1 is divided by object_2
    object_1 / object_2;

    cout << "object_1.a is " << object_1.a << "\n";
    cout << "object_2.a is " << object_2.a << "\n";
}
```

Compiling and running this program results in the following output:

```
this->a is 15
object_1.a is 2
object_2.a is 10
```

The statement

```
a = var1.a / 5;
```

can be decoded as follows:

```
object_1.a = object_2.a / 5;
```

which is equal to

```
object_1.a = 10 / 5;
```

and so `object_1.a` is set equal to 2, and `object_2.a` remains unchanged. The output should now be self-explanatory.

And now, to reinforce what you have just learned, here's another program that illustrates how operator overloading works. This time the * operator will be overloaded.

```
C:> type test15_5.cpp

//    test15_5.cpp    01/31/91 10:02 pm

#include <iostream.h>    // necessary for I/O

class assign
     {
     public:
     int a;
     // ** notice return value of overloaded function
     int operator*(assign var1);
     };

// overloaded operator function returns integer
// it takes an object of type assign as an argument
// it follows the usual function definition rules
int assign::operator*(assign var1)
{
     cout << "this->a is " << this->a << "\n";
     a = this->a * var1.a;
     return a;
}

// object_1, object_2 and object_3 are objects of type assign
assign object_1, object_2, object_3;

main(void)
{
     object_1.a = 15;
     object_2.a = 10;

     // object_3.a receives the return value
     object_3.a = object_2 * object_1;

     cout << "object_1.a is " << object_1.a << "\n";
```

```
        cout << "object_2.a is " << object_2.a << "\n";
        cout << "object_3.a is " << object_3.a << "\n";
}
```

Notice that this time the overloaded function returns an int, instead of an object of type assign. Inside the function, a is returned, this is a class member of object_2. Since an int type is being returned, main() is modified, so as to have an int type accept this value.

Compiling and running this program results in the following output:

```
this->a is 10
object_1.a is 15
object_2.a is 150
object_3.a is 150
```

The following statement:

```
        object_3.a = object_2 * object_1;
```

results in object_2 being multiplied by object_1. The * operator is overloaded. Inside the overloaded function:

```
int assign::operator*(assign var1)
{
        cout << "this->a is " << this->a << "\n";
        a = this->a * var1.a;
        return a;
}
```

object_1 is sent explicitly, and a pointer to object_2 is sent implicitly. The variables 'a' and 'this->a' belong to object_2 (they are to the left of the overloaded operator). Thus, the statement

```
        a = this->a * var1.a;
```

can be decoded as follows:

```
        object_2.a = 10 * 15;
```

Thus, the value of object_1.a remains unchanged, and object_2.a is returned via the statement:

```
        return a;
```

and assigned to object_3.a:

```
        object_3.a = object_2 * object_1;
```

The output should now be absolutely clear to you.

15.6   FRIEND FUNCTIONS

So far, member functions only have been used to illustrate how operator overloading works. *Friend functions* to the class that contains the overloaded operator function definition can also be used.

As you have seen, member functions that overload binary operators are passed only one argument; a pointer to the argument is passed implicitly through the `this` pointer. Overloaded unary operator function definitions require no arguments. In friend functions, overloaded unary operators take one argument, and binary operators take two arguments. Both arguments are passed explicitly. The `this` pointer cannot be used, since it returns the location in memory of a class member for member functions only, and a friend function does not fall into this category. Take a look at `test15_6.cpp`, which illustrates the use of a friend function that overloads an operator.

```
C:> type test15_6.cpp

//    test15_6.cpp   01/31/91 10:28 pm

#include <iostream.h>    // necessary for I/O

class assign
     {
     public:
     int a;
     // ** notice friend function
     friend int operator*(assign var1, assign var2);
     };

// overloaded operator function returns integer
// it takes an object of type assign as an argument
// it follows the usual function definition rules
// operator* is a friend function, therefore there is no
// scope resolution operator for it.
int operator*(assign var_1, assign var_2)
{
     var_2.a = var_1.a * var_2.a;
     return var_2.a;
}

// object_1, object_2 and object_3 are objects of type assign
assign object_1, object_2, object_3;

main(void)
```

```
{
    object_1.a = 15;
    object_2.a = 10;

    // object_3.a receives the return value
    object_3.a = object_2 * object_1;

    cout << "object_1.a is " << object_1.a << "\n";
    cout << "object_2.a is " << object_2.a << "\n";
    cout << "object_3.a is " << object_3.a << "\n";
}
```

Take another look at the function definition:

```
int operator*(assign var_1, assign var_2)
{
    var_2.a = var_1.a * var_2.a;
    return var_2.a;
}
```

Notice that the name of the function is not preceded by a scope resolution operator. This makes sense, since there is no scope to resolve; this is a *friend* function. Also notice that both arguments are passed explicitly.

Compiling and running this program results in the following output:

```
object_1.a is 15
object_2.a is 10
object_3.a is 150
```

Now take another look at the statement that calls the overloaded operator function:

```
        object_3.a = object_2 * object_1;
```

The object on the left of the overloaded operator *, i.e., object_2, is assigned to var1. The object on the right, i.e., object_1, is assigned to var2. Inside the function, the values of the objects themselves do not change, since copies of these objects are manipulated. The return value is assigned to object_3.a, and therefore 50 is output for this data type.

If the contents of object_1 or object_2 are to be modifed, these objects can be sent as references. Here's a program that illustrates how parameters can be sent by reference, instead of value:

```
C:> type test15_7.cpp

//    test15_7.cpp   01/31/91 10:44 pm
```

```
#include <iostream.h>    // necessary for I/0

class assign
    {
    public:
    int a;
    // ** notice friend function
    friend int operator*(assign var1, assign &var2);
    };

// overloaded operator function returns integer
// it takes an object of type assign as arguments
// it follows the usual function definition rules
// operator* is a friend function, therefore there is no
// scope resolution operator for it.
// var_2 is passed as a reference.
int operator*(assign var_1, assign &var_2)
{
    var_2.a = var_1.a * 5;
    var_2.a = var_1.a * var_2.a;
    return var_2.a;
}

// object_1, object_2 and object_3 are objects of type assign
assign object_1, object_2, object_3;

main(void)
{
    object_1.a = 15;
    object_2.a = 10;

    // object_3.a receives the return value
    object_3.a = object_2 * object_1;

    cout << "object_1.a is " << object_1.a << "\n";
    cout << "object_2.a is " << object_2.a << "\n";
    cout << "object_3.a is " << object_3.a << "\n";
}
```

Notice the function prototype for the overloaded friend function:

```
friend int operator*(assign var1, assign &var2);
```

As you can see, the first parameter is sent by value, that is, a copy of this variable is sent to the calling function. The second parameter is sent by reference.

Compiling and running this program results in the following output:

```
object_1.a is 500
object_2.a is 10
object_3.a is 500
```

The statement

```
object_3.a = object_2 * object_1;
```

results in the function call of the overloaded operator *. Inside the function, var_1 is assigned the value of object_2 (10), since it is to the left of the oveloaded operator, and var_2 is assigned the value of object_1 (15). The statement

```
var_2.a = var_1.a * 5;
```

is decoded as follows:

```
object_1.a = object_2.a * 5;
```

which results in object_1.a being set to 10 * 5, which is equal to 50.

Since object_1 is passed as a reference, its actual value is also changed to 50. The statement

```
var_2.a = var_1.a * var_2.a;
```

is decoded as follows:

```
object_1.a = object_2.a * object_1.a;
```

which is equal to

```
object_1.a = 10 * 50;
```

and so object_1.a is set equal to 500. The output should now make sense.

Friend functions make the code for overloaded operators easier to read, since all arguments sent are visible to the human eye; there are no implicit or hidden arguments involved. Whether you use class members or friend functions to overload operators is your prerogative. Regardless of your choice, remember that one day someone will more probably than not inherit your code. Make sure your overloaded function code is not impossible to penetrate, comment liberally, and don't play tricks with people's minds.

15.7   REVIEW

In this chapter, we described some additional features of overloaded operators.

- The majority of existing operators can be overloaded.
- There are some restrictions with reference to the extent to which operators can be overloaded.
- A pointer to the object on the left of a binary overloaded operator is implicitly passed to the calling function via the this pointer.
- The object to the right of the overloaded operator is passed explicitly as a parameter to the calling function.
- Binary overloaded operators are passed one argument.
- Unary overloaded operators are passed no arguments.
- Friend functions can be used to overload operators as well.
- Friend functions require that all parameters be sent to the calling function explicitly.

Turbo C++ Preprocessor Directives

16.1 INTRODUCTION

In this chapter, C++ preprocessor directives will be described. These directives allow the inclusion of files, implement simple string replacement, expand macros, and perform conditional compilation. Some directives have recently been added by the new ANSI standard that can help us in debugging the source code as well. But first, let's understand what a preprocessor is.

16.2 THE C++ PREPROCESSOR

If you are a C programmer, then you should be familiar with preprocessor control lines. Undoubtedly you have been including the header file stdio.h in your programs, so that you could utilize the prewritten I/O functions, such as printf().

C++ also comes with a standard library of functions which are normally included with the standard C++ compiler package. The rules for C++ preprocessor directives are the same as C. This chapter should serve as a review for most of you.

The preprocessor is a program that processes the source code of a program before it passes it on to the compiler. Preprocessor directives are preceded by the symbol #, and are called *preprocessor control lines*. Based on the control lines, the preprocessor performs one or more of the following functions:

1. Include files.
   Files are included when the following directive is encountered:

```
#include
```

2. **Replaces strings, expands or undefines macros.**
   The above two functions are implemented when the following directives
   are encountered:

```
#define
#undef
```

3. **Perform conditional compilation.**
   Conditional compilation is implemented through the following sets of control lines:

```
#if
#else
#endif
```

```
#if
#elif
#endif
```

```
#ifdef
#endif
```

```
#ifndef
#endif
```

4. **Aid in debugging.**
   The following control line helps debugging:

```
#pragma
```

An explanation of each directive follows.

16.3   INCLUDE FILES

We have been including the file <iostream.h> in all of our programs. Let's
take a look at what happens if this file is not included.

```
C:> type test16_1.cpp

//   test16_1.cpp 02/04/91 7:47 pm

main(void)
{
     cout << "Hi there! \n";
```

```
    printf ("Hi there again! \n");
}
```

Compiling this program results in the following error messages:

```
Error:    Undefined symbol 'cout' in function main()
Error:    Function 'printf()' should have a prototype in function
          main()
```

Obviously, iostream.h has been #included for good reason. Let's include the necessary files and recompile:

```
C:> type test16_2.cpp

//    test16_2.cpp 02/04/91 8:03 pm

#include <iostream.h>    // necessary for cout
#include <stdio.h>       // necessary for printf()

main(void)
{
    cout << "Hi there! \n";
    printf ("Hi there again! \n");
}
```

Compiling and running this program results in the following output:

```
Hi there!
Hi there again!
```

The #include directive results in the entire contents of the name of the file that follows the directive to be included in the compilation. The header file iostream.h contains the definition for cout, and stdio.h contains the definition for printf().

The #include directive can take 3 forms.

1. #include <filename>
   This is the form that you are familiar with. The name of the file inside angular brackets instructs the compiler to search for the file from the list of prearranged directories that are outside the current working directory.

2. #include "filename"
   This form instructs the compiler to search for the file inside the current working directory.

3. #include "C:\DIRNAME\FILENAME"
   This form instructs the compiler to search for the file inside the specified path. If it is not found in that directory, then the standard directories are searched.

Here's a short program that illustrates the form in which the path name is indicated.

```
C:> type test16_3.cpp

//   test16_3.cpp 02/04/91 8:35 pm

#include <iostream.h>     // necessary for cout
#include <stdio.h>  // necessary for printf()
#include "C:\WP50\fileone"

main(void)
{
    cout << "Hi there! \n";
    printf ("Hi there again! \n");
    cout << "a from fileone is " << a << "\n";
}
```

We happen to have a directory called WP50 on our computer. (As a matter of fact, this is where our word processor resides.) This is what fileone looks like:

```
int a = 5;
```

That's right. fileone is only one line long. Normally, the file that is included is quite large. In fact, that's the whole point of include files. It helps break up a large source file into logical manageable segments.

Compiling and running this program results in the following output:

```
Hi there!
Hi there again!
a in fileone is 5
```

Note that the preprocessor simply includes the file in the current source code; it is still the compiler's responsibility to check for syntax errors and the like. Unfriendly messages will be generated by the compiler if the file which is #included does not compile properly. Suppose a file called filetwo is #included, which looks like this:

```
int a = 5
```

Notice the missing semicolon. Now take a look at a program which #includes filetwo:

```
C:> type test16_4.cpp

//   test16_4.cpp 02/04/91 8:45 pm
```

```
#include <iostream.h>     // necessary for cout
#include <stdio.h>  // necessary for printf()
#include "C:\WP50\filetwo"

main(void)
{
    cout << "Hi there! \n";
    printf ("Hi there again! \n");
    cout << "a from filetwo is " << a << "\n";
}
```

Compiling this program results in five errors, the first one being:

```
Error:    Function 'main' should have a prototype
```

Slightly misleading error message, wouldn't you say? We will not list the remaining error messages, since they make no sense either. The lesson to be learned from this is make sure that your #include files will compile properly, before you include them in your source code, otherwise you may have to face a debugging nightmare.

16.4 SIMPLE STRING REPLACEMENT

Simple string replacement occurs with the #define directive. Take a look at this short program which illustrates the use of this control line.

```
C:> type test16_5.cpp

//    test16_5.cpp 02/04/91 8:55 pm

#include <iostream.h>     // necessary for I/O

#define   HELLO "Hi there! \n"

main(void)
{
    cout << HELLO ;
}
```

Compiling and running this program results in the following output:

```
Hi there!
```

HELLO is replaced by the string "Hi there! \n" each time it is encountered in the source code. The statement

```
cout << HELLO;
```

is replaced by

```
cout << "Hi there! \n";
```

and that is why you see the output

```
Hi there!
```

on your screen.

Most programmers use all caps when they use the #define control line. It is a good convention to stick to, since it clearly identifies the variables which are #defined in your program.

16.5   MACROS WITHOUT ARGUMENTS

Macro expansion is a form of string replacement. Arguments can also be specified; these will be discussed in the next section. Take a look at the following program which illustrates the expansion of a simple macro.

```
C:> type test16_6.cpp

//    test16_6.cpp    02/04/91 9:00 pm

#include <iostream.h>    // necessary for I/O

#define SQUARE_TWO 2*2

main(void)
{
    int a;
    a = SQUARE_TWO;
    cout << "a is " << a << "\n";
}
```

In the control line

```
#define SQUARE_TWO 2*2
```

#define is the control line, SQUARE_TWO is the macro template, 2*2 is the macro expansion. This is a macro definition. Compiling this program results in the following output:

```
a is 4
```

This output is achieved because the statement

```
    a = SQUARE_TWO;
```

is expanded to

```
    a = 2 * 2;
```

which, of course, is equal to 4.

Macro expansions are valuable in that they define string replacement inside a program in one location only. Suppose you have a 500-line program, in which 2 is squared 60 times. Now suppose you need to change the application to have 2 multiplied by 8, instead of 2. All you would have to do is change one line of code, the macro definition, as follows:

```
#define SQUARE_TWO  2*8
```

and all subsequent references to SQUARE_TWO will be changed accordingly.

16.6 MACROS WITH ARGUMENTS

Here's a short program that expands a macro with an argument:

```
C:> type test16_7.cpp

//   test16_7.cpp   02/04/91 9:09 pm

#include <iostream.h>    // necessary for I/O

#define ADD(X) (X + X)

main(void)
{
    int b;
    b = ADD(4);
    cout << "b is " << b << "\n";
}
```

The control line

```
#define ADD(X) (X + X)
```

is referenced in the following statement

```
    b = ADD(4);
```

which expands to

```
    b = 4 + 4;
```

Compiling and running this program results in the following output:

```
b is 8
```

Take another look at the control line.

```
#define ADD(X) (X + X)
```

Notice that there is no space between the macro template and its parameter X. If there was a space in between, then the token that follows it would become part of the macro expansion. Take a look at test16_8.cpp, which illustrates this form of expansion.

```
C:> type test16_8.cpp

//   test16_8.cpp   02/04/91 9:09 pm

#include <iostream.h>    // necessary for I/O

// notice space between macro name and parameter
#define ADD (X) (X + X)

main(void)
{
    int b;
    b = ADD(4);
    cout << "b is " << b << "\n";
}
```

Compiling this program gives the following error message.

```
Error:    Undefined symbol 'X' in function main()
```

The compiler does not understand that the 4 inside the parentheses is the parameter that is to be substituted when the string is expanded. The space acts as a delimiter of the macro template.

Now suppose we forgot to place the parentheses in the control line, as follows:

```
#define ADD(X) X + X
```

This omission can be potentially dangerous, as is illustrated by the following program:

```
C:> type test16_9.cpp
```

```
//    test16_9.cpp    02/04/91 9:31 pm

#include <iostream.h>     // necessary for I/O

// notice space between macro name and parameter
#define ADD(X) X + X

main(void)
{
    int b;
    // we multiply the result of the macro expansion by 5
    b = ADD(4) * 5;
    cout << "b is " << b << "\n";
}
```

Compiling and running this program gives the following output:

```
b is 24
```

The statement

```
    b = ADD(4) * 5;
```

was expanded as follows:

```
    b = 4 + 4 * 5;
```

and since multiplication takes precedence over addition, b was calculated as follows:

```
    b = 4 + (4 * 5);
```

However, what we wanted was this:

```
    b = (4 + 4) * 5
```

The expression was not evaluated as expected, since the parentheses are missing. Make sure you don't forget them.

16.7   UNDEFINING MACROS

Macros which have been previous #defined can be undefined with the following control line:

```
#undef
```

This control line will result in no string replacement. Take a look at test16_10.cpp, which illustrates its use.

```
C:> type test16_10.cpp

//    test16_10.cpp

#include <iostream.h>    // necessary for I/O

#define FOUR 4

main(void)
{
    int a = FOUR;
    cout << "a is " << a << "\n";

    #undef FOUR
    int b = FOUR;
    cout << "b is " << b << "\n";
}
```

Compiling this program results in the following error message:

```
Error:    Undefined symbol FOUR in function main()
```

This message is output for the following statement:

```
    int b = FOUR;
```

This is because FOUR was undefined just before this statement. The compiler no longer substitutes 4 for FOUR.

The reason for undefining a macro would be so that macro names can be localized for those sections of code in which they are needed.

16.8 CONDITIONAL COMPILATION

Conditional compilation takes place when the following keywords are encountered in the source code:

```
#if - #else - #endif
#if - #elif - #endif
#ifdef - #endif
#ifndef - #endif
```

We will discuss each.

16.8.1   #if - #endif

The #if keyword is followed by a constant expression, a block of code, and then the #endif keyword. The block of code between these two control lines is included in compilation only if the constant expression between the braces evaluates to TRUE, or a nonzero value. Take a look at test16_11.cpp, which illustrates its use.

```
C:> type test16_11.cpp

//   test16_11.cpp

#include <iostream.h>     // necessary for I/O

main(void)
{
    const int a = 5;
    const int b = 0;

    #if (a)
        cout << "a is TRUE, i.e. non-zero \n";
    #else
        cout << "a is FALSE i.e. zero \n";
    #endif

    #if (b)
        cout << "b is TRUE, i.e. non-zero \n";
    #else
        cout << "b is FALSE, i.e. zero \n";
    #endif

    cout << "This code is outside the blocks \n";
}
```

Compiling and running this program gives the following output:

```
a is TRUE
b is FALSE
This code is outside the blocks
```

The output is self-explanatory. Note that it is necessary for a constant expression to be inside the test condition. An error message will be generated if it isn't, as is illustrated by test16_12.cpp:

```
C:> type test16_12.cpp

//   test16_12.cpp
```

```
#include <iostream.h>    // necessary for I/O

main(void)
{
    int a = 5;       // a and b are declared as variables
    int b = 0;

    #if (a)
        cout << "a is TRUE, i.e. non-zero \n";
    #else
        cout << "a is FALSE i.e. zero \n";
    #endif

    #if (b)
        cout << "b is TRUE, i.e. non-zero \n";
    #else
        cout << "b is FALSE, i.e. zero \n";
    #endif

    cout << "This code is outside the blocks \n";
}
```

Compiling this program results in the following error message:

```
Error:    Constant expression required in function main()
```

The difference between the #if - #else - #endif and the regular if - else - endif control structures is that in the former case evaluation takes place before the program is compiled and run. You cannot have variables inside the test condition, since their value can change at run time.

16.8.2   #if - #elif - #endif

These control lines are equivalent to #if - #else - #endif control lines just discussed, so they will not be elaborated on any further.

16.8.3   #ifdef - #endif

The block of code between these two control lines is compiled only if the macro name that follows the directive has been previously #defined. Take a look at test16_13.cpp

```
C:> type test16_13.cpp

//    test16_13.cpp  02/04/91 10:14 pm

#include <iostream.h>    // necessary for I/O
```

```
#define   COMPILE

main(void)
{
    #ifdef COMPILE
        cout << "This code will be compiled \n";
    #endif
}
```

Compiling and running this program results in the following output:

```
This code will be compiled
```

As you can see, the macro COMPILE is #defined; hence, the code within these two control lines is compiled.

If the #define statement in the prior program is commented out, the code within the control lines will not be compiled. test16_4.cpp illustrates this.

```
C:> type test16_14.cpp

//    test16_14.cpp  02/04/91 10:14 pm

#include <iostream.h>    // necessary for I/O

// we comment out the macro definition of COMPILE
// #define    COMPILE

main(void)
{
    #ifdef COMPILE
        cout << "This code will be compiled \n";
    #endif
}
```

Compiling this program results in no output, since the macro called COMPILE is not #defined.

This preprocessor feature can be used as a debugging aid. Debug statements can be inserted for a macro name, and then this name can be commented and uncommented, in order to exclude or include the debugging statements in the source code.

16.8.4   #ifndef - #endif

These control lines are the flip side of #ifdef - #endif statements. The block of code between these control lines is included in the compilation only if the macro name is not defined.

Here's a program that illustrates just that.

```
C:> type test16_15.cpp

//    test16_15.cpp  02/04/91 10:34 pm

#include <iostream.h>      // necessary for I/O

#define   COMPILE

main(void)
{
    // the following code is compiled only if macro is not defined

    #ifndef COMPILE
        cout << "This code will be compiled \n";
    #endif
}
```

Compiling and running this program results in no output. This is because COMPILE is #defined. There would have been output if the macro control line were commented out or deleted.

16.9 #pragma

This control line allows various instructions to be given to the compiler. The specific instructions are implementation-specific. Please refer to your compiler's documentation for the #pragma directives that exist for your compiler.

16.10 REVIEW

In this chapter, we discussed the preprocessor and its directives. We learned how to

• Include files:

```
#include <fileone>

#include "fileone"

#include "c:\dir\fileone"
```

• Perform simple string replacement, by #defining macros:

```
#define HELLO hello
```

The above statement will result in HELLO being replaced by hello each time it is encountered in the source code file.

- Undefine macros, so that string replacement does not take place:

  `#undef HELLO`

- Define macros with arguments:

  `#define square(x) (x*x)`

  The above control line takes one argument, and expands it as indicated.
- Compile conditionally, through the following control lines:

  `#if - #else - #endif`

  The code between the block is compiled only if the constant expression in the test condition evaluates to TRUE, or a nonzero value.

  `#if - #elif - #endif`

  These directives are equivalent to `#if - #else - #endif` **directives.**

  `#ifdef - #endif`

  The code between the block is compiled only if the macro name that follows the directive has been previously `#defined`.

  `#ifndef - #endif`

  The code between the control lines is compiled only if the macro name is not `#defined`.
- Use of the `#pragma` directive, which issues instructions to the compiler. This directive is implementation-dependent.

3

Object-Oriented Approach Applied to C++

Object-Oriented Analysis

17.1 INTRODUCTION

It is now time to put all of the pieces together and to forge ahead armed with the tools that C++ provides you, and which you have learned in Parts 1 and 2 of the book. In this chapter, we will describe object-oriented analysis of a problem. In the next chapter, our analysis will be synthesized into object-oriented program design. The methodology described will be translated into a sample C++ application. Then, the ease with which the code can be revised, enhanced, and expanded will be illustrated. The true power of an object-oriented environment will be apparent to you as you conclude this section of the book.

17.2 WHAT IS OBJECT-ORIENTED ANALYSIS?

Take your eyes off this book just for a moment and look up directly at any object before you. . . . Did you notice how your eyes focused on that object and everything else faded, almost out of view? Out of all possible objects, your eyes focused on a specific one, because that was the object that held relevance for you at the time.

Undoubtedly, at work, there must have been occasions when you were required to perform a set number of tasks before the start of the next business day. However, due to limitations of time and prior commitments, you realized that it would be impossible to perform all assigned tasks as necessary. Assuming that you are of stable and sane mind, you probably proceeded as follows:

1. Prioritized the tasks.

2. Analyzed how the top priority tasks were to be performed.

3. Implemented these tasks.

4. Disregarded (at least for the time being) those tasks that had no crucial relevance.

This was your way of handling the complexity at hand, and your method of simplifying it in order to resolve the current problem. Well, what you did (without perhaps even realizing it) was apply the principle of abstraction to resolve a problem. Rather than trying to comprehend and resolve the complete complexity of the problem right away, you chose to concentrate only on a part of it that was considered more relevant at the time.

If you take a moment to think about what we have just said, you will realize that abstraction is a method that we use constantly and consistently as we live our day-to-day lives. Life is too complex. In order to understand it, it has to be broken up into simpler components that are comprehensible and more relevant at any particular time.

Abstraction lies at the very core of object-oriented analysis. With this introduction, we now proceed to describe how this methodology can be applied to formulate an efficient, manageable, and powerful system.

17.2.1 Understand the problem

The first step in the design of a system is to understand what the system is required to do. The best place to start is with the user or the client.

Users are almost always vague in their perception of what they want (they are almost never vague about how soon they want it ... tomorrow, or next week, at the latest!). It is unlikely that they understand the relationships between what they want, and how it can be implemented.

Suppose that you are required to implement a system which maintains a file of customer records. Users are to be given the capability of being able to browse, add, change, and delete records from this file.

Talk to the user. Find out how he or she currently stores the data and manipulates it. Try to get a feeling for what the user really requires from this system. How will he or she search for customers? Will it be through customer name and address, or through a preassigned customer number? What information is required to be retrieved? Is there a system currently in use? What are its shortcomings? How can it be improved? Immerse yourself in the world of the user.

17.2.2 Identify objects

Consider an object to be simply a package of information and knowledge of how that information can be manipulated. Based upon the requirements stated in the prior section, the following objects can be identified:

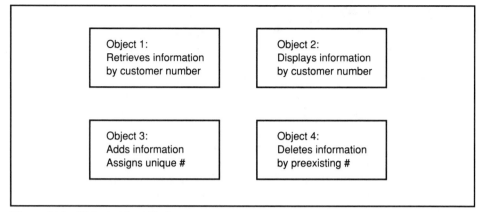

Figure 17.1   Objects identified.

1. An object that retrieves information for current customers.

2. An object that displays information for customers on the screen.

3. An object that adds customers to the file.

4. An object that deletes customers from the file.

We will assume that a unique identifying number is assigned to each customer, and all searches and manipulation of data are based upon this key.

Figure 17.1 illustrates these objects.

Notice that customers may come and go, and the information required to be stored for each customer may vary over time. However, the functionality of each object will more or less remain the same. Objects are relatively stable. Of course, new requirements may emerge, such as the storage and retrieval of customer responses to a survey. But this would mean the creation of a new self-contained object that will have a functionality all its own. It should be no problem fitting this new object into the current schema, since it will be self-contained, and hence will not interfere with the working of other objects. This is the beauty of object-oriented analysis. It results in a framework which can be easily expanded and modified.

Let's continue with the analysis.

17.2.3   Identify common attributes

Try to identify those attributes which apply to every single occurrence of the objects that you have formulated. In our example, we can safely state that the customer number is common to all objects.

17.2.4   Identify common services

In our example, the functionality of each object can be differentiated as follows:

Object	Function
1	Retrieves information for customers.
	Searches for the existence of a customer number, before it allows Object 2 to display it.
	Searches for the existence of a duplicate customer number, before it allows Object 3 to add a new record.
	Searches for the existence of customer number, before it allows Object 4 to delete it.
2	Displays information for customers.
	Searches the customer file for a customer number.
	If it finds the number, it displays relevant information for it. Otherwise, it displays a message stating customer not found.
3	Adds customers.
	Searches the customer file for a customer number.
	If it finds the number, it disallows the transaction, since the customer already exists.
	It allows the transaction if it does not find the customer number.
4	Deletes customers.
	Searches the customer file for a customer number.
	If it does not find the number, it disallows the transaction, since the customer does not exist.
	It allows the transaction if the customer number is found.

Based upon this analysis, it appears that the service that is common to all objects is the retrieval of a record by customer number.

What each object does with it after it is retrieved is unique to it.

17.2.5   Identify structure

Try to identify those objects from your list that are the most generalized. Then, list the ones that are specialized cases. This step of the analysis will allow you to form class hierarchies. Attributes and services which are common

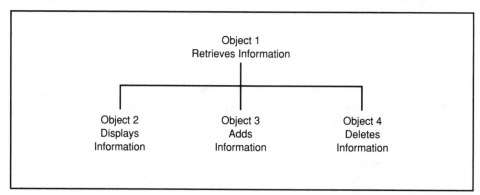

Figure 17.2   Object hierarchy.

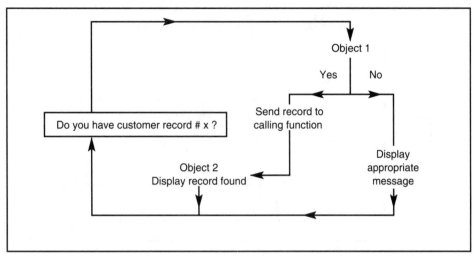

Figure 17.3 Message flow between objects 1 and 2.

to all classes will be placed at the top of the hierarchy. The lower levels will be derived from the ones at the higher levels. In our example, Object 1, which maintains customer information, seems to contain the data and functionality that is required by the remaining objects. Hence, this object is a good candidate to be placed at the top of the hierarchy. All other objects will derive their functionality from it, and add a unique functionality of their own.

Figure 17.2 illustrates the object hierarchy.

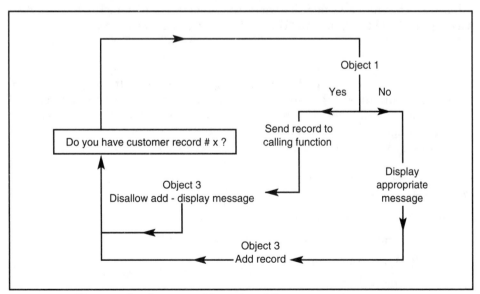

Figure 17.4 Message flow between objects 1 and 3.

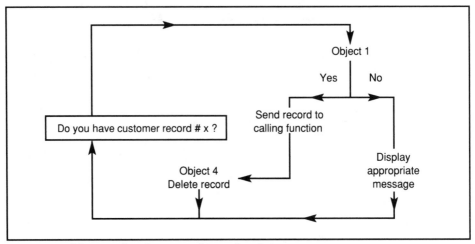

Figure 17.5 Message flow between objects 1 and 4.

17.2.6   Identify object dependency

Identify those objects that are dependent on others. Identify those objects which need to access others, in order to implement the functionality assigned to them. In our example, objects 2, 3, and 4 depend on the accurate functioning of object 1.

17.2.7   Identify message flow of objects

Identify the communication pattern between each object. The message pattern can be classified as inbound or outbound. Figures 17.3, 17.4, and 17.5 illustrate the message flow between the objects identified. Proceed to read the figures from the question "Do you have customer record #x?"

17.3   REVIEW

In this chapter, we learned how to design a system using object-oriented analysis techniques. We realized that abstraction lies at the very core of object-oriented analysis. Abstraction is a method by which those aspects of a subject are ignored which are not relevant to the current purpose, in order to concentrate on those that are. Our analysis was broken down as follows:

1. Understand the problem.
2. Identify objects.
3. Identify common attributes.
4. Identify common services.
5. Identify structure.
6. Identify object dependency.
7. Identify message flow between objects.

Chapter

18

Object-Oriented Program Design

18.1 INTRODUCTION

In the previous chapter, an object-oriented approach was used to analyze the requirements for a system that maintains and updates customer information. In this chapter, object-oriented program design will be described, and some parts of the resulting code will also be developed. As you proceed through the remaining chapters in this book, you will notice that code developed in prior chapters will be redisplayed, as new code is added to it. This is done so as to reinforce concepts that you may have missed at the time that the code was originally developed. It will also help you see the resulting complete program all in one place, thereby saving you the trouble of having to flip through the pages, if you need to refer back to the code for any reason. New code will always be indicated via comments.

18.2 WHAT IS OBJECT-ORIENTED PROGRAM DESIGN?

Object-oriented programs have the remarkable capability of being able to be continually modified, expanded, and refined, with minimal changes to the basic structure of the program. The best way for you to understand the power that can be derived from object-oriented programs is by implementing the design itself. Let's begin.

18.3 A BRIEF REVIEW

A brief review is presented of the problem and the results of the analysis in the prior chapter.

18.3.1 Requirements

We were required to design a system which would maintain information for customers, and display and update this information on an as-needed basis.

18.3.2 Objects identified

Four objects were identified:

Object 1:   Retrieves customer information
Object 2:   Displays information
Object 3:   Adds information
Object 4:   Deletes information

18.3.3 Attributes identified

The following attribute was found to be common to all objects: *customer number.*

18.3.4 Services identified

The following services were found to be common between objects:

Object	Service
1, 2, 3, 4	Retrieve customer information via customer record number.

18.4 PROGRAM DESIGN

Let's analyze the data at hand.

18.4.1 Formulate classes

Upon review, we find that there is enough information to design the structure of each object. In Part 2 of the book, you learned how to declare and define classes. Recall that a class contains both data and code. The next step would be to translate the objects that have been identified into classes. Each class will be given a meaningful name. The name `del` instead of `delete` will be given to the class that will delete information, since `delete` is a reserved keyword.

For the sake of simplicity, assume that customer information comprises only customer number. We are more interested in the design of the program, rather than those details that do not affect the design in any way. The following elements are common to all classes:

1. Customer number
2. Retrieval of customer information via customer number.

For now, assume that the class member functions take no parameters, and return no value. Here's the first draft of each class:

```
class retrieve
    {
    int customer_numbers;

    void search(void);
    };

class display
    {
    int customer_numbers;

    void search(void);
    };

class add
    {
    int customer_numbers;

    void search(void);
    };

class del
    {
    int customer_numbers;

    void search(void);
    };
```

Upon further analysis, you may realize that modification of records has not been incorporated in any of the classes. It appears that the best resort would be to allow modification of current records by the class retrieve only. In this way, the possibility of data being erroneously modified by some other unsuspecting class will be minimized. The classes display, add, and del are distinguished from each other by these very functions. Take a look at the new declarations of the classes:

```
class retrieve
    {
    int customer_numbers;

    void search(void);
    void modify(void);
    };

class display
    {
```

```
        int customer_numbers;

        void search(void);
        void display_info(void);
        };

  class add
        {
        int customer_numbers;

        void search(void);
        void add_info(void);
        };

  class del
        {
        int customer_numbers;

        void search(void);
        void delete_info(void);
        };
```

Now take a closer look at the data types of the parameters that will be passed to and returned from the member functions.

The function `search()` is required to do so based on customer number, which will be unique, and is the key field. This function will be called by the remaining classes, and sent a customer number to search for. This customer number may or may not exist. If it exists, we can have this function return the customer number found to the calling function. If it does not exist, it can return a 0.

The function `modify()` will take the customer number as a parameter, and continue to return `void`, since it has nothing else to do. The prototypes for these functions will change inside each class as follows:

```
  class retrieve
        {
        int customer_numbers;

        int search(int);
        void modify(int);
        };

  class display
        {
        int customer_numbers;
```

```
        int search(int);
        void display_info(void);
        };

class add
        {
        int customer_numbers;

        int search(int);
        void add_info(void);
        };

class del
        {
        int customer_numbers;

        int search(int);
        void delete_info(void);
        };
```

An analysis of the remaining functions follows:

1. `display_info()`
   This function will assess the value sent back from `search()` member function of the class `retrieve`. If it is a 0, it means that no corresponding record was found. This function will do nothing, since the message stating as such will be displayed by the class `retrieve`. If a valid number was returned by `retrieve`, then the customer record will be displayed on the screen. Therefore, this function will take the customer number returned from `search()` as a parameter. It will still return `void`, since it has nothing else to do but display or not display the record. The prototype for `display_info()` will change as follows:

   ```
   void display_info( int );
   ```

2. `add_info()`
   This function will also access the value returned by `search()`. If it is a 0, it means that a corresponding record was not found. Hence, it is OK to add the current record. If a nonzero value is returned, it means that the customer record already exists, and an attempt is being made to add a duplicate. The transaction will not be allowed. If a duplicate exists, then it will suffice to output a message stating as such. If the transaction is to be allowed, then all that has to be done is to insert the value in the next available slot of customer numbers. This function will take the customer number to be added as a parameter. It will return no value either. The prototype for `add_info()` will be as follows.

```
void add_info( int );
```

3. delete_info()

This function, like add_info(), will check the value sent back from search(). If it is a 0, it means that no corresponding record was found. This function will do nothing, since the message which indicates as such will be output within the class retrieve itself. If a nonzero value is returned, then the customer record can be deleted, and this function will display a message indicating as such. Hence, the function will take the customer number as a parameter. It will return no value. The prototype will look as follows:

```
void delete_info( int );
```

Our class objects are now starting to take shape. Here's how they look:

```
class retrieve
    {
    int customer_numbers;

    int search(int);
    void modify(int);
    };

class display
    {
    int customer_numbers;

    int search(int);
    void display_info(int);
    };

class add
    {
    int customer_numbers;

    int search(int);
    void add_info(int);
    };

class del
    {
    int customer_numbers;

    int search(int);
    void delete_info(int);
    };
```

Let's take a breather and review our progress. It seems like we have

1. Figured out the different types of objects required to implement the required system.
2. Figured out the data and member functions each object requires.
3. Know the data types of the return values and the arguments of the member functions.

Now it's time to incorporate the member access specifiers `private`, `public`, and, if necessary, `protected`, into the class definitions. This will allow us to "encapsulate" data, "hide information," or whatever else you may like to call it. An analysis of each class follows:

1. retrieve
   The following conclusions can be made about this class:

   a) Customer number will be accessed by all classes. Hence, it should be made public.
   b) The `modify()` function should be the only function that is permitted to modify existing records. No other class object should be allowed to access this function. Therefore, it should be private.
   c) The `search()` function is accessed by all other classes. Hence, it should be public.

This class with the appropriate access specifiers now looks as follows:

```
class retrieve
    {
    private:
    void modify(int);

    public:
    int customer_numbers;
    int search(int number);
    };
```

2. display
   The function `display_info()` is a general-purpose function which simply displays the appropriate customer record. There is no need to make this function private. Here's the declaration:

```
class display
    {
    public:
    int customer_numbers;
```

```
int search(int);
void display_info( int );
};
```

3. add

The function `add_info()` adds data to the current file. It has a specialized function to perform. However, we plan to implement all of our processing inside `main()`. Therefore, this function should be accessible from it. This function will be public.

```
class add
    {
    public:
    int customer_numbers;
    int search(int);
    void add(int);
    };
```

4. delete

The function `delete_info()` deletes data from the current file. This function will be declared as public for the same reasons as `add_info()`. Here's the subsequent class declaration:

```
class del
    {
    public:
    int cutomer_no;
    int search(int);
    void delete_info(int);
    };
```

18.4.2 Identify structure

In Chap. 17, the object hierarchy was identified. Figure 18.1 redisplays this hierarchy in terms of the class objects formulated.

Based on this hierarchy, we can say that `retrieve` is the base class, and `display`, `add`, and `del` are derived from it. The following data items are common to all classes:

```
int customer_numbers;
int search(int);
```

Hence, these will be the common elements in `retrieve`, which will be derived by the remaining classes. Take a look at the class declarations:

```
class retrieve
```

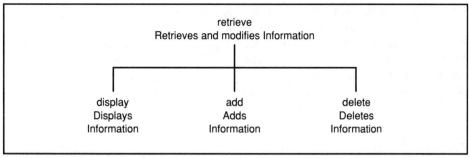

Figure 18.1   Object hierarchy.

```
    {
    private:
    void modify(int);

    public:
    int customer_numbers;
    int search(int);
    };

class display : public retrieve
    {
    public:
    int customer_numbers;
    void display_info(int);
    };

class add : public retrieve
    {
    public:
    int customer_numbers;
    void add_info(void);
    };

class del : public retrieve
    {
    public:
    int customer_numbers;
    void delete_info(int);
    };
```

Notice that the classes are being publicly derived. This results in the public members of the base class retrieve becoming public members of each class derived from it. This is fine, since the body of the code will be placed inside main(), and functions such as search() will be accessed from here.

Remember, however, that the private members of retrieve, i.e., the function modify(), will continue to remain private to it. Other class objects will not be allowed to access this member. This is exactly what we want. It would be much too dangerous to allow any function to inadvertently change the information for the customer records, except those designated to do so—only the *private* member function modify() is given that capability.

18.4.3   Identify object dependency

Through the course of the discussion, the classes display, add, and del were found to be dependent on retrieve.

18.4.4   Identify message flow between objects

Through the course of the program design, the communication pattern between objects was identified. This communication pattern is based on the parameters sent to and returned from class member functions. Please refer to Figs. 17.3, 17.4, and 17.5 if you need to review the communication pattern. We will have each function output a response. A simple print() function in each class will be used to display the response. These print functions will be declared as public; there is no need to make them private. Here's the modified class declarations:

```
class retrieve
    {
    private:
    void modify(int);

    public:
    int customer_numbers;
    int search(int);
    void print(void);
    };

class display : public retrieve
    {
    public:
    void display_info(int);
    void print(void);
    };

class add : public retrieve
    {
    public:
    void add_info(int);
    void print(void);
    };
```

```
class del : public retrieve
    {
    public:
    void delete_info(int);
    void print(void);
    };
```

18.4.5 Introduce polymorphism/virtual functions

It seems that each step of the analysis stage has been translated into code, except for main(). Let's take another look at the class declarations, and see if they can somehow be refined further. You will notice that each class has a function called print(), which outputs a simple response. The name, parameters, and return value of this function are the same for all classes. However, the output will vary, based on the class object that will invoke it. Sounds like a perfect candidate for a virtual function. Here's the final template for each class:

```
class retrieve
    {
    private:
    void modify(int);

    public:
    int cutomer_no;
    int search(int);
    virtual void print(void);
    };

class display : public retrieve
    {
    public:
    void display_info(int);
    void print(void);
    };

class add : public retrieve
    {
    private:
    void add_info(int);
    void print(void);
    };

class delete : public retrieve
    {
    private:
```

```
void delete_info(int);
void print(void);
};
```

The function is declared as *virtual* inside the base class. The appropriate response for each class will be determined at run time, based on which class object is being pointed to at the time. The class declarations are now complete.

18.5   DEFINITION OF MEMBER FUNCTIONS

We are now ready to define each member function. In the next section, the code for `main()` will be implemented. The following class member functions have to be defined; they are listed by class name.

1. The class *retrieve*:

```
void modify(int);
int search(int);
virtual void print(void);
```

2. The class *display*:

```
void display_info(int);
void print(void);
```

3. The class *add*

```
void add_info(int);
void print(void);
```

4. The class *del*

```
void delete_info(int);
void print(void);
```

For now, to keep things simple, the class members `search()`, `print()`, and `display()` only will be defined. In the next two chapters, the code for the remaining member functions will be presented. This will help you understand how easy it is to expand and modify object-oriented programs. However, in order for the program to compile properly, function definitions must exist. Therefore, for now, a statement identifying the class member will be output.

In order to simplify things further, the list of valid customer numbers will be placed inside an array called `customer_numbers[]`. In the real world, customer number and information would be kept inside a file, which would need to be opened, read, updated, and modified as required. But this would mean getting into file I/O functions; they would just make the code longer, and add unnecessary details. (These functions will be covered in Part 4 of the book.) For now, we are more interested in program design. You may have noticed that each class member function accesses `customer_numbers[]`, and contains a variable with the same class name. However, just as a file is globally available to any function in a program that tries to access it, the same location in memory that contains the relevant information must be accessible to each class. Therefore, the declaration of `customer_numbers[]` will be moved outside of the class declarations, thereby enabling it to be a globally accessible array.

Here are the definitions. Comments and identifying statements have been added for your convenience:

```
// valid customer numbers are delimited by a 0
int customer_numbers[6] = {100, 200, 300, 400, 500, 0};

// modify takes the customer number to modify as a parameter.
// it returns no value.
void retrieve::modify(int)
{
    cout << "Inside modify \n";
}


// retrieve takes the customer number to search for as a paramter.
// it returns the customer number if found.
// it returns 0 if customer number is not found.
int retrieve::search(int number)
{
    int i = 0;
    cout << "Inside search \n";

    while (customer_numbers[i] != 0)
        {
        if (number != customer_numbers[i])
            {
            i++;
            }
        else
            {
            // print() is a virtual function.
            // Based on the object which is accessing
            // search(), the appropriate print()
            // function will be called.
             print();
             number = customer_numbers[i];
```

```
                    return number;
                }
            }
    // if a corresponding record is not found, then the print()
    // statement for the base class will be called.
    retrieve::print();
    return 0;
}


void retrieve::print(void)
{
    cout << "Record not found!! \n";
}


// display_info takes the customer number returned from search()
// as a parameter.
// It has nothing to return.
void display::display_info(int temp)
{
    cout << "Inside display_info \n";
    cout << "Customer number is " << temp << " \n";
}


void display::print(void)
{
    cout << "Here's a copy of the record! \n";
}


void add::add_info(void)
{
    cout << "Inside add_info \n";
}


void add::print(void)
{
    cout << "Attempt to add duplicate record! \n" <<
            "Transaction disallowed!! \n";
}


void del::delete_info(int)
{
    cout << "Inside delete_info \n";
}


void del::print(void)
```

```
{
     cout << "Record ready to be deleted! \n";
}
```

18.6 main()

It is now time to implement the code for main(). Remember that the display function will request search() to find a customer record. If found, display_info() will display it. If not, the appropriate message will be displayed. The remaining functions will be developed in the next two chapters. Here's the code for main():

```
main(void)
{
     int temp, number;
     retrieve retrieve_customer;
     display display_customer;
     add add_customer;
     del delete_customer;

     // search for customer number 100
     number = 100;
     temp = display_customer.search(number);
     if (temp > 0)
     {
          display_customer.display_info(temp);
     }
}
```

And for your convenience, the complete program is displayed in one place, so that you can see the logical progression of object-oriented analysis into object-oriented program design.

```
C:> type test18_1.cpp

// test18_1.cpp          02/17/90  2:28 pm

#include <iostream.h>     // necessary for I/O

int customer_numbers[6] = {100, 200, 300, 400, 500, 0};

// retrieve is the base class
class retrieve
     {
     private:
     void modify(int);
```

```
      public:
      int search(int number);
      virtual void print(void);
      };

// display is publicly derived from retrieve
class display : public retrieve
      {
      public:
      void display_info(int temp);
      void print(void);
      };

// add is publicly derived from retrieve
class add : public retrieve
      {
      public:
      void add_info(void);
      void print(void);
      };

// del is publicly derived from retrieve
class del : public retrieve
      {
      public:
      void delete_info(int);
      void print(void);
      };

// modify takes the customer number to modify as a parameter.
// it returns no value.
void retrieve::modify(int)
{
      cout << "Inside modify \n";
}

// search() takes the customer number to search for as a paramter.
// it returns the customer number if found.
// it returns 0 if customer number is not found.
int retrieve::search(int number)
{
      int i = 0;
      cout << "Inside search \n";
      while (customer_numbers[i] != 0)
            {
            if (number != customer_numbers[i])
```

```
                         {
                         i++;
                         }
                  else
                         {
                         // print() is a virtual function.
                         // Based on the object which is accessing
                         // search(), the appropriate print()
                         // function will be called.
                          print();
                          number = customer_numbers[i];
                          return number;
                          }
                  }
       // if a corresponding record is not found, then the print()

       // statement for the base class will be called.
       retrieve::print();
       return 0;
}

void retrieve::print(void)
{
       cout << "Record not found!! \n";
}


// display_info takes the customer number returned from search()
// as a parameter.
// It has nothing to return.
void display::display_info(int temp)
{
       cout << "Inside display_info \n";
       cout << "Customer number is " << temp << " \n";
}

void display::print(void)
{
       cout << "Here's a copy of the record! \n";
}

void add::add_info(void)
{
       cout << "Inside add_info \n";
}


void add::print(void)
```

```
     {
          cout << "Attempt to add duplicate record! \n" <<
               "Transaction disallowed!! \n";
     }

void del::delete_info(int)
     {
          cout << "Inside delete_info \n";
     }

void del::print(void)
     {
          cout << "Record ready to be deleted! \n";
     }

main(void)
     {
          int temp, number;
          retrieve retrieve_customer;
          display display_customer;
          add add_customer;
          del delete_customer;

          // search for customer number 100
          // display it, if found
               number = 100;
          temp = display_customer.search(number);
          if (temp > 0)
          {
               display_customer.display_info(temp);
          }
     }
```

Compiling and running this program gives the following output:

```
Inside search
Here's a copy of the record
Inside display_info
Customer number is 100
```

The output should be self-explanatory. Notice the invocation of the virtual print() **function inside** search(). **Inside main, the following code:**

```
          else
               {
               // print() is a virtual function.
```

```
              // Based on the object which is accessing
              // search(), the appropriate print()
              // function will be called.
               print();
```

resulted in the following statement being output:

```
Here's a copy of the record!
```

This is the print() function version of the class display.

In those instances where the search() function fails to find a record, the print() function for the base class retrieve will be called:

```
          // statement for the base class will be called.
          retrieve::print();
```

Test18_1.cpp will now be modified to illustrate the search for a nonexistent customer number:

```
C:> type test18_2.cpp

// test18_2.cpp          02/17/90  2:28 pm

#include <iostream.h>     // necessary for I/O

int customer_numbers[6] = {100, 200, 300, 400, 500, 0};

// retrieve is the base class
class retrieve
    {
    private:
    void modify(int);

    public:
    int search(int number);
    virtual void print(void);
    };

// display is publicly derived from retrieve
class display : public retrieve
    {
    public:
    void display_info(int temp);
    void print(void);
    };

// add is publicly derived from retrieve
```

```
class add : public retrieve
    {
    public:
    void add_info(void);
    void print(void);
    };

// del is publicly derived from retrieve
class del : public retrieve
    {
    public:
    void delete_info(int);
    void print(void);
    };

// modify takes the customer number to modify as a parameter.
// it returns no value.
void retrieve::modify(int)
{
    cout << "Inside modify \n";
}


// search() takes the customer number to search for as a paramter.

// it returns the customer number if found.
// it returns 0 if customer number is not found.
int retrieve::search(int number)
{
    int i = 0;
    cout << "Inside search \n";
    while (customer_numbers[i] != 0)
        {
        if (number != customer_numbers[i])
            {
            i++;
            }
        else
            {
            // print() is a virtual function.
            // Based on the object which is accessing
            // search(), the appropriate print()
            // function will be called.
            print();
            number = customer_numbers[i];
            return number;
            }
```

```
        }
    // if a corresponding record is not found, then the print()

    // statement for the base class will be called.
    retrieve::print();
    return 0;
}

void retrieve::print(void)
{
    cout << "Record not found!! \n";
}

// display_info takes the customer number returned from search()

// as a parameter.
// It has nothing to return.
void display::display_info(int temp)
{
    cout << "Inside display_info \n";
    cout << "Customer number is " << temp << " \n";
}

void display::print(void)
{
    cout << "Here's a copy of the record! \n";
}

void add::add_info(void)
{
    cout << "Inside add_info \n";
}

void add::print(void)
{
    cout << "Attempt to add duplicate record! \n" <<
        "Transaction disallowed!! \n";
}

void del::delete_info(int)
{
    cout << "Inside delete_info \n";
}

void del::print(void)
{
```

```
          cout << "Record ready to be deleted! \n";
    }


main(void)
{
     int temp, number;
     retrieve retrieve_customer;
     display display_customer;
     add add_customer;
     del delete_customer;

     // search for non-existent customer number 10
     // display it, if found
     number = 10;
     temp = display_customer.search(number);
     if (temp > 0)
     {
          display_customer.display_info(temp);
     }
}
```

Compiling and executing this program results in the following output:

```
Inside search
Record not found!!
```

The output should be self-explanatory.

18.7 REVIEW

In this chapter the object-oriented analysis of a problem was synthesized into the object-oriented design of a sample C++ application. Each step of the analysis was translated into code, as follows:

Object-Oriented Analysis	Object-Oriented Program Design
1. Identify objects	-> Formulate classes
2. Identify attributes	-> Formulate class data members
3. Identify services	-> Formulate class member functions
	-> Include access specifiers
4. Identify structure	-> Formulate base and derived classes
5. Identify message flow	-> Formulate the code for main()
6. Identify object dependency	-> Formulate the code for main()
	-> Introduce virtual functions, if possible

Chapter 19

Expansion of Object-Oriented Programs—Part 1

19.1 INTRODUCTION

In this chapter, the prewritten code for the system that was analyzed and designed in Chaps. 17 and 18 will be expanded. This chapter will develop the code for the `modify()` function. The next two chapters will develop the code for the `add_info()` and `delete_info()` functions.

19.2 THE modify() FUNCTION

For your convenience, the `retrieve` class is redisplayed. The `modify()` function is a private member of this class.

```
class retrieve
    {
    private:
    int modify(int);

    public:
    int search(int number);
    virtual void print(void);
    };
```

We are interested in somehow encapsulating the modification of existing customer records to one function only. That was why this function was made private in the first place, thereby being inaccessible to any object other than that of type `retrieve`. After reviewing the class declaration, it is obvious that only `search()` can access this function, because this is the only other class member function in the class. But the functionality of `search()` is unique; the idea is not to incorporate any further logic into it. `search()` is required to search for the existence or nonexistence of a customer record, and return an appropriate value, and that's it. It seem like a new function will have to be created within the class `retrieve`. This function would have to be *public*, so that it is accessible from `main()`. Here's the revised template:

```
class retrieve
    {
    private:
    int modify(int);

    public:
    int search(int number);
    virtual void print(void);
    void modify_record(int);
    };
```

The function `modify_record` will do a search on the customer number that is to be modified. If the number is found, the private function `modify()` will be called, with the customer number to be modified as an argument. `modify()` will return the modified customer number to `modify_record()`.

However, it seems that we neglected to take into account that `retrieve` is a base class for `display`, `add`, and `del`. All public members of `retrieve` will become public members of the derived classes. Therefore, a class object of either one of these classes will be able to access `modify_record()`, like this:

```
display_customer.modify_record(100);
```

or

```
add_customer.modify_record(200);
```

and thereby gain access to the function `modify()`. This is not at all desirable. So how will this problem be resolved? Well, recall those friendly friend functions? We can make `modify_record` a friend function of the class retrieve. A friend function has the capability of accessing the private members of a class. But, at the same time, it is not a part of the class that it is a friend of. Therefore, it cannot be a derived member for any classes derived from the base class that it is a friend of. This is exactly what we want. Here's the code. First, the class declarations:

```
C:> type test19_1.cpp

// test19_1.cpp            02/17/90   6:47 pm

#include <iostream.h>     // necessary for I/O

int customer_numbers[6] = {100, 200, 300, 400, 500, 0};

// retrieve is the base class
class retrieve
     {
     private:
     int modify(int);

     public:
     int search(int number);
     friend void modify_record(int number);
     virtual void print(void);
     };

// display is publicly derived from retrieve
class display : public retrieve
     {
     public:
     void display_info(int temp);
     void print(void);
     };

// add is publicly derived from retrieve
class add : public retrieve
     {
     public:
     void add_info(void);
     void print(void);
     };

// del is publicly derived from retrieve
class del : public retrieve
     {
     public:
     void delete_info(int);
     void print(void);
     };
```

Next, the class definitions. We are obliged to move the declaration of an instance of a class of type retrieve before the definition of modify(), since

modify() references it. Failure to do so would result in an error message from
the compiler stating that the object retrieve_customer is undefined.

```cpp
retrieve retrieve_customer;

// modify_record calls modify().
// it takes the customer number to be modified as a parameter.
// it returns no value.
// it is a friend function of the class retrieve.
// This enables this function and this function alone to modify the
// customer record.
void modify_record(int number)
{
    int i = 0;
    cout << "Inside modify_record \n";
    while (customer_numbers[i] != 0)
        {
        if (number != customer_numbers[i])
            {
            i++;
            }
        else
            {
            customer_numbers[i] =
               retrieve_customer.modify(customer_numbers[i]);
            return;
            }
        }
    cout << "Record not found! \n";
}


// modify takes the customer number to be modified as a parameter.
// it returns the modified value to the calling function.
int retrieve::modify(int number)
{
    cout << "Inside modify \n";
    number = number + 55;
    cout << "Record modified \n";
    return number;
}


// search() takes the customer number to search for as a parameter.
// it returns the customer number if found.
// it returns 0 if customer number is not found.
int retrieve::search(int number)
```

```
{
    int i = 0;

    cout << "Inside search \n";
    while (customer_numbers[i] != 0)
        {
        if (number != customer_numbers[i])
            {
            i++;
            }
        else
            {
            // print() is a virtual function.
            // Based on the object which is accessing
            // search(), the appropriate print()
            // function will be called.
             print();
             number = customer_numbers[i];
             return number;
             }
        }
    // if a corresponding record is not found, then the print()
    // statement for the base class will be called.
    retrieve::print();
    return 0;
}


void retrieve::print(void)
{
    cout << "Record not found!! \n";
}


// display_info takes the customer number returned from search()

// as a parameter.
// It has nothing to return.
void display::display_info(int temp)
{
    cout << "Customer number is " << temp << " \n";
}


void display::print(void)
{
    cout << "Here's the record! \n";
}
```

```
void add::add_info(void)
{
     cout << "Inside add_info \n";
}


void add::print(void)
{
     cout << "Attempt to add duplicate record! \n" <<
          "Transaction disallowed!! \n";
}


void del::delete_info(int)
{
     cout << "Inside delete_info \n";
}


void del::print(void)
{
     cout << "Record ready to be deleted! \n";
}
```

And finally, the code for `main()`. The customer array is output so that you can see how it was modified:

```
main(void)
{
     int temp, i, number;

     display display_customer;
     add add_customer;
     del delete_customer;

     // search for customer number 200
     number = 200;
     temp = display_customer.search(number);
     if (temp > 0)
     {
          display_customer.display_info(temp);
     }

     // modify customer number 200
     modify_record(number);

     for (i = 0; i < 6; i++)
          {
```

```
        cout << "cusotomer_numbers[" << i << "] is " <<
            customer_numbers[i] << "\n";
        }
    }
```

Compiling and running this program results in the following outptut:

```
Inside search
Here's the record
Customer number is 200
Inside modify_record
Inside modify
Record modified
Customer_numbers[0] is 100
Customer_numbers[1] is 255
Customer_numbers[2] is 300
Customer_numbers[3] is 400
Customer_numbers[4] is 500
Customer_numbers[5] is 0
```

Customer number 200 is searched for and displayed, via display_info().
Then, this record is modified by adding 55 to its current value. The output
should be self-explanatory.

19.3   MODIFICATION OF NONEXISTENT CUSTOMER RECORD

Let's try to modify a nonexistent customer record. As usual, first the class
declarations and definitions:

```
C:> type test19_2.cpp

// test19_2.cpp          02/18/90  3:55 pm

#include <iostream.h>    // necessary for I/0

int customer_numbers[6] = {100, 200, 300, 400, 500, 0};

// retrieve is the base class
class retrieve
    {
    private:
    int modify(int);

    public:
    int search(int number);
    friend void modify_record(int number);
```

```
        virtual void print(void);
        };

// display is publicly derived from retrieve
class display : public retrieve
        {
        public:
        void display_info(int temp);
        void print(void);
        };

// add is publicly derived from retrieve
class add : public retrieve
        {
        public:
        void add_info(void);
        void print(void);
        };

// del is publicly derived from retrieve
class del : public retrieve
        {
        public:
        void delete_info(int temp);
        void print(void);
        };


retrieve retrieve_customer;

// modify_record calls modify().
// it takes the customer number to be modified as a parameter.
// it returns no value.
// it is a friend function of the class retrieve.
// This enables this function and this function alone to modify the
// customer record.
void modify_record(int number)
{
        int i = 0;
        cout << "Inside modify_record \n";
        while (customer_numbers[i] != 0)
            {
            if (number != customer_numbers[i])
                {
                i++;
                }
            else
```

```
            {
            customer_numbers[i] =
              retrieve_customer.modify(customer_numbers[i]);
            return;
            }
        }
    cout << "Record not found! \n";
}


// modify takes the customer number to be modified as a parameter.
// it returns the modified value to the calling function.
int retrieve::modify(int number)
{
    cout << "Inside modify \n";
    number = number + 55;
    cout << "Record modified \n";
    return number;
}


// search() takes the customer number to search for as a paramter.
// it returns the customer number if found.
// it returns 0 if customer number is not found.
int retrieve::search(int number)
{
    int i = 0;

    cout << "Inside search \n";
    while (customer_numbers[i] != 0)
        {
        if (number != customer_numbers[i])
            {
            i++;
            }
        else
            {
            // print() is a virtual function.
            // Based on the object which is accessing
            // search(), the appropriate print()
            // function will be called.
             print();
             number = customer_numbers[i];
             return number;
             }
        }
    // if a corresponding record is not found, then the print()
    // statement for the base class will be called.
```

```
        retrieve::print();
        return 0;
}

void retrieve::print(void)
{
        cout << "Record not found!! \n";
}

// display_info takes the customer number returned from search()
// as a parameter.
// It has nothing to return.
void display::display_info(int temp)
{
        cout << "Customer number is " << temp << " \n";
}

void display::print(void)
{
        cout << "Here's the record! \n";
}

void add::add_info(void)
{
        cout << "Inside add_info \n";
}

void add::print(void)
{
        cout << "Attempt to add duplicate record! \n" <<
             "Transaction disallowed!! \n";
}

void del::delete_info(int)
{
        cout << "Inside delete_info \n";
}

void del::print(void)
{
        cout << "Record ready to be deleted! \n";
}
```

And here's the code for main():

```
main(void)
{
```

```
    int temp, i, number;

    display display_customer;
    add add_customer;
    del delete_customer;

    // search for non-existent customer number 250
    number = 250;
    temp = display_customer.search(number);
    if (temp > 0)
    {
        display_customer.display_info(temp);
    }
    // modify non-existent customer number 250
    modify_record(number);
    for (i = 0; i < 6; i++)
        {
        cout << "cusotomer_numbers[" << i << "] is " <<
            customer_numbers[i] << "\n";
        }
}
```

Compiling and running this program gives the following output:

```
Inside search
Record not found!!
Inside modify_record
Record not found!
customer_numbers[0] is 100
customer_numbers[1] is 200
customer_numbers[2] is 300
customer_numbers[3] is 400
customer_numbers[4] is 500
```

The output should be self-explanatory.

19.4   ACCESSING modify() VIA NONMEMBER CLASS OBJECTS

And now, let's try to have some other class object access modify(). Here's the code:

```
C;> type test19_3.cpp

// test19_3.cpp        02/17/90  4:00 pm

#include <iostream.h>    // necessary for I/O
```

```
int customer_numbers[6] = {100, 200, 300, 400, 500, 0};

// retrieve is the base class
class retrieve
    {
    private:
    int modify(int);

    public:
    int search(int number);
    friend void modify_record(int number);
    virtual void print(void);
    };

// display is publicly derived from retrieve
class display : public retrieve
    {
    public:
    void display_info(int temp);
    void print(void);
    };

// add is publicly derived from retrieve
class add : public retrieve
    {
    public:
    void add_info(void);
    void print(void);
    };

// del is publicly derived from retrieve
class del : public retrieve
    {
    public:
    void delete_info(int);
    void print(void);
    };

retrieve retrieve_customer;

// modify_record calls modify().
// it takes the customer number to be modified as a parameter.
// it returns no value.
// it is a friend function of the class retrieve.
// This enables this function and this function alone to modify the
```

```
// customer record.
void modify_record(int number)
{
    int i = 0;
    cout << "Inside modify_record \n";
    while (customer_numbers[i] != 0)
        {
        if (number != customer_numbers[i])
            {
            i++;
            }
        else
            {
            customer_numbers[i] =
              retrieve_customer.modify(customer_numbers[i]);
            return;
            }
        }
    cout << "Record not found! \n";
}

// modify takes the customer number to be modified as a parameter.
// it returns the modified value to the calling function.
int retrieve::modify(int number)
{
    cout << "Inside modify \n";
    number = number + 55;
    cout << "Record modified \n";
    return number;
}

// search() takes the customer number to search for as a paramter.
// it returns the customer number if found.
// it returns 0 if customer number is not found.
int retrieve::search(int number)
{
    int i = 0;

    cout << "Inside search \n";
    while (customer_numbers[i] != 0)
        {
        if (number != customer_numbers[i])
            {
            i++;
            }
        else
```

```
                              {
                              // print() is a virtual function.
                              // Based on the object which is accessing
                              // search(), the appropriate print()
                              // function will be called.
                               print();
                               number = customer_numbers[i];
                               return number;
                               }
                        }
        // if a corresponding record is not found, then the print()
        // statement for the base class will be called.
        retrieve::print();
        return 0;
}


void retrieve::print(void)
{
        cout << "Record not found!! \n";
}


// display_info takes the customer number returned from search()
// as a parameter.
// It has nothing to return.
void display::display_info(int temp)
{
        cout << "Customer number is " << temp << " \n";
}


void display::print(void)
{
        cout << "Here's the record! \n";
}


void add::add_info(void)
{
        cout << "Inside add_info \n";
}


void add::print(void)
{
        cout << "Attempt to add duplicate record! \n" <<
            "Transaction disallowed!! \n";
}


void del::delete_info(int)
```

```
{
     cout << "Inside delete_info \n";
}

void del::print(void)
{
     cout << "Record ready to be deleted! \n";
}

main(void)
{
     int temp, i, number;

     display display_customer;
     add add_customer;
     del delete_customer;

     // search for customer number 200
     number = 200;
     temp = display_customer.search(number);
     if (temp > 0)
     {
         display_customer.display_info(temp);
     }

     // modify customer number 200
     // try to invoke modify as an instance of display_customer
     display_customer.modify(number);
     for (i = 0; i < 6; i++)
         {
         cout << "cusotomer_numbers[" << i << "] is " <<
             customer_numbers[i] << "\n";
         }
}
```

Inside `main()`, `modify()` is accessed as follows:

```
display_customer.modify(number);
```

But `modify()` is a private function; not only can no other class access it, but the function itself cannot be invoked from `main()`. Compiling this version yields the following unfriendly message from the compiler:

```
Error: retrieve::modify() is not accessible in function main()
```

Perfect! Just what we wanted. We have successfully encapsulated the functionality of the `modify()` function.

By now you must have noticed a few choice features about the sample programs and output:

1. None of the existing class definitions was required to be modified, save for the addition of code for the function that was developed.
2. Therefore, if the preexisting classes worked before the insertion of the new code, they must work even now.
3. Therefore, there is no need to retest their functionality.

19.5   REVIEW

In this chapter, we expanded the code for an existing program, and in the process realized the power that can be derived from object-oriented programs. The basic structure (given that you took the time to design it as best as you could in the first place), remains unaltered. Preexisting code for existing classes does not have to be retested. Functionality of each object is encapsulated. Debugging becomes a cinch for this very reason.

Expansion of Object-Oriented Programs—Part 2

20.1 INTRODUCTION

In this chapter, the system designed in Chap. 17, and developed in Chaps. 18 and 19, will be expanded. Now the code for the `delete` function will be developed.

20.2 THE delete_info() FUNCTION

To start things off, `search()` will be invoked to search for the customer number that is to be deleted. If it is found, `delete_info()` will proceed to delete it. In our example, the appropriate slot will simply be set to 0. The remaining elements of the array will be moved up one slot, so that all existing customer record numbers are contiguous. If customer record is not found, the appropriate message will be displayed by `search()`. Here's the code:

```
C:> type test20_1.cpp

// test20_1.cpp          02/18/90  4:47 pm

#include <iostream.h>    // necessary for I/O

int customer_numbers[6] = {100, 200, 300, 400, 500, 0};

// retrieve is the base class
```

```
class retrieve
     {
     private:
     int modify(int);

     public:
     int search(int number);
     friend void modify_record(int number);
     virtual void print(void);
     };

// display is publicly derived from retrieve
class display : public retrieve
     {
     public:
     void display_info(int temp);
     void print(void);
     };

// add is publicly derived from retrieve
class add : public retrieve
     {
     public:
     void add_info(void);
     void print(void);
     };

// del is publicly derived from retrieve
class del : public retrieve
     {
     public:
     void delete_info(int temp);
     void print(void);
     };


retrieve retrieve_customer;

// modify_record calls modify().
// it takes the customer number to be modified as a parameter.
// it returns no value.
// it is a friend function of the class retrieve.
// This enables this function and this function alone to modify the
// customer record.
void modify_record(int number)
{
     int i = 0;
```

```
        cout << "Inside modify_record \n";
        while (customer_numbers[i] != 0)
            {
            if (number != customer_numbers[i])
                {
                i++;
                }
            else
                {
                customer_numbers[i] =
                  retrieve_customer.modify(customer_numbers[i]);
                return;
                }
            }
        cout << "Record not found! \n";
}


// modify takes the customer number to be modified as a parameter.
// it returns the modified value to the calling function.
int retrieve::modify(int number)
{
        cout << "Inside modify \n";
        number = number + 55;
        cout << "Record modified \n";
        return number;
}


// search() takes the customer number to search for as a paramter.
// it returns a copy of the customer number if found.
// it returns 0 if customer number is not found.
int retrieve::search(int number)
{
        int i = 0;

        cout << "Inside search \n";
        while (customer_numbers[i] != 0)
            {
            if (number != customer_numbers[i])
                {
                i++;
                }
            else
                {
                // print() is a virtual function.
                // Based on the object which is accessing
                // search(), the appropriate print()
```

```
                    // function will be called.
                     print();
                     number = customer_numbers[i];
                     return number;
                     }
               }
         // if a corresponding record is not found, then the print()

         // statement for the base class will be called.
         retrieve::print();
         return 0;
}


void retrieve::print(void)
{
     cout << "Record not found!! \n";
}


// display_info takes the customer number returned from search()
// as a parameter.
// It has nothing to return.
void display::display_info(int temp)
{
     cout << "Customer number is " << temp << " \n";
}


void display::print(void)
{
     cout << "Here's the record! \n";
}


void add::add_info(void)
{
     cout << "Inside add_info \n";
}


void add::print(void)
{
     cout << "Attempt to add duplicate record! \n" <<
          "Transaction disallowed!! \n";
}
```

So far, the code is the same. The code for `del::delete_info()` is developed
next:

```
void del::delete_info(int temp)
```

```
{
    cout << "Inside delete_info \n";
    int i = 0;
    while (customer_numbers[i] != 0)
        {
        if (temp != customer_numbers[i])
            {
            i++;
            }
        else
            {
            customer_numbers[i] = 0;
            // move remaining array in by 1
            while (customer_numbers[i+1] != 0)
                {
                customer_numbers[i] = customer_numbers[i+1];

                i++;
                }
            // zero out the previous last element
            customer_numbers[i] = 0;
            return;
            }
        }
    retrieve::print();
}

void del::print(void)
{
    cout << "Record ready to be deleted! \n";
}
```

And finally, the code for `main()`. The code developed previously is intact.

```
main(void)
{
    int temp, i, number;

    display display_customer;
    add add_customer;
    del delete_customer;

    // search for customer number 200
    number = 200;
    temp = display_customer.search(number);
    if (temp > 0)
```

```
        {
              display_customer.display_info(temp);
        }
        // modify customer number 200
        modify_record(number);

        // search for customer number 300
        // if found, delete it.
        temp = delete_customer.search(300);
        if (temp > 0)
        {
              delete_customer.delete_info(temp);
        }

        for (i = 0; i < 6; i++)
            {
            cout << "customer_numbers[" << i << "] is " <<
                    customer_numbers[i] << "\n";
            }
}
```

Compiling and running this program results in the following output:

```
Inside search
Here's the record!
Customer number is 200
Inside modify_record
Inside modify
Record modified
Inside search
Record ready to be deleted!
Inside delete_info
customer_numbers[0] is 100
customer_numbers[1] is 255
customer_numbers[2] is 400
customer_numbers[3] is 500
customer_numbers[4] is 0
customer_numbers[5] is 0
```

The output should be self-explanatory.

20.3   DELETION OF NONEXISTENT CUSTOMER RECORD

Let's try to delete a record that does not exist in customer_numbers[]. Here's the code:

```
C:> type test20_2.cpp

// test20_2.cpp           02/18/90  5:25 pm

#include <iostream.h>     // necessary for I/O

int customer_numbers[6] = {100, 200, 300, 400, 500, 0};

// retrieve is the base class
class retrieve
    {
    private:
    int modify(int);

    public:
    int search(int number);
    friend void modify_record(int number);
    virtual void print(void);
    };

// display is publicly derived from retrieve
class display : public retrieve
    {
    public:
    void display_info(int temp);
    void print(void);
    };

// add is publicly derived from retrieve
class add : public retrieve
    {
    public:
    void add_info(void);
    void print(void);
    };

// del is publicly derived from retrieve
class del : public retrieve
    {
    public:
    void delete_info(int temp);
    void print(void);
    };

retrieve retrieve_customer;
```

```
// modify_record calls modify().
// it takes the customer number to be modified as a parameter.
// it returns no value.
// it is a friend function of the class retrieve.
// This enables this function and this function alone to modify the
// customer record.
void modify_record(int number)
{
    int i = 0;
    cout << "Inside modify_record \n";
    while (customer_numbers[i] != 0)
        {
        if (number != customer_numbers[i])
            {
            i++;
            }
        else
            {
            customer_numbers[i] =
              retrieve_customer.modify(customer_numbers[i]);
            return;
            }
        }
    cout << "Record not found! \n";
}


// modify takes the customer number to be modified as a parameter.
// it returns the modified value to the calling function.
int retrieve::modify(int number)
{
    cout << "Inside modify \n";
    number = number + 55;
    cout << "Record modified \n";
    return number;
}


// search() takes the customer number to search for as a parameter.
// it returns the customer number if found.
// it returns 0 if customer number is not found.
int retrieve::search(int number)
{
    int i = 0;

    cout << "Inside search \n";
    while (customer_numbers[i] != 0)
```

```
            {
        if (number != customer_numbers[i])
            {
            i++;
            }
        else
            {
            // print() is a virtual function.
            // Based on the object which is accessing
            // search(), the appropriate print()
            // function will be called.
             print();
             number = customer_numbers[i];
             return number;
             }
        }
    // if a corresponding record is not found, then the print()

    // statement for the base class will be called.
    retrieve::print();
    return 0;
}


void retrieve::print(void)
{
    cout << "Record not found!! \n";
}


// display_info takes the customer number returned from search()
// as a parameter.
// It has nothing to return.
void display::display_info(int temp)
{
    cout << "Customer number is " << temp << " \n";
}


void display::print(void)
{
    cout << "Here's the record! \n";
}


void add::add_info(void)
{
    cout << "Inside add_info \n";
}
```

```
void add::print(void)
{
    cout << "Attempt to add duplicate record! \n" <<
        "Transaction disallowed!! \n";
}


void del::delete_info(int temp)
{
    cout << "Inside delete_info \n";
    int i = 0;
    while (customer_numbers[i] != 0)
        {
        if (temp != customer_numbers[i])
            {
            i++;
            }
        else
            {
            customer_numbers[i] = 0;
            // move remaining array in by 1
            while (customer_numbers[i+1] != 0)
                {
                customer_numbers[i] = customer_numbers[i+1];
                i++;
                }
            // zero out the previous last element
            customer_numbers[i] = 0;
            return;
            }
        }
    retrieve::print();
}


void del::print(void)
{
    cout << "Record ready to be deleted! \n";
}


main(void)
{
    int temp, i, number;

    display display_customer;
    add add_customer;
    del delete_customer;
```

```
// search for customer number 200
number = 200;
temp = display_customer.search(number);
if (temp > 0)
{
    display_customer.display_info(temp);
}

// modify customer number 200
modify_record(number);

// search for nonexistent customer number 350
// if found, delete it.
temp = delete_customer.search(350);
if (temp > 0)
{
    delete_customer.delete_info(temp);
}

for (i = 0; i < 6; i++)
    {
    cout << "customer_numbers[" << i << "] is " <<
            customer_numbers[i] << "\n";
    }
}
```

Compiling and running this program gives the following output:

```
Inside search
Here's the record!
Customer number is 200
Inside modify_record
Inside modify
Record modified
Inside search
Record not found!
customer_numbers[0] is 100
customer_numbers[1] is 255
customer_numbers[2] is 300
customer_numbers[3] is 400
customer_numbers[4] is 500
customer_numbers[5] is 0
```

As you can see, the array of customer numbers remains unchanged. The output is self-explanatory.

20.4   ACCESS OF delete_info() BY NONCLASS MEMBER

Finally, a nonclass member attempts to delete a customer number. Here's the code:

```
C:> type test20_3.cpp

// test20_3.cpp          02/18/90  5:25 pm

#include <iostream.h>     // necessary for I/O

int customer_numbers[6] = {100, 200, 300, 400, 500, 0};

// retrieve is the base class
class retrieve
     {
     private:
     int modify(int);

     public:
     int search(int number);
     friend void modify_record(int number);
     virtual void print(void);
     };

// display is publicly derived from retrieve
class display : public retrieve
     {
     public:
     void display_info(int temp);
     void print(void);
     };

// add is publicly derived from retrieve
class add : public retrieve
     {
     public:
     void add_info(void);
     void print(void);
     };

// del is publicly derived from retrieve
class del : public retrieve
     {
     public:
     void delete_info(int temp);
```

```
        void print(void);
        };


retrieve retrieve_customer;

// modify_record calls modify().
// it takes the customer number to be modified as a parameter.
// it returns no value.
// it is a friend function of the class retrieve.
// This enables this function and this function alone to modify the

// customer record.
void modify_record(int number)
{
     int i = 0;
     cout << "Inside modify_record \n";
     while (customer_numbers[i] != 0)
          {
          if (number != customer_numbers[i])
                {
                i++;
                }
          else
                {
                customer_numbers[i] =
                   retrieve_customer.modify(customer_numbers[i]);
                return;
                }
          }
     cout << "Record not found! \n";
}


// modify takes the customer number to be modified as a parameter.
// it returns the modified value to the calling function.
int retrieve::modify(int number)
{
     cout << "Inside modify \n";
     number = number + 55;
     cout << "Record modified \n";
     return number;
}


// store takes the customer number to search for as a paramter.
// it returns the customer number if found.
// it returns 0 if customer number is not found.
int retrieve::search(int number)
```

```
{
      int i = 0;

      cout << "Inside search \n";
      while (customer_numbers[i] != 0)
          {
          if (number != customer_numbers[i])
                {
                i++;
                }
          else
                {
                // print() is a virtual function.
                // Based on the object which is accessing
                // search(), the appropriate print()
                // function will be called.
                 print();
                 number = customer_numbers[i];
                 return number;
                 }
          }
      // if a corresponding record is not found, then the print()
      // statement for the base class will be called.
      retrieve::print();
      return 0;
}

void retrieve::print(void)
{
      cout << "Record not found!! \n";
}


// display_info takes the customer number returned from search()
// as a parameter.
// It has nothing to return.
void display::display_info(int temp)
{
      cout << "Customer number is " << temp << " \n";
}

void display::print(void)
{
      cout << "Here's the record! \n";
}


void add::add_info(void)
```

```
{
     cout << "Inside add_info \n";
}


void add::print(void)
{
     cout << "Attempt to add duplicate record! \n" <<
          "Transaction disallowed!! \n";
}


void del::delete_info(int temp)
{
     cout << "Inside delete_info \n";
     int i = 0;
     while (customer_numbers[i] != 0)
          {
          if (temp != customer_numbers[i])
               {
               i++;
               }
          else
               {
               customer_numbers[i] = 0;
               // move remaining array in by 1
               while (customer_numbers[i+1] != 0)
                    {
                    customer_numbers[i] = customer_numbers[i+1];

                    i++;
                    }
               // zero out the previous last element
               customer_numbers[i] = 0;
               return;
               }
          }
     retrieve::print();
}


void del::print(void)
{
     cout << "Record ready to be deleted! \n";
}


main(void)
{
     int temp, i, number;
```

```
display display_customer;
add add_customer;
del delete_customer;

// search for customer number 200
number = 200;
temp = display_customer.search(number);
if (temp > 0)
{
    display_customer.display_info(temp);
}

// modify customer number 200
modify_record(number);

// search for customer number 300
// if found, delete it.
temp = delete_customer.search(300);
if (temp > 0)
{
// object display_customer attempts to access
// delete_info().
    display_customer.delete_info(temp);
}

for (i = 0; i < 6; i++)
    {
    cout << "customer_numbers[" << i << "] is " <<
        customer_numbers[i] << "\n";
    }
}
```

Compiling this program results in the compiler issuing an error message:

```
Error:    'delete_info' is not a member of 'display' in function
          main()
```

Perfect! Just what we wanted! We have successfully used derivation to encapsulate the delete function to objects of type `del` only.

20.5   REVIEW

This chapter incorporated the code for the `delete_info()` function into the program designed and developed in the prior three chapters. Once again, the ease with which object-oriented programs can be expanded was illustrated.

Expansion of Object-Oriented Programs—Part 3

21.1 INTRODUCTION

Last but not least, the code for add_info() will be developed and incorporated into the application designed and implemented in the prior four chapters.

21.2 THE add_info() FUNCTION

First, the customer record that is to be added will be searched. If the record is found, then an attempt is being made to add a duplicate record, and the transaction will be disallowed. The record will be added if search() outputs "Record not found!". Here's the code:

```
C;> type test21_1.cpp

// test21_1.cpp          02/18/90  4:47 pm

#include <iostream.h>     // necessary for I/O

int customer_numbers[6] = {100, 200, 300, 400, 500, 0};

// retrieve is the base class
class retrieve
    {
```

```
        private:
        int modify(int);

        public:
        int search(int number);
        friend void modify_record(int number);
        virtual void print(void);
        };

// display is publicly derived from retrieve
class display : public retrieve
        {
        public:
        void display_info(int temp);
        void print(void);
        };


// add is publicly derived from retrieve
class add : public retrieve
        {
        public:
        void add_info(int temp);
        void print(void);
        };

// del is publicly derived from retrieve
class del : public retrieve
        {
        public:
        void delete_info(int temp);
        void print(void);
        };


retrieve retrieve_customer;

// modify_record calls modify().
// it takes the customer number to be modified as a parameter.
// it returns no value.
// it is a friend function of the class retrieve.
// This enables this function and this function alone to modify the
// customer record.
void modify_record(int number)
{
     int i = 0;
     cout << "Inside modify_record \n";
     while (customer_numbers[i] != 0)
```

```
            {
            if (number != customer_numbers[i])
                {
                i++;
                }
            else
                {
                customer_numbers[i] =
                  retrieve_customer.modify(customer_numbers[i]);
                return;
                }
            }
        cout << "Record not found! \n";
}


// modify takes the customer number to be modified as a parameter.
// it returns the modified value to the calling function.
int retrieve::modify(int number)
{
    cout << "Inside modify \n";
    number = number + 55;
    cout << "Record modified \n";
    return number;
}


// retrieve takes the customer number to search for as a paramter.
// it returns the customer number if found.
// it returns 0 if customer number is not found.
int retrieve::search(int number)
{
    int i = 0;

    cout << "Inside search \n";
    while (customer_numbers[i] != 0)
        {
        if (number != customer_numbers[i])
            {
            i++;
            }
        else
            {
            // print() is a virtual function.
            // Based on the object which is accessing
            // search(), the appropriate print()
            // function will be called.
             print();
```

```
                    number = customer_numbers[i];
                    return number;
                    }
            }
        // if a corresponding record is not found, then the print()

        // statement for the base class will be called.
        retrieve::print();
        return 0;
    }


void retrieve::print(void)
{
    cout << "Record not found!! \n";
}


// display_info takes the customer number returned from search()
// as a parameter.
// It has nothing to return.
void display::display_info(int temp)
{
    cout << "Customer number is " << temp << " \n";
}


void display::print(void)
{
    cout << "Here's the record! \n";
}
```

The code for add_info **is short and simple:**

```
void add::add_info(int temp)
{
    cout << "Inside add_info \n";
    int i = 0;
    // find the slot to add to
    while (customer_numbers[i] != 0)
        {
        i++;
        }
    customer_numbers[i] = temp;
}


void add::print(void)
{
    cout << "Attempt to add duplicate record! \n" <<
```

```
                "Transaction disallowed!! \n";
}


void del::delete_info(int temp)
{
     cout << "Inside delete_info \n";
     int i = 0;
     while (customer_numbers[i] != 0)
          {
          if (temp != customer_numbers[i])
               {
               i++;
               }
          else
               {
               customer_numbers[i] = 0;
               // move remaining array in by 1
               while (customer_numbers[i+1] != 0)
                    {
                    customer_numbers[i] = customer_numbers[i+1];

                    i++;
                    }
               // zero out the previous last element
               customer_numbers[i] = 0;
               return;
               }
          }
     retrieve::print();
}


void del::print(void)
{
     cout << "Record ready to be deleted! \n";
}


main(void)
{
     int temp, i, number;

     display display_customer;
     add add_customer;
     del delete_customer;

     // search for customer number 200
     number = 200;
```

```
temp = display_customer.search(number);
if (temp > 0)
{
    display_customer.display_info(temp);
}

// modify customer number 200
modify_record(number);

// search for customer number 300
// if found, delete it.
temp = delete_customer.search(300);
if (temp > 0)
{
    delete_customer.delete_info(temp);
}

// search for customer number 600
// if not found, add it.
temp = add_customer.search(600);
if (temp == 0)
{
    add_customer.add_info(600);
}

for (i = 0; i < 6; i++)
    {
    cout << "customer_numbers[" << i << "] is " <<
            customer_numbers[i] << "\n";
    }
}
```

The output for this program follows:

```
Inside search
Here's the record
Customer number is 200
Inside modify_record
Inside modify
Record modified
Inside search
Record ready to be deleted!
Inside delete_info
Inside search
Record not found!
Inside add_info
```

```
customer_numbers[0] is 100
customer_numbers[1] is 255
customer_numbers[2] is 400
customer_numbers[3] is 500
customer_numbers[4] is 600
customer_numbers[5] is 0
```

Even though the output is self-explanatory, it won't hurt to briefly overview it anyway. (Feel free to skip over to the next section if you understand it thoroughly.)

First, a search for customer record number 200 is initiated. The record is found and displayed by `display_info`. Following is the output for this segment of code:

```
Inside search
Here's the record
Customer number is 200
```

Next, record number 200 is modified, by adding 55 to its current value. The corresponding output for this segment of code is:

```
Inside modify_record
Inside modify
Record modified
```

Ideally, a duplicate search should have been issued for the modified record, but we just wanted to keep things as simple as possible.

Next, record number 300 is successfully deleted. Output follows:

```
Inside search
Record ready to be deleted!
Inside delete_info
```

And then, record number 600 is added:

```
Inside search
Record not found!
Inside add_info
```

And after all has been said and done, here's the resulting array of customer numbers:

```
customer_numbers[0] is 100
customer_numbers[1] is 255
customer_numbers[2] is 400
customer_numbers[3] is 500
```

```
customer_numbers[4] is 600
customer_numbers[5] is 0
```

21.3   ADDITION OF DUPLICATE RECORD

Let's try to add a record which already exists in the array:

```
C:> type test21_2.cpp

// test21_2.cpp          02/18/90  6:23 pm

#include <iostream.h>     // necessary for I/O

int customer_numbers[6] = {100, 200, 300, 400, 500, 0};

// retrieve is the base class
class retrieve
    {
    private:
    int modify(int);

    public:
    int search(int number);
    friend void modify_record(int number);
    virtual void print(void);
    };

// display is publicly derived from retrieve
class display : public retrieve
    {
    public:
    void display_info(int temp);
    void print(void);
    };

// add is publicly derived from retrieve
class add : public retrieve
    {
    public:
    void add_info(int temp);
    void print(void);
    };

// del is publicly derived from retrieve
class del : public retrieve
```

```
        {
        public:
        void delete_info(int temp);
        void print(void);
        };

retrieve retrieve_customer;

// modify_record calls modify().
// it takes the customer number to be modified as a parameter.
// it returns no value.
// it is a friend function of the class retrieve.
// This enables this function and this function alone to modify the
// customer record.
void modify_record(int number)
{
        int i = 0;
        cout << "Inside modify_record \n";
        while (customer_numbers[i] != 0)
                {
                if (number != customer_numbers[i])
                        {
                        i++;
                        }
                else
                        {
                        customer_numbers[i] =
                          retrieve_customer.modify(customer_numbers[i]);
                        return;
                        }
                }
        cout << "Record not found! \n";
}


// modify takes the customer number to be modified as a parameter.
// it returns the modified value to the calling function.
int retrieve::modify(int number)
{
        cout << "Inside modify \n";
        number = number + 55;
        cout << "Record modified \n";
        return number;
}


// retrieve takes the customer number to search for as a parameter.
// it returns the customer number if found.
```

```cpp
// it returns 0 if customer number is not found.
int retrieve::search(int number)
{
    int i = 0;

    cout << "Inside search \n";
    while (customer_numbers[i] != 0)
        {
        if (number != customer_numbers[i])
            {
            i++;
            }
        else
            {
            // print() is a virtual function.
            // Based on the object which is accessing
            // search(), the appropriate print()
            // function will be called.
             print();
             number = customer_numbers[i];
             return number;
             }
        }
    // if a corresponding record is not found, then the print()
    // statement for the base class will be called.
    retrieve::print();
    return 0;
}


void retrieve::print(void)
{
    cout << "Record not found!! \n";
}


// display_info takes the customer number returned from search()
// as a parameter.
// It has nothing to return.
void display::display_info(int temp)
{
    cout << "Customer number is " << temp << " \n";
}


void display::print(void)
{
    cout << "Here's the record! \n";
}
```

```
void add::add_info(int temp)
{
    cout << "Inside add_info \n";
    int i = 0;
    // find the slot to add to
    while (customer_numbers[i] != 0)
        {
        i++;
        }
    customer_numbers[i] = temp;
}


void add::print(void)
{
    cout << "Attempt to add duplicate record! \n" <<
        "Transaction disallowed!! \n";
}


void del::delete_info(int temp)
{
    cout << "Inside delete_info \n";
    int i = 0;
    while (customer_numbers[i] != 0)
        {
        if (temp != customer_numbers[i])
            {
            i++;
            }
        else
            {
            customer_numbers[i] = 0;
            // move remaining array in by 1
            while (customer_numbers[i+1] != 0)
                {
                customer_numbers[i] = customer_numbers[i+1];

                i++;
                }
            // zero out the previous last element
            customer_numbers[i] = 0;
            return;
            }
        }
    retrieve::print();
}
```

```
void del::print(void)
{
    cout << "Record ready to be deleted! \n";
}

main(void)
{
    int temp, i, number;

    display display_customer;
    add add_customer;
    del delete_customer;

    // search for customer number 200
    number = 200;
    temp = display_customer.search(number);
    if (temp > 0)
    {
        display_customer.display_info(temp);
    }

    // modify customer number 200
    modify_record(number);

    // search for customer number 300
    // if found, delete it.
    temp = delete_customer.search(300);
    if (temp > 0)
    {
        delete_customer.delete_info(temp);
    }

    // try to add duplicate customer record 500
    temp = add_customer.search(500);
    if (temp == 0)
    {
        add_customer.add_info(500);
    }

    for (i = 0; i < 6; i++)
        {
        cout << "customer_numbers[" << i << "] is " <<
            customer_numbers[i] << "\n";
        }
}
```

The output for this program follows:

```
Inside search
Here's the record
Customer number is 200
Inside modify_record
Inside modify
Record modified
Inside search
Record ready to be deleted!
Inside delete_info
Inside search
Attempt to add duplicate record!
Transaction disallowed!!
customer_numbers[0] is 100
customer_numbers[1] is 255
customer_numbers[2] is 400
customer_numbers[3] is 500
customer_numbers[4] is 0
customer_numbers[5] is 0
```

You should be keying in on the following output:

```
Inside search
Attempt to add duplicate record!
Transaction disallowed!!
```

21.4   ACCESS OF add_info() BY NONCLASS MEMBER

And finally, we will have a nonmember class object, such as retrieve_cus-tomer **access** add_info(). Here's the code:

```
C:> type test21_3.cpp

// test21_3.cpp          02/18/90  6:35 pm

#include <iostream.h>    // necessary for I/O

int customer_numbers[6] = {100, 200, 300, 400, 500, 0};

// retrieve is the base class
class retrieve
    {
    private:
    int modify(int);
```

```cpp
public:
int search(int number);
friend void modify_record(int number);
virtual void print(void);
};

// display is publicly derived from retrieve
class display : public retrieve
    {
    public:
    void display_info(int temp);
    void print(void);
    };

// add is publicly derived from retrieve
class add : public retrieve
    {
    public:
    void add_info(int temp);
    void print(void);
    };

// del is publicly derived from retrieve
class del : public retrieve
    {
    public:
    void delete_info(int temp);
    void print(void);
    };

retrieve retrieve_customer;

// modify_record calls modify().
// it takes the customer number to be modified as a parameter.
// it returns no value.
// it is a friend function of the class retrieve.
// This enables this function and this function alone to modify the
// customer record.
void modify_record(int number)
{
    int i = 0;
    cout << "Inside modify_record \n";
    while (customer_numbers[i] != 0)
        {
        if (number != customer_numbers[i])
            {
```

```
                i++;
                }
        else
            {
            customer_numbers[i] =
              retrieve_customer.modify(customer_numbers[i]);
            return;
            }
        }
    cout << "Record not found! \n";
}


// modify takes the customer number to be modified as a parameter.
// it returns the modified value to the calling function.
int retrieve::modify(int number)
{
    cout << "Inside modify \n";
    number = number + 55;
    cout << "Record modified \n";
    return number;
}


// retrieve takes the customer number to search for as a paramter.
// it returns the customer number if found.
// it returns 0 if customer number is not found.
int retrieve::search(int number)
{
    int i = 0;

    cout << "Inside search \n";
    while (customer_numbers[i] != 0)
        {
        if (number != customer_numbers[i])
            {
            i++;
            }
        else
            {
            // print() is a virtual function.
            // Based on the object which is accessing
            // search(), the appropriate print()
            // function will be called.
             print();
             number = customer_numbers[i];
             return number;
             }
```

```
                }
        // if a corresponding record is not found, then the print()

        // statement for the base class will be called.
        retrieve::print();
        return 0;
}


void retrieve::print(void)
{
        cout << "Record not found!! \n";
}


// display_info takes the customer number returned from search()
// as a parameter.
// It has nothing to return.
void display::display_info(int temp)
{
        cout << "Customer number is " << temp << " \n";
}


void display::print(void)
{
        cout << "Here's the record! \n";
}


void add::add_info(int temp)
{
        cout << "Inside add_info \n";
        int i = 0;
        // find the slot to add to
        while (customer_numbers[i] != 0)
                {
                i++;
                }
        customer_numbers[i] = temp;
}


void add::print(void)
{
        cout << "Attempt to add duplicate record! \n" <<
                "Transaction disallowed!! \n";
}


void del::delete_info(int temp)
{
```

```
            cout << "Inside delete_info \n";
            int i = 0;
            while (customer_numbers[i] != 0)
                  {
                  if (temp != customer_numbers[i])
                        {
                        i++;
                        }
                  else
                        {
                        customer_numbers[i] = 0;
                        // move remaining array in by 1
                        while (customer_numbers[i+1] != 0)
                              {
                              customer_numbers[i] = customer_numbers[i+1];

                              i++;
                              }
                        // zero out the previous last element
                        customer_numbers[i] = 0;
                        return;
                        }
                  }
            retrieve::print();
}

void del::print(void)
{
      cout << "Record ready to be deleted! \n";
}

main(void)
{
      int temp, i, number;

      display display_customer;
      add add_customer;
      del delete_customer;

      // search for customer number 200
      number = 200;
      temp = display_customer.search(number);
      if (temp > 0)
      {
            display_customer.display_info(temp);
      }
```

```
        // modify customer number 200
        modify_record(number);

        // search for customer number 300
        // if found, delete it.
        temp = delete_customer.search(300);
        if (temp > 0)
        {
            delete_customer.delete_info(temp);
        }

        // search for customer number 500
        // if not found, add it.
        temp = add_customer.search(500);
        if (temp == 0)
        {
            retrieve_customer.add_info(500);
        }

        for (i = 0; i < 6; i++)
            {
            cout << "customer_numbers[" << i << "] is " <<
                customer_numbers[i] << "\n";
            }
    }
```

You can probably already anticipate the result of compiling this version. That's right—the error message (as per your anticipation) is as follows:

```
Error:    'add_info' is not a member of 'retrieve' in function
          main().
```

This is good. We have successfully encapsulated the add function as well.

21.5   REVIEW

Object-oriented programs are powerful and efficient, at the cost of perhaps being a little more difficult to design. But if you follow the simple methodology outlined in Part 3 of this book, and utilize the tools that C++ makes available, you will be able to design your own set of classes that can be utilized to build other classes.

And so the power of object-oriented analysis and design should now be apparent to you, and you should feel comfortable and capable of implementing, modifying, and expanding your very own system.

Some Handy Classes

Designing Classes

22.1 INTRODUCTION

In this chapter and Part 4 of the book, we will design some very simple classes that you may reuse and customize, if necessary. Each step of the design process will be explained. The reuse of code will be illustrated, as existing classes will be used to derive new ones.

22.2 DESIGNING A LIBRARY OF CLASSES

A set of classes will be designed and implemented that will perform the following functions:

1. Create a text window. A text window is a rectangular area on the PC which is divided into cells, each cell consisting of a character and an attribute. The character is displayed in ASCII format, while the attribute specifies how that character will be displayed (background and foreground color, intensity, blink on or off, and so on). Text can be manipulated in a variety of ways in the active text window.

2. Paint the window. A numeric value will specify the color.

3. Specify foreground color, or the color in which the ASCII characters will display.

4. Write text at specified coordinates inside the window.

5. Have the text blink on and off.

The first two classes will be developed in this chapter. The remaining classes will be developed in the next chapter. Each will be developed in sequence, and moved to a separate file called `classes.h` after it has been tested and debugged. This file will be `#included` in various programs that will require using their functionality.

22.3   THE BASE AND DERIVED CLASSES

Since all classes deal with a text window, the base class will be used to create this. All subsequent classes will be derived from this class. Public derivation will be utilized. You may use this base class and derive your own set, to implement functions customized to your needs. For example, you may use this window to output help text for a program, utilize it as a little electronic notepad to jot down notes, send your program's output to it, pop up other windows inside this window, and so on.

22.4   CREATING A WINDOW

The name of the base class which will create a text window will be `make_window`. In order to create a window, you need two sets of coordinates which will identify top left corner (top row, starting column) and bottom right corner (bottom row, ending column). Since a class is a collection of data, and functions which will manipulate this data, a function is also required. This function will be called display(). A class should be designed in such a way that it offers as much flexibility as possible. When a window is created, it is possible that the coordinates may be specified. If no coordinates are specified, then it means that the programmer is leaving the size of the window up to the good faith of the class designer, who, hopefully, wrote code to implement a window using default coordinates. The class `make_window` will take this possibility into consideration, and overload the function `display()` to take four parameters or none. If four arguments are sent to this function, then it implies that coordinates have been specified. If no arguments are sent, then the window will be created using default parameters.

The default parameters in `make_window` are row 5, column 12 and row 20, column 70. You may customize this class and specify different values, if necessary.

Here's the code for `make_window`:

```
class make_window
     {
     int x;    // left corner
     int y;    // top row
     int a;    // right corner
     int b;    // bottom row
     public:
     void display(void);
```

```
        void display(int x1, int y1, int a1, int b1);
        };
```

As you can see, the function `display()` is overloaded. The compiler will know which version to call based on the type of parameters sent to this function.

The implementation for the two functions follows:

```
// This function draws a window at the default coordinates, since
// none are specified

void make_window::display(void)
{
        int i;

        // set default coordinates, if none exist
        x = 12;
        y = 5;
        a = 70;
        b = 20;

        window(x, y, a, b);     // draw window at default coordinates

        gotoxy(x, y);           // position cursor at top left
        clrscr();                // clear screen
}


// This function draws a window at the specified coordinates

void make_window::display(int x1, int y1, int a1, int b1)
{
        int i;

        x = x1;
        y = y1;
        a = a1;
        b = b1;

        window(x, y, a, b); // draw window with given coordinates
        gotoxy(x,y);        // position cursor at top left
        clrscr();            // clear to bottom of text window
}
```

The functions `window()`, `gotoxy()`, and `clrscr()` are all library routines that are grouped together in `conio.h` file, which is part of the standard libraries. There are a host of other functions that you may use to perform a variety of tasks. Refer to your compiler's reference manual for a description of the ones available with your system. Please note that the functions `window()`, `gotoxy()`, and `clrscr()` work with IBM PCs and compatibles only.

`gotoxy(x, y)` positions the cursor within the current text window at the specified coordinates. `clrscr()` clears the current window, and positions the cursor at row 1, column 1. The call to `gotoxy()` is unnecessary, since the cursor will be positioned automatically via `clrscr()`, but it has been included to illustrate its use, for those times when `clrscr()` is not called.

Now all that is needed is the code for `main()`. Here's the program, all in one place:

```
C:> type test22_1.cpp

// test22_1.cpp
// make_window draws a window at the specified or default //
coordinates
// and clears it

class make_window
    {
    int x;     // left corner
    int y;     // top row
    int a;     // right corner
    int b;     // bottom row
    public:
    void display(void);
    void display(int x1, int y1, int a1, int b1);
    };

#include <conio.h>

main(void)
{
    make_window object_1;
    object_1.display();
}
// This function draws a window at the default coordintes,
// since none are specified
void make_window::display(void)
{
    int i;

    // set default coordinates, if none exist
    x = 12;
    y = 5;
    a = 70;
    b = 20;
```

```
    window(x, y, a, b);      // draw window at default coordinates

    gotoxy(x, y);            // position cursor at top left
    clrscr();      // clear screen
}


// This function draws a window at the specified coordinates
void make_window::display(int x1, int y1, int a1, int b1)
{
    int i;

    x = x1;
    y = y1;
    a = a1;
    b = b1;

    window(x, y, a, b); // draw window with given coordinates
    gotoxy(x,y);            // position cursor at top left
    clrscr();        // clear to bottom of text window
}
```

main() is only two lines long. An object of type make_windows is created, and the window is created via display(). Notice that the window is created using default coordinates, void make_window::display(void) is called, and a text window is created where the top left corner is row 5, column 12, and bottom right corner is row 20, column 70.

We will modify test22_1.cpp by moving the class declaration and implementation to a separate header file called classes.h, and #including that file. Here's the modified version:

```
C:> type test22_2.cpp

// test22_2.cpp
// This program illustrates how to #include a header file, which
// contains a library of classes, and use one of the classes
// defined.

#include <conio.h>
#include "classes.h"      // contains some class definitions

main(void)
{
    make_window object_1;

    // draw a window at the default coordintes
    object_1.display();
}
```

This program produces the same output as test22_1.cpp.

Let's specify the coordinates for the window this time. Here's the modified version of the program:

```
C:> type test22_3.cpp

// test22_3.cpp
// This program illustrates how to #include a header file, which
// contains a library of classes, and use one of the classes //
defined.

#include <conio.h>
#include "classes.h"      // contains some class definitions

main(void)
{
    make_window object_1;

    // draw a window at specified coordinates
    // Top row 1, column 3, bottom row 22, column 75
    object_1.display(1, 3, 22, 75);
}
```

Compiling and running this program creates a window at the specified coordinates. Note that if you run this program on your PC, you may not see any output. This is because the text window has not been colored yet, and blends in with the remainder of your console background. We will now develop a class that will color this window.

22.5   PAINTING A WINDOW

The class color_window will be created. This class will be publicly derived from make_window. This will result in its inheriting the protected and public members of make_window, with no change in their access privileges. The data and function that will uniquely identify color_window from make_window will be color, an integer value, and color_it(). The function color_it() will be overloaded so as to provide three implementations for it. The first implementation will take no parameters. This will result in a window being created using the default coordinates, and painted a default color; we have chosen blue. The second implementation will take one integer argument, which will specify the color. The window will continue to be created using the default values. The third implementation will take five arguments, which will specify the position of the window, and the color that it is to be painted. You may edit this class to create further implementations of color_it(), or to change the current default settings. The code and implementation of make_window remains unchanged. Here's the code, presented in logical segments, for your convenience:

```
C:> type test22_4.cpp

// test22_4.cpp
// This program illustrates how a class can be used to draw a
// window at the specified or default coordinates, and then color
// it.
// The classes are not #included in a header file.

// make_window draws a window at the specified or default
// coordinates,
// and clears that portion of the screen
class make_window
    {
    protected:
    int x;    // left corner
    int y;    // top row
    int a;    // right corner
    int b;    // bottom row
    public:
    void display(void);
    void display(int x1, int y1, int a1, int b1);
    };
```

The code for make_window is untouched. What this implies for you as a programmer is that you don't have to debug it again; it worked the first time; it's going to work again.

```
class color_window: public make_window
    {
    int color;        // numeric value of color
    public:
    void color_it(void);
    void color_it(int color);
    void color_it(int x1, int y1, int a1, int b1, int color);
    };
```

The function color_it() is overloaded; it contains three implementations, as explained previously. The include file conio.h contains symbolic names for the colors available. Each color can also be specified by a numeric value. If you are working with a monochrome monitor, the colors obviously will not be visible, but variations such as underscores, highlights, reverse video, and shading will be visible. The following colors are available as background and foreground colors:

Symbolic Name	Numeric Value
BLACK	0
BLUE	1
GREEN	2
CYAN	3
RED	4
MAGENTA	5
BROWN	6
LIGHTGRAY	7

The following colors are available for foreground only:

Symbolic Name	Numeric Value
DARKGRAY	8
LIGHTBLUE	9
LIGHTGREEN	10
LIGHTCYAN	11
LIGHTRED	12
LIGHTMAGENTA	13
YELLOW	14
WHITE	15
BLINK	128

The symbolic constant BLINK can be added (e.g., "BLACK + BLINK") to have the character blink on and off. Let's continue with the code for main().

```
#include <conio.h>

main(void)
{
    color_window object_1;

    object_1.color_it();
}
```

main() is once again only two lines long. This time an object of type color_window is created, and color_it() is called. Notice that we don't create the window via display(), although we could have. Since color_window inherits all public members of make_window, it inherits this function as well. The implementation of the classes follows:

```
// This function draws a window at the default coordinates
void make_window::display(void)
{
    int i;

    // set default coordinates
    x = 12;
    y = 5;
```

```
    a = 70;
    b = 20;

    window(x, y, a, b); // draw window
}


// This function draws a window at the specified coordinates
void make_window::display(int x1, int y1, int a1, int b1)
{
    int i;

    x = x1;
    y = y1;
    a = a1;
    b = b1;

    window(x, y, a, b); // draw window with given coordinates
}
```

The implementation of the functions for make_window remains untouched.
Following are the three implementations for color_it():

```
// This function draws a window at the default coordinates,
// and colors it blue
void color_window::color_it(void)
{
    int i, j;
    // set default setting for window
    display();
    color = 1;
    j = 5;

    while (j < 20)
        {
        for (i = 12; i <= 70; i++)
            {
            textbackground(color);
            cprintf(" ");
            }
        j++;
        }
}
```

Inside color_it, a call to display() creates the text window using default
coordinates. color is set to 1, which is the numeric representation of the color
BLUE. The functions textbackground() and cprintf() are used to paint the

text window. j is set to 5, which is the starting row of the window. 20 rows, columns 12 through 70, are painted with the background color. The function `textbackground()` selects the new text background color. `cprintf()` writes formatted output to the screen, a blank " " does the job. Following are the remaining two implementations of `color_it()`:

```
// This function draws a window at the default coordinates
// It colors the window with the specified color
void color_window::color_it(int color)
{
      int i, j;

      // set default setting of window
      display();

      j = 5;
      // color it in specified color
      while (j < 20)
          {
          for (i = 12; i<= 70; i++)
              {
              textbackground(color);
              cprintf(" ");
              }
          j++;
          }
}
```

Here you see that the value of `color` is sent as an argument; it is specified. The next implementation requires specification of coordinates and `color`:

```
// This function draws the window at the specified coordinates
// It colors the window with the specified color
void color_window::color_it(int x1, int y1, int a1, int b1,
                                     int color)
{
      int i, j;

      display(x1, y1, a1, b1);

      while (y1 < b1)
          {
          for (i = x1; i <= a1; i++)
              {
              textbackground(color);
              cprintf(" ");
```

```
            }
      y1++;
      }
}
```

Notice that the second implementation of display() is used to create the text window. You should now be able to understand how existing code can be reused inside a derived class, and how it helps speed up development time, since it does not have to be retested. Remember, the idea is to use one class as a building block for another, to create a hierarchy of classes, and to design the hierarchy in such a way that the creation of new objects is facilitated for expected future projects. So far, we have been successful in achieving this end.

Compiling and running this program results in a window being created at the default coordinates. This window is painted blue. The prior program will now be modified to move the class declarations and implementation inside classes.h. Here's the result:

```
C:> type test22_5.cpp

// test22_5.cpp
// This program illustrates how a class can be used to draw a
// window at default coordinates, and then colored.
// The classes are #included in a header file.

#include <conio.h>
#include "classes.h"      // contains some class definitions

main(void)
{
    color_window object_1;

    // draw window at default coordinates and
    // color it with the default color.
    object_1.color_it();
}
```

This program produces the same output as the prior program.

Suppose color_it() is called with a list of arguments for which there is no implementation. Here's the code:

```
C:> type test22_6.cpp

// test22_6.cpp
// This program illustrates how a class can be used to draw
// a window at default coordinates, and then colored.
// The classes are #included in a header file.
```

```
#include <conio.h>
#include "classes.h"      // contains some class definitions

main(void)
{
     color_window object_1;

     // draw window at specified coordinates and
     // color it with the default color.

     object_1.color_it(20, 1, 70, 24);
}
```

Compiling this version results in the following error message:

```
Error:    Could not find a match for 'color_window::color_it(int,
          int, int, int) in function main().
```

Of course, nothing is stopping you from creating and adding your own implementation.

The original program will be modified one more time, in which all parameters will be specified. Here's the code:

```
C:> type test22_7.cpp


// test22_7.cpp
// This program illustrates how a class can be used to draw a //
window at default coordinates, and then colored.
// The classes are #included in a header file.

#include <conio.h>
#include "classes.h"      // contains some class definitions

main(void)
{
     color_window object_1;

     // draw window at specified coordinates and
     // color it with a specified color.

     object_1.color_it(1, 20 , 70, 24, 3);
}
```

Compiling and running this program results in a window starting at row 20, column 1 through row 24, column 70. This window is painted cyan (numeric value of 3).

22.6   REVIEW

In this chapter, we created a base class, and derived a class from it. The advantages of code reuse and ease of maintenance of existing classes was illustrated along the way.

Extending Classes

23.1 INTRODUCTION

In this chapter, we will build upon the classes designed in the prior chapter, and add a few new ones which will perform the following functions:

1. Specify a default foreground color, and display text in the window.

2. Write text to the window in a specified color, instead of the default.

3. Make the text blink on and off.

23.2 HEADER FILE CONTAINING LIBRARY OF CLASSES

For your convenience, the header file `classes.h`, developed in the prior chapter, is now redisplayed. The three classes that will be developed in this chapter will also be incorporated in this header file.

```
C:> type classes.h

// classes.h
// This file contains a library of classes.
// It can be customized, as necessary.
// New classes can be derived, or created, from existing ones.

// make_window draws a window at the specified or default
// coordinates,
// and clears that portion of the screen
```

```
class make_window
    {
    protected:
    int x;      // left corner
    int y;      // top row
    int a;      // right corner
    int b;      // bottom row
    public:
    void display(void);
    void display(int x1, int y1, int a1, int b1);
    };

class color_window: public make_window
    {
    protected:
    int color;      // numeric value of color
    public:
    void color_it(void);
    void color_it(int color);
    void color_it(int x1, int y1, int a1, int b1, int color);
    };


// This function draws a window at the default coordinates
void make_window::display(void)
{
    int i;

    // set default coordinates
    x = 12;
    y = 5;
    a = 70;
    b = 20;

    window(x, y, a, b); // draw window
}

// This function draws a window at the specified coordinates
void make_window::display(int x1, int y1, int a1, int b1)
{
    int i;

    x = x1;
    y = y1;
    a = a1;
    b = b1;
```

```
        window(x, y, a, b); // draw window with given coordinates
}


// This function draws and colors a window at the default
// coordinates,
// and with the default color of blue
void color_window::color_it(void)
{
        int i, j;
        // set default setting for window
        display();
        color = 1;
        j = 5;

        while (j < 20)
          {
          for (i = 12; i <= 70; i++)
                {
                textbackground(color);
                cprintf(" ");
                }
          j++;
          }
}


// This function draws a window at the default coordinates
// It colors the window with the specified color
void color_window::color_it(int color)
{
        int i, j;

        // set default setting of window
        display();

        j = 5;
        // color it in specified color
        while (j < 20)
          {
          for (i = 12; i<= 70; i++)
                {
                textbackground(color);
                cprintf(" ");
                }
          j++;
          }
}
```

```
// This function draws the window at the specified coordinates
// It colors the window with the specified color
void color_window::color_it(int x1, int y1, int a1, int b1, int
color)
{
    int i, j;

    display(x1, y1, a1, b1);

    while (y1 < b1)
        {
        for (i = x1; i <= a1; i++)
            {
            textbackground(color);
            cprintf(" ");
            }
        y1++;
        }
}
```

23.3   SPECIFYING FOREGROUND COLOR

A new class called color will be designed that will specify a default foreground color of cyan. This class will be publicly derived from color_window, which was in turn derived from the class make_window. The class make_window created a text window at the default or specified coordinates. color_window painted it in the default or specified color. Thus, the new class color will inherit all of these functions from the prior classes.

Three functions will be implemented in this class. Their function names will be overloaded so as to provide flexibility to the program. One function will draw a window at the default coordinates and specify default background color of blue, and foreground color of cyan, and display a "Hello" at Row 2, column 2. The next will allow the specification of the foreground color. All other specifications will remain the same. The last function will allow for the specification of coordinates of the window, background and foreground colors.

You may edit the implementation of this class per your own needs. You may change the default settings, the text that is displayed, etc. Here's the class declaration:

```
class color:public color_window
    {
    protected:
    int color_fg;      // numeric value of foreground color
    public:
    void color_f(void);
```

```
        void color_f(int color);
        void color_f(int x1, int y1, int a1, int b1, int color_a,
              int color_b);
        };
```

and here's the implementation of the three functions:

```
// This function draws a window at the default coordinates.
// It colors the window's background and foreground with the
// default colors.

void color::color_f(void)
{
    // set background color
    color_it();

    // set foreground color to cyan
    textcolor(3);
}

// This function draws a window at the default coordinates
// It colors the window with the default color of blue
// It colors the foreground in the specified color

void color::color_f(int color_fg)
{
    int color = 1;

    // set background to default color of blue
    color_it(color);
    // set foreground to specified color
    textcolor(color_fg);
    // display some text, to see how it looks
    gotoxy(2, 2);
    cprintf ("Hello");
}

// This function draws the window at the specified coordinates
// It colors the foreground and background window with the
// specified color

void color::color_f(int x1, int y1, int a1, int b1,
                                int color_1, int color_2)
{
    // draw window at specified coordinates
    // color background as indicated
```

```
        color_it(x1, y1, a1, b1, color_1);

        // color foreground and display some text
        textcolor(color_2);
        gotoxy(2, 2); // position cursor
        cprintf("Hello");
    }
```

And now, here's one program that illustrates the use of the class just developed:

```
C:> type test23_1.cpp

// test23_1.cpp

// This program illustrates how to set the foreground color
// of a window via a class.
// The classes are #included in a header file.

#include <conio.h>
#include "classes.h"      // contains some class definitions

main(void)
{
    color object_1;

    // draw window at specified coordinates and
    // color the background and foreground with the
    // default colors

    object_1.color_f();
}
```

Running and executing this program produces no text output. This is because the function color::color_f() does not use any console I/O (i.e., cprintf()) to display the result of the default settings. Results will be obvious to the eye if an output statement is added inside main(), like this:

```
C:> type test23_2.cpp

// test23_2.cpp
// This program illustrates how to set the foreground color
// of a window via a class.
// The classes are #included in a header file.

#include <conio.h>
```

```
#include "classes.h"       // contains some class definitions

main(void)
{
    color object_1;

    // draw window at specified coordinates and
    // color the background and foreground with the
    // default colors

    object_1.color_f();
    gotoxy(2,2);
    cprintf (" Hello ");
}
```

The function gotoxy() sets the cursor at row 2, column 2 in the current text window. cprintf() displays "Hello" at that location. As you can see, in this program, the position and contents of the text displayed inside the window are not hard-coded inside the class. The only time you would wish to hard code some values inside a class would be if you expect this text to be displayed frequently inside your program, or consistently under a certain set of conditions. You may edit this class, or create a new one, to display default text, if none is sent to it as a parameter.

test23_3.cpp displays text inside the window, in a color specified explicitly. Here's the code:

```
C:> type test23_3.cpp

// test23_3.cpp
// This program illustrates how to set the foreground color
// of a window via a class.
// The classes are #included in a header file.

#include <conio.h>
#include "classes.h"       // contains some class definitions

main(void)
{
    color object_1;

    // draw window at specified coordinates and
    // color the background and foreground with
    // a specified color

    object_1.color_f(14);
    gotoxy(2,2);
```

```
        cprintf (" Hello ");
}
```

Compiling and running this program results in "Hello" being output at row 2, column 2, in the color yellow, on a background window which is blue.

In the next program, the window coordinates are specified along with the background and foreground colors. The display of the text in this program is coded right into the class itself. Here's the code:

```
C:> type test23_4.cpp


// test23_4.cpp
// This program illustrates how to set the window size,
// background and foreground colors
// of a window via a class.
// The classes are #included in a header file.

#include <conio.h>
#include "classes.h"      // contains some class definitions

main(void)
{
    color object_1;

    // draw window at specified coordinates and
    // color the background and foreground with the
    // specified colors

    object_1.color_f(1, 20, 70, 24, 3, 5);
}
```

Compiling and running this program results in the creation of a window whose top right corner is row 20, column 1, and bottom left corner is row 24, column 70. The window is painted cyan. Hello displays at row 2, column 2 inside the text window in magenta.

23.4   BLINKING FOREGROUND COLORS

The numerical value of 128 can be added to any specified foreground color to make it blink. This particular feature can be incorporated within the code presented in the prior programs, or a new set of classes can be built. We will illustrate each possibility.

A class called colorblink will be created, which will contain all of the functionality of the class color, in addition to having the foreground characters blink. Here's the code for the class:

```
class colorblink:public color_window
     {
     protected:
     int color_fg;  // numeric value of foreground color
     public:
     void color_fb(void);
     void color_fb(int color);
     void color_fb(int x1, int y1, int a1, int b1, int color_a,

             int color_b);
     };
```

And here's the implementation:

```
// This function draws a window at the default coordinates
// It colors the window's background and foreground with the
// default colors of blue and cyan
// The foreground text blinks.

void color::color_fb(void)
{
     // set background color
     color_it();

     // set foreground color to cyan
     // and make it blink
     textcolor(3 + 128);
}

// This function draws a window at the default coordinates
// It colors the window with the default color of blue
// It colors the foreground in the specified color
// and makes it blink
void color::color_fb(int color_fg)
{
     int color = 1;

     // set background to default color of blue
     color_it(color);
     // set foreground to specified color
     textcolor(color_fg + 128);
     // display some text, to see how it looks
     gotoxy(2, 2);
     cprintf ("Hello");
}
```

```
// This function draws the window at the specified coordinates
// It colors the foreground and background window with the
// specified color
void color::color_fb(int x1, int y1, int a1, int b1,
                                   int color_1, int color_2)
{
    // draw window at specified coordinates
    // color background as indicated
    color_it(x1, y1, a1, b1, color_1);

    // color foreground and display some text
    textcolor(color_2 + 128);
    gotoxy(2, 2); // position cursor
    cprintf("Hello");
}
```

Here's a program that uses the original class color to blink the text in the window:

```
C:> type test23_5.cpp

// test23_5.cpp
// This program illustrates how to set the foreground color
// of a window via a class.
// The classes are #included in a header file.

#include <conio.h>
#include "classes.h"      // contains some class definitions

main(void)
{
    color object_1;

    // draw window at specified coordinates and
    // color the background and foreground with
    // a specified color
    // Make the text output blink

    object_1.color_f(14 + 128);
    gotoxy(2,2);
    cprintf (" Hello ");
}
```

Notice that 128 is added to the foreground color:

```
    object_2.color_f(14 + 128);
```

This is all that is required to make the text blink.
Here's an example of a program that uses the class colorblink.

```
C:> type test23_6.cpp

// test23_6.cpp
// This program illustrates how to set the window size,
// background and foreground colors
// of a window via a class.
// The classes are #included in a header file.

#include <conio.h>
#include "classes.h"      // contains some class definitions

main(void)
{
    colorblink object_1;

    // draw window at specified coordinates and
    // color the background and foreground with the
    // specified colors
    // The blinking characters are incorporated inside the class

    // implementation

    object_1.color_fb(1, 20, 70, 24, 3, 5);
}
```

Compiling and running this program results in a window being drawn at the specified coordinates, painted cyan, and the letters "Hello" blinking in row 2, column 2, in magenta.

23.5   REVIEW

In this chapter, a few new classes were derived from the classes developed in Chap. 22. This chapter was intended to help you understand how new classes can be developed from existing ones, and existing classes can be modified to suit your needs. Undoubtedly, by now, you must have a few ideas of your own of some common classes that you would like to develop, build a library, and store into a header file for future use in all subsequent projects.

I/O Class Libraries in C++

24.1 INTRODUCTION

In this chapter, we will describe a few handy classes that perform I/O on files. These classes are prewritten for you, and they can be utilized simply by incorporating the header files which contain them in your program.

24.2 STREAMS

In C, as you are aware, input and output are accomplished through the use of prewritten library functions. One of the systems defined for both C and C++ is the *buffered file system* (also called *high-level* or *formatted*). This system is defined by the ANSI C standard, and is designed to work with a variety of devices. Each device is converted into a logical device, and is called a *stream*. Streams form the common interface between the program, the device, and the user.

24.3 FILES

In the buffered file system, a *file* can be a disk file, or any other kind of peripheral. A stream becomes associated with a file upon successful implementation of an open operation. A stream becomes disassociated with a file upon a close operation, or termination of your program. The structure of files can vary with devices, but streams always behave the same.

In C and C++, files are considered nothing more than streams of bytes; the programmer need concern himself or herself only with streams.

24.4   I/O IN C++

All I/O functions available in C are supported by C++ as well. However, as we have seen consistently throughout this book, in addition to what C provides, C++ adds a few unique features of its own. C++ has its own I/O system, and this is what we will discuss in the remainder of the chapter.

24.5   PREDEFINED STREAMS

The following C++ streams are opened automatically as a program begins execution:

1. cin—This is the standard input stream.

2. cout—This is the standard output stream.

3. cerr—This is the standard error stream; it is unbuffered.

4. clog—This is also a standard error stream; it is buffered.

   C++ standard streams are linked to the console by default. However, they can be redirected to other files or devices as necessary.

   The following classes exist to allow a programmer to relate to streams; they exist in the header file `iostream.h`:

1. streambuf—This class contains the basic functions that allow buffering of data. It allocates a buffer for the file, and keeps track of the current position in the buffer.

2. istream—This class creates an input stream, and contains the actual operations that perform I/O.

3. ostream—This class creates an output stream, and also contains the actual operations that perform I/O.

   The `cin` stream is of type `istream`. The `cout` stream is of type `ostream`. `cerr` is also of type `ostream`.

   The I/O streams in C++ can be used to support output of, or input to, user-defined objects, such as structures and classes, in addition to the usual predefined types, like char, int, float, etc. This is a feature which is not available in C. The << operator is overloaded to put to or insert characters to a stream, while the >> operator is overloaded to get from, or extract characters from a stream. We will discuss the << operator first.

24.6   THE << OPERATOR

You have encountered this operator throughout this book. What you may have noticed is that contrary to the usual `printf()` statement, which requires the specification of the data type that is being output, if it is to function correctly:

```
printf ("This is an_int %d \n", an_int);
```

no such specification is required when outputting a stream via `cout`:

```
cout << "This is an_int " << an_int << "\n";
```

If the variable `an_int` was a `float`, a `char`, or any other data type, the output of the prior statement would still be correct, without having to modify it in any way. This is true because this operator has already been overloaded in the header file `iostream.h` to operate correctly on any of the built-in data types. In order to output the contents of user-defined types, you may further overload this operator to create your own implementation. For example, if a class is declared as follows:

```
class one
    {
    int a;
    char b;
    float c;
    public:
    one (int x, char y, float z)
        {
        a = x;
        b = y;
        c = z;
        }
    };
```

and defined in `main()` like this:

```
main(void)
{
    one object_one(10, 'a', 20.5), object_two(25, 'b', 30.5);
}
```

then the contents of each class defined can be output inside main() as follows:

```
cout << "object_one: " << object_one << "\n"
     << "object_two: " << object_two << "\n";
```

given that the << operator is overloaded to output the contents of your class, as follows:

```
ostream& operator<<(ostream& stream, one object)
{
    stream << object.a << " ,";
    stream << object.b << " ,";
    stream << object.c << " \n";
```

```
        return stream;
}
```

It would be necessary for this operator to be declared as a friend of the class one, so that it can access its private members *a, b,* and *c.* The class definition would be modified as follows:

```
class one
    {
    int a;
    char b;
    float c;
    public:
    one (int x, char y, float z)
        {
        a = x;
        b = y;
        c = z;
        }
    friend ostream& operator<<(ostream& stream, one object);
    };
```

Take a moment to understand the overloaded operator function. Notice that it returns a *reference* to an object of type ostream. Recall that a reference is used when the actual variable, instead of a copy of it, is to be utilized. A reference is required so that several << operators may be strung together. Failure to do so would result in an error. The function itself takes two parameters; the first is another reference to the stream that occurs on the left side of the << operator, and the second is an object of the type of class that is to be output. Inside the function, stream is returned. Here's the complete program, and its output:

```
C:> type test24_1.cpp

// test24_1.cpp          4/10/91  11:05 pm

#include<iostream.h>     // necessary forI/O

class one
    {
    int a;
    char b;
    float c;
    public:
    one (int x, char y, float z)
```

```
            {
                a = x;
                b = y;
                c = z;
            }
        friend ostream& operator<<(ostream& stream, one object);
        };

ostream& operator<<(ostream& stream, one object)
{
        stream << object.a << " ,";
        stream << object.b << " ,";
        stream << object.c << " \n";
        return stream;
}


main(void)
{
        one object_one(10, 'a', 20.5), object_two(25, 'b', 30.5);

        cout << "object_one: " << object_one << "\n"
            << "object_two: " << object_two << "\n";
}
```

Compiling and running this program gives the following output:

```
object_one: 10, a, 20.5
object_two: 25, b, 30.5
```

24.7   THE OUTPUT FUNCTIONS put() AND flush()

There are two output functions that are members of the ostream class: *put()* and *flush()*. A description of each follows:

1. put() outputs a single character to the specified device. It is accessed as follows:

    ```
    cout.put(x);
    ```

    where x is predeclared as a character. cout is an object of the ostream class. Since put() is a member function, this is the standard way of accessing it.

2. flush() clears the output buffer of anything that may be contained in it. It is accessed as follows:

```
        cout.flush();
```

flush() is automatically called when an ostream object is destroyed, hence there is often no need to place an explicit call to it.

Here's a short program that illustrates their use:

```
C:> type test24_2.cpp

// test24_2.cpp           04/13/91 8:45 pm

#include <iostream.h>

main(void)
{
        char x = 'X';

        cout.put(x);
        cout.flush();
}
```

Compiling and executing this program produces the output:

```
X
```

on the terminal.

24.8   THE >> OPERATOR

The >> operator is the counterpart of the << operator. It reads in a string until the first occurrence of white space. It offers the same flexibility as the << operator just discussed. A variable can be input to a stream like this:

```
        int an_int;
        cin >> an_int;
        cout << "an_int is " << an_int;
```

The statement above reads in user input and stores it in the predefined variable an_int, which is an integer. The variable entered is output via the cout statement. The << is also overloaded for each supported data type.

24.9   THE INPUT FUNCTION get()

The get() function is a member of the istream class. This function is designed to retrieve a complete string of input, including white spaces. It performs no conversions; it simply takes what it finds and puts it in the specified variable. This function has three implementations; its most general prototype looks like this:

```
get(char *var, int len, char terminator);
```

where var is a character string, len is the expected maximum length of the input string, and the terminator is the character that will terminate output. The carriage return ('\n') is the default terminator.

24.10   FORMATTED OUTPUT

C++ allows you to format output, much like a printf() statement, in 2 ways:

1. By setting and unsetting flags preset in the ios class, which is available by #including <iostream.h>.
2. By using special functions which are declared and defined in the header file <iomanip.h>.

First, a description of the use of flags available in ios follows.

Flags in the ios class can be set via the setf() function. This function can be used to format output like this:

```
cout.setf(ios::flag);
```

where ios is the class inside which flag is defined. Execution of the above statement will turn on the flag specified. One or more flags can be or'ed to get the desired result. (Please note that setf() can be used to format input as well; the name of the stream that it would be used with would be cin, instead of cout.)

A description of some of the more commonly used flags available for controlling output follows:

Flag	Description
left	Left justifies
right	Right justifies
dec	Output in decimal
oct	Output in octal
hex	Output in hexadecimal
showpoint	Display decimal point and trailing 0's for floating point numbers
showpos	Displays a leading + sign before positive numbers
uppercase	Display characters in uppercase
scientific	Display floating point numbers in scientific notation
fixed	Display floating point numbers in regular notation

Now, a description of some of the functions available in `<iomanip.h>`:

Function	Description
dec	Formats numeric data in decimal
ends	Output null in the position indicated
hex	Output numeric data in hexadecimal
oct	Output numeric data in octal
setfill(int num)	Set the fill character to num
setprecision(int num)	Set precision to num
setw(int num)	Set field width to num

And now, a short program that outputs format, using the methods just described.

```
C:> type test24_3.cpp

// test24_3.cpp          04/13/91 8:50 pm

#include <iostream.h>
#include <iomanip.h>

main(void)
{
    // right justify and set field width to 25
    cout.setf(ios::right);
    cout << setw(25) << "Make it right!\n";

    // unset flag set previously to right justify
    cout.unsetf(ios::right);
    cout << "Now make it left. \n";

    // display in scientifc notation
    // display leading plus sign
    float b = 40.009876;
    cout.setf(ios::scientific | ios::showpos);
    cout << "40.009876 in scientific notation is " << b << "\n";


    // display in octal
    int c = 50;
    cout.setf(ios::oct);
    cout << "50 in octal is " << c << "\n";

    // set precision, without resetting flags
    cout << setprecision(3) << 20.1234 << "\n";

    // unset scientific notation and setpos flag
```

```
    cout.unsetf(ios::scientific | ios::showpos);
    cout << setprecision(3) << 20.1234 << "\n";

    // flush input buffer
    cout.flush();
}
```

Compiling and running this program gives the following output:

```
        Make it right!
Now make it left
40.009876 in scientific notation is +4000988e+01
50 in octal is 62
+2.012e+01
20.123
```

The output should be self-explanatory.
The following rules are common to all of the above functions:

1. Output is right-justified.

2. If the specified width is too small, it will be automatically expanded to accommodate the additional characters.

24.11   FILE I/O STREAMS

The following functions are generally required to manipulate a file:

1. Open a file

2. Read and write to a text file

3. Read and write binary data to a file

4. Detect EOF

5. Close a file

Each will be discussed. But first, we need to talk some more about streams.

In C++, just like C, a file is linked to a stream when it is opened, accessed, read or written to, and closed. After a file is opened, it must be attached to a stream. A file can be attached to the following three streams:

1. ifstream—when a file is opened for input

2. ofstream—when a file is opened for output

3. fstream—when a file is opened for both input and output

We will begin with the open() function.

24.12   OPENING A FILE

In C, a file is opened and attached to a stream as follows:

```
#include <stdio.h>

FILE *stream_a;      /* stream pointer to FILE */

main(void)
{
    stream_a = fopen("file1", "r"); /* open file1 for reading */

    if (stream_a)
    {
        printf ("Successful open!! \n");
    }
    else
    {
        printf ("Unsuccessful open!! \n");
    }
}
```

Compiling and running the above program will result in the statement

```
Successful open!!
```

being output upon a successful open of the file called file1, or if a non-null
pointer is returned by fopen(). Otherwise, the statement

```
Unsuccessful open!!
```

will be output.

As you can see, stream_a is a stream pointer to FILE. FILE is a structure
which is defined in stdio.h, and it contains I/O routines that store information about a file stream upon opening, reading, or writing of a file.

In C++, the name attached to the particular stream itself contains the
function being accessed. The prototype of the open() function looks like this:

```
stream_name.open(char *file_name, mode, access)
```

stream_name is the name attached to the type of stream being accessed.

file_name is a character string which contains the file name; it can contain
the path specification.

mode can be one of the following values:

0   Input only
1   Output only
2   Append only

access **can be one of the following:**

0	Open access to normal file, this is the default
1	Read-only
2	Hidden file
3	System file

The following program illustrates the use of open() in a C++ program:

```
C:> type test24_4.cpp

// test24_4.cpp          04/13/91 12:17 pm

#include <iostream.h>    // necessary for I/O
#include <fstream.h>     // necessary for file I/O

main(void)
{
    ifstream stream_a;  // attach stream to ifstream

    stream_a.open("file1", 0, 0); // open file1 for reading

    if (stream_a)  // stream_a is not zero
    {
        cout << "Successful open!! \n";
    }
    else
    {
        cout << "Unsuccessful open!! \n";
    }
}
```

Compiling this program will result in one or the other of the statements being output, depending on the condition of the open. Take a moment to note a few salient features of this program. First, a stream is attached to ifstream, implying that an input stream will be opened. Next, the file itself is opened by attaching the name of the stream to the function:

```
    stream_a.open("file1", 0, 0);
```

The file is opened in read mode, with open access. A nonzero value is returned to the stream upon a successful open; a zero is returned if the open() fails.

The above program may be modified to open the file like this:

```
C:> type test24_5.cpp
```

```
// test24_5.cpp          04/13/91 12:34 am

#include <iostream.h>     // necessary for I/O
#include <fstream.h>      // necessary for file I/O

main(void)
{
    ifstream stream_a("file1");

    if (stream_a)  // stream_a is not zero
    {
        cout << "Successful open!! \n";
    }
    else
    {
        cout << "Unsuccessful open!! \n";
    }
}
```

This is because the stream classes ifstream, ofstream, and fstream all contain constructor functions which automatically open the file for you. This is a kind of short-cut method.

24.13 READING AND WRITING TEXT FILES

C++ allows you to read from and write to files simply by applying the << and >> operators to the stream opened. Here is a short program that writes to a file:

```
C:> type test24_6.cpp

// test24_6.cpp          04/13/91 12:31 am

#include <iostream.h>     // necessary for I/O
#include <fstream.h>      // necessary for file I/O

main(void)
{
    ofstream stream_b("file3");

    if (stream_b)
    {       // file opened successfully
        stream_b << "Give me " << 10 << " kisses \n";
        stream_b << "Not " << 5.5 << "!!! \n";
    }
    else
```

```
    {    // file did not open successfully
        cout << "Unable to open file3 \n";
    }
}
```

Assuming that a file with the name of `file3` exists, compiling and executing this program will give no output. Obviously, this is because a file has been written to; it has not been read yet.

Let's read it using the DOS command `type`:

```
C:> type file3

Give me 10 kisses
Not 5.5!!!
```

24.14   READING AND WRITING BINARY DATA TO FILES

There are two functions available that read and write bytes of data from a file. Their prototype, description and use follows:

1. istream& get(char &var)

   The `get()` function reads a byte of data from the stream associated with the file opened, and puts the value into `var`. It returns the stream.

2. ostream& put(char var)

   The `put()` function writes a byte of data to the stream, and also returns the stream. The following short program writes a string to a file:

```
C:> type test24_7.cpp

// test24_7.cpp

#include <iostream.h>      // necessary for I/O
#include <fstream.h>       // necessary for file I/O

main(void)
{
    char *string = "This is still not the end.";

    ofstream write("file3");

    if (write)
        {    // successfuly open of file
        while (*string != <\#39>\0')
            {
            write.put(*string++);
            }
        }
```

```
        else
            {
            cout << "Unable to open file3 \n";
            }
    }
```

Once again, assuming that `file1` exists, compiling and running this program produces no visible output. Here's a short program that reads and displays what was written.

```
C:> type test24_8.cpp

// test24_8.cpp

#include <iostream.h>     // necessary for I/O
#include <fstream.h>      // necessary for file I/O

main(void)
{
    char var1;

    ifstream read("file3");

    if (read)
        {    // successfuly open of file
        while (read != '\0')
            {
            read.get(var1);
            cout << var1;
            }
        }
    else
        {
        cout << "Unable to open file3 \n";
        }
}
```

Compiling and running this program gives the following output:

```
This is still not the end.
```

Notice the statement

```
        while (read != '0')
```

The stream is set to 0 when the EOF is detected. Thus, the stream is read, one byte or character at a time, and output, until the end of file is reached.

24.15   DETECTING EOF

The end of a file can be detected via the function *eof()*. Its prototype looks as follows:

```
int eof();
```

This function returns a nonzero value when the end of file is detected. It returns a zero in all other cases. We can modify the prior program to include the eof() function:

```
C:> type tst24_9.cpp

// test24_9.cpp

#include <iostream.h>      // necessary for I/O
#include <fstream.h>       // necessary for file I/O

main(void)
{
     char var1;

     ifstream read("file3");

     if (read)
          {     // successful open of file
          while (!read.eof())
               {
               read.get(var1);
               cout << var1;
               }
          }
     else
          {
          cout << "Unable to open file3 \n";
          }

}
```

24.16   CLOSING A FILE

A file is closed via the function close(), which is linked to the stream that was associated with a file when it was opened. The prototype for the close function looks like this:

```
void close(void)
```

Note that there is no need for explicit calls to this function, since files are automatically closed upon normal termination of a program. Here's a short program that simply opens and closes a file:

```
C:> type tst24_10.cpp

// test24_10.cpp

#include <iostream.h>    // necessary for I/O
#include <fstream.h>     // necessary for file I/O

main(void)
{
     ifstream stream_a("file3");   // open file

     if (stream_a)  // stream_a is not zero
     {
         cout << "Successful open!! \n";
     }
     else
     {
         cout << "Unsuccessful open!! \n";
     }

     stream_a.close();   // close file
}
```

This program would output

```
Successful open!!
```

and then gracefully exit the program after closing the file opened.

24.17   REVIEW

In this chapter, we discussed how streams are used to accomplish I/O in C++. Streams form the common interface beween the program, the device, and the user. Here's a synopsis of the main features discussed.

- A stream becomes associated with a file when it is opened. The same stream is used to perform any subsequent I/O on that file.
- All I/O functions available in C are available in C++ as well.
- C++ complements what C has by providing its own I/O system as well.
- The following streams are opened automatically when a program starts to execute: `cin, cout, cerr, clog`.
- The following classes attach operations to streams: `streambuf, istream, ostream`.

- The << operator can be used to output contents of predefined as well as user-defined data types.

- The >> operator can be used to input to predefined or user-defined types.

- Several functions are available that allow the formatting of data.

- Files can also be read and written to using the >> and << operators.

- Several functions are available that read, write, and perform various functions on text and binary files.

Glossary of Terms

Abstract Classes. A base class which has a member that is a pure virtual function. Abstract classes can be used only as base classes that are to be inherited by subsequent classes.

Binding. The occurrence of the event in which the address of a procedure is given to the caller. See Early Binding and Late Binding as well.

C++. An object-oriented language developed by Bjarne Stroustrup in the mid-1980s, a successor of C.

Classes. A definition of an object which can contain members and access privileges of these members to specific functions or methods within the declaration.

Constructor. A method or function which automatically initializes objects when they are created. The C++ compiler calls constructors implicitly if an explicit definition is not supplied.

Data Hiding. A mechanism by which data for members declared as private is hidden from all functions except those that are declared within the class.

Destructor. A method or function used to deallocate memory that may have been allocated to objects through constructors. The C++ compiler calls destructors implicitly, if an explicit definition is not supplied.

Dynamic Binding. Late binding. The occurrence of the determination of events that are to take place at the time that a program is run. The addresses of procedures or functions are determined at run time. Late binding makes polymorphism possible.

Early Binding. The occurrence of the determination of events that are to take place at the time that a program is compiled. The addresses of procedures or functions are determined at compile/link time.

Encapsulation.   The mechanism by which data and functions that are allowed to manipulate this data are bound together within an object definition.

Extensibility.   A feature which is provided by object-oriented languages which allows the extension of existing code without knowledge (or need for) the existing source. Extension of code allows the creation of new objects from existing ones.

Free Store Objects.   Objects which are created dynamically by the operator new from the "free store" or heap. Free store is the pool of unallocated memory that is provided to a program when it is run.

Friend Functions.   A function within a class which is not a member of that class. However, it has full access to the private and protected members of that class.

Information Hiding.   See Encapsulation.

Inheritance.   The property by which one class derives all data members and function definitions from one or more other classes (except private members), without having to restate them. This allows the creation of new objects from existing ones, resulting in a logical hierarchy of objects.

Inline Functions.   Member Functions or methods which are defined within the class itself. The compiler compiles the code for inline functions at the time that the keyword inline is encountered. This results in a reduction of processing and function call overhead for the program.

Instance.   The existence of a predefined object.

Late Binding.   See Dynamic Binding.

Member Function.   A method within a class. A method is nothing more than a function prototype within the declaration of a class. This function may or may not be inline (i.e., defined).

Method.   See Member Function.

Multiple Inheritance.   The feature by which one object inherits data and functions from two or more base classes. See also Inheritance.

Object.   An instance or occurrence of a class.

Object-Oriented.   The term given to languages which allow the collection of individual blocks of code into hierarchies of classes, thereby allowing code reuse and code extension without redefinition.

Operator Overloading.   A feature which allows the meaning of most unary and binary operators to be changed.

Polymorphism.   The property by which virtual functions are invoked using pointers to base classes, resulting in each object within the hierarchy implementing a method specific to its own requirements.

Private.   The feature which allows the encapsulation of data and functions within that class alone. Data and functions within an object are private by default. See also Protected and Public.

Privately Derived Classes.   Classes which are preceded by the keyword *private* at the time that they are derived from a base class. This results in public and protected members of the base becoming private for the derived. Private members of the base class continue to remain private to it.

Protected.   The feature which allows the encapsulation of functions within that class and derived classes only. See also Private and Public.

Public.   The feature which allows the accessibility of data elements and functions to derived classes and the remainder of the application.

Publicly Derived Classes.   Classes which are preceded by the keyword *public* at the time that they are derived from a base class. This results in public and protected members of the base becoming public and protected for the derived. Private members of the base class continue to remain private to it.

Reusability.   See Object-Oriented.

this.   An invisible identifier which automatically points to the object for which it exists, and exists for each instance of that object. It is passed implicitly to overloaded operator functions.

Virtual Function or Method.   A virtual function is usually a group of functions which have identical names but different implementation. The appropriate function is invoked based on the address of the particular object that is pointed to at the time. Virtual functions are implemented with Dynamic Binding. See also Dynamic Binding and Polymorphism.

C++ Syntax

Format Notation:

- Syntactic definitions will be followed by a colon.
- Alternatives will follow on the next line.
- Optional elements will be enclosed within angle brackets (<..>).

Declaration Syntax

```
declaration:
    <declaration_specifiers><declaration_list>

declaration_specifiers:
    storage_class_specifier
    type_specifer
    function_specifier

declaration_list:
    declaration

storage_class_specifiers:
    auto
    register
    static
```

```
        extern

type_specifiers:
    type_name
    class_specifier
    enum_specifier
    const
    volatile

function_specifiers:
    inline
    virtual
    friend

type_names:
    class_name
    typedef_name
    char
    short
    int
    long
    signed
    unsigned
    float
    double
    void

class_specifiers:
    class
    struct
    union

enum_specifiers:
    enum <identifier>{enum_list}

enum_list:
    identifier
    identifier = constant_expression
```

Expression Syntax

```
expression:
    primary_expression
    expression binary_operator expression
    expression_list
```

```
operators:
    =    *=    /=    %=    +=    -=    <<=  >>=
    &=   ^=    |=    +     -     <<    >>    <
    <=   >     >=    ==    !=    &     ^     |
    &&   ||    ?=
```

```
primary_expression:
    constant
    string
    this
    ::identifier
    ::operator_function_name
    name
```

```
name:
    identifier
    operator_function_name
    class_name::identifier
    class_name::operator_function_name
    class_name::class_name
    class_name::~class_name
```

```
allocation_expression:
    <::> new <expression_list> type_specifier <initializer>
```

```
deallocation_expression:
    <::> delete expression
```

Class Declaration Syntax

```
class_specifier:
    base_specifier { member_list }
```

```
base_specifier:
    class_name
    virtual <access_specifier> class_name
    friend class_name
```

```
member_list:
    member_declaration <member_list>
```

```
access_specifiers:
    private
    public
    protected
```

```
member_declarations:
    <declaration_specifiers><member_list>
    function_definitions

member_list:
    member_declaration <member_list>
    access_specifier:<member_list>

operator_function_name:
    operator operator

operators:
    +     -     *     /     %     ^
    &     |     ~     !     =     <>
    +=    -=    *=    /=    %=    ^=
    &=    |=    <<    >>    <<=   >>=
    ==    !=    <=    >=    &&    ||
    ++    --    ,     ->*   ->    ()
    []    new   delete    sizeof
```

Index

DISK WARRANTY